Government and Politics
of the United States

WILLIAM C. HAVARD

Harper & Row, Publishers
New York, Evanston, and London

LIBRARY OF CONGRESS CATALOG CARD NUMBER: 65-11703

Contents

Preface

The teaching of American government and politics is continually being enriched by the availability of an increasing number of excellent paperbacks on particular areas of the subject. The wealth of inexpensive monographs makes it feasible to offer a brief, general, and interpretative volume as a coordinating basis for these specialized materials. A book such as this may also have some attraction for the general audience that desires a brief overview of the American governmental system.

There may also be some utility in a small book for a foreign audience. The idea was suggested to me while I was a Fulbright visiting professor in the University of Munich in 1960–1961. In point of fact the genesis of three or four of the chapters in this volume consisted of several lectures given in Germany under the auspices of the United States Information Service and other organizations. Accordingly, I should like to express my appreciation to all those persons, official and non-official and too numerous to single out individually, who arranged the lectures or who served as audience and discussion groups for what may be called an early try-out of some of the ideas of the manuscript.

The effort to serve these several purposes in so small a volume could not have been undertaken without the encouragement and aid of friends and colleagues. Professors Peter J. Fliess, René Williamson, Loren P. Beth, Eric Voegelin, and Robert J. Steamer have read the manuscript either in part or in its entirety and have offered many useful suggestions. I have been exceptionally fortunate in having as editors two perceptive and exacting critics, Professor William A. Robson and Dr. Rollin B. Posey, both of whom nicely balanced the rigor of their corrective guidance with encouragement and restraint. The extent to which the book fulfills the intentions with which it was written is due in no small part to advice from all these persons—advice which I almost invariably tried to follow in the processes of revision. The shortcomings in facts or interpretation which remain are the responsibility of the writer. Finally, I should like to add a note of appreciation to Miss Josephine Scurria for the patience, speed, and accuracy with which she typed several versions of the manuscript.

WILLIAM C. HAVARD

Amherst
January, 1965

GOVERNMENT AND POLITICS
OF THE UNITED STATES

The Constitution:
Its Origins and Content

THE SYMBOL AND THE INSTRUMENT

One of the most distinguished students of the United States Constitution, Professor Edward S. Corwin, has made a useful distinction between the functions of the Constitution as symbol and as instrument. The symbolic role of the Constitution in American political life can hardly be exaggerated; the Constitution is revered as the perfect expression of the unity, continuity, and purpose of the American nation. In this capacity it is truly a common determinant superior, above politics and beyond criticism, an oracle which upon appeal speaks nothing less than ultimate truth with respect to the fundamental principles of American political order. There may be disagreement on the meaning of the Constitution, but there can be no division on the idea of the Constitution itself. In the folklore of American politics, the Constitution may be changed in its written detail, but its spirit may not be impeached. In some cases politicians may accuse one another of malevolently altering its meaning to suit nefarious purposes of their own, but the purity of the Constitution itself is not impaired by this usurpation by men of a government founded on law.

Thus the most unreconstructed southern politician, fighting his grimly uncompromising battle for the "Southern way of life" in opposition to racial integration, will argue that one or more of the Civil War amendments (numbers XIII, XIV, and XV) were illegally imposed and that the federal government is arbitrarily encroaching on the authority of the states, but his arguments will invariably appeal to the Constitution or against the Court rather than to extra-constitutional sanctions. The most persuasive appeal in such a politician's store of fine rhetoric is not for the abolition of the Constitution, but for a "return to the Constitution" or a "restoration of constitutional government." An effort is required to imagine any public figure today following in the steps of William Lloyd Garrison, who publicly burned a copy of the Constitution as part of his dramatic agitation against slavery.

The symbolic function of the Constitution has on occasion been compared to the Monarchy in Britain; it is a representation of the majesty and historical persistence of the society on a more ethereal level than the pragmatic representative institutions by which a country is actually governed. In this sense the Constitution is an abiding, concrete expression of the self-interpretation or self-perception of the American society as a body politic. And this is a function which can hardly be dispensed with, much less despised, for it furnishes a point of reference for the unarticulated consensus that is necessary to the perpetuation of an ordered community in a world of relentless change. The steps recently taken to preserve the original Declaration of Independence and the Constitution against deterioration by sealing them in specially constructed cases is a direct manifestation of their importance as physical symbols of the national spirit; it is no sacrilege to suggest that these parchments have been treated in a manner befitting the sacred national relics into which they have gradually been transmuted.

The symbolic position that the Constitution has come to occupy permeates the national consciousness and produces habitual responses to a wide variety of social and governmental situations. No other society, for example, seems quite so addicted to the habit of constitution-making. Constitutional practice is second nature to Americans. If a motley collection of schoolboys band together to form a club, their first step almost invariably will be to draft and adopt a constitution of some sort. In this and countless other ways the esteem in which the national constitution is held exerts a strong influence over everyday practical life. The conditioning of the American public through the practice of democratic constitutionalism in so many of their public and private affairs immeasurably eases the problem of adjusting conflicts arising from human coexistence. Americans generally have great confidence (among other things) in their capacity to set and reach collective goals for themselves at many levels of cooperation because they are so well versed in their general domestic style of politics. And their constitution-mindedness furnishes the metes and bounds for this field of action.

The instrumental side of the Constitution is another matter altogether. In outlining the organization of the institutions through which the American people are governed, in assigning the powers, setting the limitations and prescribing the procedures through which these institutions are to function, the Constitution has to be concerned with men and society as they are rather than as they ideally should be. In its symbolic aspects the Constitution presents to the American public a vision of the fully formed or best government of which man is capable and promises a basic law so sound that the arbitrary will of man cannot alter or corrupt it. And these ideals have had an important effect on the way in which the United States has developed politically. Despite this complementary relation between the Constitution as symbol and the Constitution as instrument, the working Constitution has a more pedestrian character and a more checkered past than the symbolic Constitution. The instrumental Constitution was, as John Quincy Adams expressed it, ". . . extorted from the grinding necessity of a reluctant nation." The fundamental arrangements of government which it embodied were a product of compromise and adjustment of conflicting ideas and interests; and, since even the best of laws are inaugurated, administered, and changed by men, the Constitution has continued to develop in response to the aspirations of the American people, the conflicts which arise within as well as outside the country, and the successes and failures of various administrations, economic policies, and social experiments. The meaning of the Constitution has expanded and contracted with the shifting tides of men's affairs. Although certain basic principles of the Constitution and some of its institutional characteristics are abiding, no Constitution can be written to cover all contingencies in the affairs of men. Paradoxical as it may seem, if the living American society had not been able to sustain its superiority over the fixed text of the Constitution, the Constitution itself could hardly have survived to become the revered symbol that it is.

FRAMING THE INSTRUMENT

The relation between the role of the Constitution as a symbol and its function as an instrument can be understood only in terms of the origin of the document, for the American nation was effectively generated and much of its political tone was set in the struggle to frame and adopt the Constitution. In 1787 the political problem that faced what had formerly been a considerable portion of British North America was precisely the problem that has confronted so many areas of the world in the nineteenth and twentieth centuries—how does one create a unified, viable, political entity out of the human and geographical material at hand? Independence had been secured, but political cohesion was lacking. The cooperation among the colonies which the Revolutionary War had sustained had almost totally disappeared in peace, and the arguments and slogans of the Revolution, based as they were (particularly in the later phases) on the rationalistic ideals of the Enlightenment, appeared to be weak and visionary when measured in terms of the necessities of an independent national order.

The crisis was grave indeed; some even regarded it as comparable to the darkest days of the winter of Valley Forge. Alexander Hamilton was later to give an explicit analysis of the condition in *The Federalist*. He noted that America was suffering from a national humiliation which weighed upon the country both internally and externally. Foreign and domestic debts were outstanding against the United States which the government had no means of paying; valuable posts and territories were in the hands of foreigners in contravention of treaties (here Hamilton was referring to the retention by the British in clear violation of the Treaty of 1783 of a chain of military and trading posts within the river and lake boundaries of the United States in the Great Lakes region); our ambassadors had no status in many of the countries to which they were assigned, being the "mere pageants of mimic sovereignty," and the country's economic plight was reflected in the depression of land values and the drying up of sources of domestic credit.

These specific conditions, however, merely reflected what Hamilton recognized to be the general weakness of the whole governing system of the Confederation, whose primary deficiency was the absence of a central government that would be adequate to the tasks of external defense, preservation of internal order, and adjustment of the national economy. Shortly after the Declaration of Independence was signed on July 4, 1776, the committee which had earlier been appointed to prepare a form of confederation reported its plan to the Continental Congress. Although this plan was discussed and amended for over a year in Congress, it took three additional years to secure ratification by all 13 states. Even before the Articles of Confederation (the "first" American constitution) went into effect in 1781, however, Congress seems to have brought its own practices into conformity with the requirements of the pertinent provisions of the plan. The difficulties which this meager effort at national unity encountered are sufficient to indicate the obstacles to further national consolidation that confronted the 13 former colonies when they later moved toward the preparation of the Constitution. It should be remembered that the colonies had enjoyed a considerable measure of practical, if not theoretical, autonomy under British rule. These 13 separate jurisdictions had further consolidated their respective local sovereignties in the period between 1776 and 1781, and the appearance of the Articles of Confederation did little to arrest this trend toward governmental separation.

The governments of the individual states were for the most part predicated on the former colonial governments (in some cases the charters were unchanged), but the intensification of the emotional attachment to the doctrines that were used to justify revolution hardened popular sentiment against any suggestion of strong central government, even at the state level. It was during this period that the propensity towards grassroots democracy, which has been a dominant feature of government along the frontier throughout American history and is a recurrent phenomenon in American politics today, became so pronounced. The major attitudes toward the problem of government which this situation brought out included an almost anarchic individualism; representation based on strict equality, with the representative acting under an instructed rather than a free mandate; minimization of governmental power, especially in the executive branch; and a concentration of those limited powers which were delegated to government in the local units closest to the people, with a constant diminution of powers as the levels of government became further removed from the public subject to their authority. It was also in this period that a special type of representative body, the constitutional convention, was developed as a device which would most nearly approach a full assembly of the sovereign people of the state for the purpose of preparing their fundamental instrument of government.

The national government under the Articles of Confederation mirrored these conceptions. The sole national institution under the Articles was a Congress in which each state had a single vote, although states might send from two to seven delegates each to the Congress. The delegates were appointed each year by any method chosen by the state legislatures, they were paid by their respective states, and they were subject to recall at any time by the states they represented. The main powers of the Congress (e.g., the power to engage in war, enter into treaties, coin money, determine expenditures, appropriate money, borrow, and raise armies and navies) could not be exercised except on approval of 9 of the 13 states. Having no power to tax, Congress had to requisition funds for support of national activities from the states, and it had no means of enforcing its requisitions when the states were derelict. The government under the

Articles had no executive other than committees which it formed from its own membership and no judiciary except for congressionally appointed courts to deal with certain types of maritime cases and disputes between the states. The central government was thus little more than a league of independent states; even the Articles contained the specific stipulation that "Each state retains its sovereignty, freedom and independence . . ." The individual states could defy or disrupt the union with impunity since the Confederation had neither the authority nor the governmental agencies to act directly on the people of the United States. The Confederation was not, as Hamilton was careful to point out, a government in the true sense because it was not applicable to men; it was an attempt to regulate the affairs of bodies politic or communities or states, in relation to which the only effective sanction would be coercion by arms.

The actual method by which the Constitutional Convention of 1787 came into being attests the failure of the Articles of Confederation to provide a means for resolving the most serious problems of the union. Virginia and Maryland held conferences at least as early as 1785 and, in contravention of the Articles which required the consent of the Congress to agreements among the states, settled their conflicting interests over the navigation of the Chesapeake Bay. Acting on the basis of the effectiveness of this arrangement, Virginia promoted a plan for a general trade convention of the states to be held at Annapolis, Maryland, in the fall of 1786. Although the proposal seemed to be favored and at least nine state governments appointed delegates, only five states were actually represented. This was too small a number to act, but the opportunity was seized for recommending that another convention of even broader scope be called for the year following. The delegates to the Annapolis Convention reported to their respective states that there were defects in the existing system of government serious enough to render the situation of the United States critical and to justify the calling of a convention for the sole purpose of determining the nature of these defects and providing a plan for remedying them. The reports further suggested that the states to which they were addressed should attempt to secure the concurrence of the other states in the specific proposal to appoint commissioners to meet at Philadelphia in May, 1787, where they would draft provisions necessary to render the constitution adequate ". . . to the exigencies of the Union . . ." and then report this action to the Congress for its approval and transmittal to the state legislatures for confirmation.

By one of those odd quirks of history, an abortive uprising of debt-ridden farmers in Massachusetts in the fall of 1786, known as Shays' Rebellion, created grave apprehension about the security of persons and property throughout the country and greatly stimulated interest in the proposed convention. Virginia was the first state to act on the proposal by appointing a delegation modeled on its congressional delegation. Several other states quickly followed this example, and in February the Congress finally put the capstone on the plan by approving it. The congressional resolution specified, however, that the recommendations of the Convention would require approval by the Congress and confirmation of all the state legislatures in accordance with the provisions of the Articles of Confederation before becoming effective.

Much scholarly controversy has been generated over such questions as the extra-legal character of the Philadelphia Convention, the conservative predisposition of the framers, the economic motivation behind the drafting of the Constitution, and the procedure adopted by the Convention for ratification of a document which, after all, went far beyond the limits of the mandate under which the Convention operated. When the heat of all this controversy is allowed to diminish somewhat, it is possible for almost all parties to unite in agreeing that the Convention was remarkably successful in providing a Constitution which not only solved many of the immediate problems of a union that appeared to be crumbling, but at the same time has proved to be adaptable to historical exigencies of the Union which could not possibly have been foreseen in the eighteenth century.

The Convention met throughout the hot summer of 1787, completing its work with the signing of the Constitution on September 17. Although a number of delegates who were nominated to the Convention did not attend, 55 men did put in appearances during the course of the meetings and 39 members signed the final draft. Rhode Island was the only state which did not appoint delegates. Even when due reservation is made for the hallowing effect produced by the passage of time, the assembly was a remarkable one. The education and experience of its members were unusual: over half were lawyers, 29 were university graduates, about three-fourths had served in the Congress, a number of them had been state governors, and 8 had signed the Declaration of Independence. Among them were men who either already had exhibited a wide variety of talents in statesmanship or administration or were soon to do so. These included that earlier prototype of a rising middle-class energy and ingenuity, Benjamin Franklin, at 81 the oldest member of the assembly; George Washington, the idol of his country and virtually an automatic choice as presiding officer; Alexander Hamilton, the administrative genius of Washington's administration; James Madison, who kept careful notes that were destined to become the most important record of the Convention and whose distinction as a statesman still rests heavily on his work in that body; Edmund Randolph, the brilliant young governor of Virginia; Gouverneur Morris, the final draftsman of the Constitution; James Wilson; the Pinckneys of South Carolina; John Dickinson; William Patterson and several others of this high caliber. A large proportion of these men were quondam scholars and had read the ancient classics on politics as well as the seventeenth-century English republicans (especially Harrington and Locke) and eighteenth-century writers such as Montesquieu.

The opposite side of the coin has also been displayed, most conspicuously in Charles A. Beard's *Economic Interpretation of the Constitution of the United States*, first published in 1913. Beard stressed the economic background of the delegates in order to suggest the connection between the material interests of the framers of the Constitution and the type of document they produced. The Convention was made up of the propertied middle class who were holders of public securities and were also creditors in the private sector of the economy; included also were a number of land speculators, merchants, manufacturers, and slaveowners. Negatively, the Convention was conspicuous by the absence of delegates who were identified with the radical democratic ideology of the American Revolution, especially figures such as Tom Paine, Samuel Adams, Patrick Henry, John Hancock, Thomas Jefferson, and even John Adams who, while already moving in the direction of the Federalist "right" which eventually claimed him completely, was widely regarded as one of the active fomentors of the Revolution. There was not a single worker, frontiersman, or small farmer in the Convention.

Despite this appearance of upper middle-class solidarity and the tendencies that it yielded for creating a strong national government with a primary emphasis on a national policy to make property secure, more recent scholarship has questioned Beard's single-factor analysis. By reworking available materials along lines outlined by Beard himself, several historians have indicated that the questions which divided the framers (including some fundamental economic issues) were apparently more important than the external personal characteristics by which they seemed to be united. Regional questions, conflicting forms of economic productivity, slavery, international trade, and large-state versus small-state interests had already made their weight felt in diversifying the American population and geographic sectors, and these factors were centers of controversy in the Convention. The evidence further indicates that the views expressed by individual members of the Convention contradicted the apparent personal interests of the spokesmen almost as frequently as they supported them. If there were time-servers and special pleaders in the assembly, there were also statesmen and men of emancipated intellect. Furthermore, the accessibility of property and the spread of liberal doctrine had already encouraged the assimilation by virtually the entire American population of the middle-class image as the appropriate ideal of the good life, and this condition made the framers a much more representative body than they might otherwise have been.

The reasons for calling the Philadelphia Convention, the records of the meetings, and the structure and content of the Constitution itself point to a wide area of agreement among the delegates on the need for a greatly strengthened central government and for an adequate machinery through which that government might be operated. The achievement of this felt necessity of the time is reflected in several features of the new Constitution. The founders created a national representative assembly which was vested with substantial powers in finance, the regulation of interstate and international commerce, the issuance of currency, and several other functional areas. They also established a strong independent executive who could take the initiative in the field of foreign policy as well as manage the internal administrative affairs of the government. They laid the constitutional basis for a national judicial system that was soon to become a more important branch than the founding fathers had envisaged. Perhaps most important of all, the framers included in Article VI the declaration known as the "Supreme Law of the Land Clause" which made the Constitution, laws of the United States made in pursuance thereof, and treaties made under the authority of the United States prevail over all other legal enactments in the country.

Although the Convention seems to have been generally agreed on a bicameral (or two-chambered) Congress, the greatest single controversy that arose was over the method of representation. This question was one which touched the whole problem of more effective national unity; in its details it was a struggle between large and small states, with the latter fearing that they would be overwhelmed by the larger states in a "national" government. The "Virginia Plan" for revision, which was submitted very early in the Convention and tended in the direction of a national government that would go far beyond an amendment of the Articles, called for the apportionment of both houses of the legislative assembly on the basis of the monetary contribution or the numbers of free inhabitants of the states, or both. Under this plan the lower house was to be elected by the people within the several states and the upper house was to be chosen by the lower house from candidates nominated by the state legislatures. This proposal was eventually countered by the "New Jersey Plan," which hewed closer to the line of simply revising the Articles and by implication left representation among the states in Congress on a basis of equality. After prolonged consideration, the so-called "Great Compromise" or Connecticut Compromise was effected whereby the lower house was popularly elected and its seats apportioned on the basis of population, with slaves to be reckoned at three-fifths of their actual number in making this calculation and in apportioning direct taxes. Under the compromise the upper house (Senate), over which most of the contention arose, was apportioned on the basis of equal representation of the states (two from each) and its members were to be selected by the legislatures of the respective states.

Other compromises were reached throughout the deliberations, up to and including the stage at which the document was being drafted in its final form. Among the most important was the final settlement on a single-head chief executive who would be indirectly elected and would be assigned extensive, general powers to administer foreign and domestic affairs. The resolution of another key issue that was to have great future importance was the double-barreled concession to the southern states under which the importation of slaves would not be interfered with prior to 1808 and no taxes would be levied on exports.

The founding fathers were bold in their innovation; they had gone beyond their mandate in preparing a constitution that radically altered the existing form of government. Having done so, they took it upon themselves to provide a method of ratification that violated the requirement in the Articles of Confederation that alterations be agreed to by the Congress and then confirmed by the legislatures of every state. The delegates realized the impossibility of securing the approval of the legislatures of all 13 states, so Article VII provided that "The ratification of the *conventions* of *nine* States shall be sufficient for the establishment of this Constitution between the States so ratifying the same." (Italics supplied.) As a practical matter the new union probably could not have survived unless all the colonies had entered it, but in taking the extra-legal (or in relation to the near anarchic libertarianism of the Declaration of Independence, the *counter*revolutionary) action that they did, the framers provided a means for simultaneously bringing some sort of union into effect and inducing the few states that might have held out under the unanimous requirement to enter the federation. Late in September of 1787 the Congress assented to the plan of ratification proposed by the Convention and the issue was thrown open to national debate.

The struggle over ratification by the states was intense. Some of the strongest opposition came from the conventions in the three large states of Massachusetts, Virginia, and New York. Failure in any one of these three might well have wrecked the proposed union. Despite the fact that rigid suffrage requirements, problems of getting to the polls, and general lethargy kept the number of voters to an estimated 25 percent of the free male adult population, a sizable opposition gathered in the state conventions. For the most part the opponents of ratification were an amalgam of debt-ridden small farmers, frontiersmen, and laborers in the towns. Other more favorably situated persons remained in doubt, too; northerners and southerners were divided over the question whether too many or too few concessions had been made to slaveholders; paper-money advocates were disturbed at the curb on state-issued bills of credit; and some commercial interests feared the new taxing powers. The leadership around which these groups coalesced were the more radically democratic figures of the Revolution such as Samuel Adams and John Hancock (a later supporter) in Massachusetts and Patrick Henry of Virginia.

Two outstanding features of the American political heritage appeared as part of the persuasive effort and concessions necessary to secure the general adoption of the Constitution. One was *The Federalist*, which was a series of 85 papers appearing in the leading newspapers of New York over the pen name *Publius*. Written by Alexander Hamilton, James Madison, and John Jay, *The Federalist* has frequently been cited as America's single entry among the lists of outstanding works in political philosophy; without doubt it remains the most important interpretation of what the men who drafted the Constitution intended the document to be. Whether these papers actually turned the tide of the New York opposition is open to conjecture, but that state's convention did ratify the Constitution by the narrow margin of two votes on July 26, 1788, more than three weeks after Congress had announced that the required ninth state had approved.

With New York's approval, only 2 of the 13 states, North Carolina and Rhode Island, remained outside the union. However, many of the ratifying conventions of the other states had registered dissatisfaction with the absence from the document of a specific bill of rights, as was attested by the proposal in those conventions of more than 100 amendments, most of which were concerned with matters appropriate to such a reservation of individual rights. This reaction produced the second great development of the ratification period—the creation of the Bill of Rights. The newly-organized Congress undertook to submit to the states a series of 10 proposed constitutional amendments in the effort to meet the objections against a Constitution which did not specifically reserve certain individual liberties against governmental action. The inclusion of a bill of rights was in accordance with the practice that characterized most state constitutions. Following this action, which was to have incalculably important consequences for American political history, North Carolina approved the Constitution late in 1789 and Rhode Island finally ratified in the spring of 1790. In the meantime, the government under the new Constitution had completed its organization in April, 1789.

SOURCES AND STRUCTURE

In form, the Constitution of the United States is brief, simple, and logical in structure and admirably clear in syntax. These features are especially pronounced when one considers the complexity of the theoretical sources and the breadth of experience out of which the document was conceived. Although leavened by the necessity for compromise that the wisdom of experience demanded, a few concepts stand out as basic principles. Two of these, the notion of popular sovereignty and the idea of bestowal of governmental powers, were united in the attempt to achieve the fundamental purpose of constitutionalism—a limited and responsible government. The idea of popular sovereignty early established a tenacious hold on the American mind, and this outlook was strengthened by the success of the American Revolution. The rationalist, natural-law, natural-rights philosophers of sixteenth- and seventeenth-century Europe were secularizing politics and elaborating the contract theory of government during the initial period of America's settlement. By implication in its early phases and specifically in its later development, especially in John Locke's *Second Treatise on Civil Government* (1690), the contract theory stressed consent as the basis for the establishment of government, the welfare of the people who made up the political community as the proper end of government, and majoritarianism as the appropriate means of reaching governmental decisions.

In opposing the Puritan theocracy of New England in the seventeenth century, early American forerunners of democratic thought such as Thomas Hooker, John Wise, and Roger Williams relied explicitly or implicitly upon natural law and the contract theory. Of equal if not greater importance is the fact that Hooker in Connecticut and Williams in Rhode Island established political regimes that substantially reflected the principles of a covenanted or contracted association, virtually universal adult male participation in politics, and governmental institutions that served as "stewards" or agents of the popular will. The pattern of settlement of British North America (in small, isolated communities), easy accessibility to property, the great distance from the seat of central power at Westminister, and the relative lack of rigid social class stratification resulted in political institutions that were veritable models of the contractual theory.

A century of experience with this style of politics brought about an enormous gulf between the political arrangements of the imperial government and the domestic institutions of the North American colonies. However influential the Glorious Revolution of 1688–1689 was in foreclosing the idea that government derived its authority from some source outside society, it did not provide the institutions of a prescriptive British Constitution with a popular basis. The sovereignty which was subtly proclaimed in 1689 was the sovereignty of Parliament, not of the people; the British Constitution still functioned as a "mixt aristocracie." and even the royal prerogative, while muted, was not crudely repressed. America was practicing popular government while England was still sloughing off the vestiges of the divine right of monarchy. The American Revolution, precipitated largely by these divergencies in practice, intensified the latently democratic proclivities of the American colonies because Lockean doctrine provided so much of its ideological justification.

Even though the American Constitution was generated in part as a reaction against the excesses of democracy and many harsh expressions against the evils of *demos* were heard in the Convention, no delegate seriously challenged the idea that government rested on the consent of the governed. However, this did not prevent the delegates in Philadelphia from drafting a legal instrument that placed elaborate restraints on the popular will or even from including in the document certain institutional provisions that drew heavily on arrangements more characteristic of aristocracy and monarchy than of democracy. Thus despite the Lockean presumption that the people were the sole possessors of rights and only the government had obligations, prior American experience with constitutional restraints on the power of the governed and the government alike influenced the drafting of the Constitution. The "higher law" which the Constitution represented might have its only source in the people themselves, but its content nonetheless reflected the idea of a legal self-limitation of the popular will as well as a carefully circumscribed allocation of power to the governmental authorities created by the Constitution.

The governmental power was restrained not only by a strict definition (bestowal) of powers and by an equally carefully delineated set of specific limitations on governmental authority, but also by the elaborate structural arrangement for checks against usurpation which are discussed more fully below. The limitations on the power of the public, on the other hand, were implicit in the idea of the written Constitution itself, with its fixed superior legal rules which though subject to change by popular process, are based on a consensus that goes beyond a simple plebiscite. Popular sovereignty, then, was expressed most completely in the act of drafting and adopting the Constitution. Although the instrumental parts of the Constitution have been gradually democraticized through a combination of formal amendment and usage (in themselves historical applications of the principle of popular sovereignty), the restrictions to the rules of the game implied by the original act of constitutional creation continue to prevail in practice. The tension between the notion of a sovereign people and a persisting self-limitation of popular power through a written constitution was clearly expressed (and perhaps partially resolved) in the following words of James Wilson, one of the most distinguished delegates to the 1787 Convention: "After the lapse of six thousand years since the creation of the world, America now presents the first instance of a people assembled to weigh deliberately and calmly, and to decide leisurely and peaceably, upon the form of government by which they will bind themselves and their posterity."

The structural features of the Constitution reflect the attempt to implement a government based on consent, limited in its powers, and responsive to popular controls within a constitutional framework. The Constitution contains three main parts: (1) an organizational part which provides for the major institutions of government, and outlines their main powers, limitations, and procedures; (2) the Bill of Rights; and (3) a provision for piecemeal amendment. Each of these elements of the Constitution has its own complex history. Much of the discussion in the chapters which follow is concerned with the functioning of the organizational part of the Constitution, but it is important to outline the basic character of all three parts as a background to the analysis of the government in action.

ORGANIZATION OF THE GOVERNMENT

The organizational part of the Constitution has three marked characteristics. First, the Constitution creates a *federal* government; second, the national (or central) government is organized on the basis of the doctrine of the separation of powers; and finally, the Constitution was originally designed to reflect some aspects of a "mixed" constitution. The development of a federal as opposed to a unitary form of government complicated the problem of constitution making. Federalism is based on the idea of a divided or dual sovereignty. Professor K. C. Wheare notes in his *Federal Government* that the main factor which is necessary for the establishment of the federal principle is that " . . . each government should be limited to its own sphere and, within that sphere, should be independent of the other." Although it may be contended that federalism in this rigorous sense no longer exists in practice in the United States because of the difficulty of identifying any substantial sphere of governmental power in which the states are completely independent of Washington, the dual sovereignty conception of federalism was central to the aims of the draftsmen of the Constitution. And as Wheare is also careful to point out, the United States determined the content of the modern idea of federalism.

Because it is the supreme law of the land and as such seeks to assign separate spheres of legitimate governmental authority to a central government and to the constituent geographical units called "states," the American Constitution is really three constitutions in one. First, there is the national constitution, which outlines the organization, powers, and limitations of the central government; second there is the constitution of the states, which consists mainly of specific limitations on the power of states; and finally, there are provisions which might be called the constitution of the whole, consisting of those parts of the constitution which seek

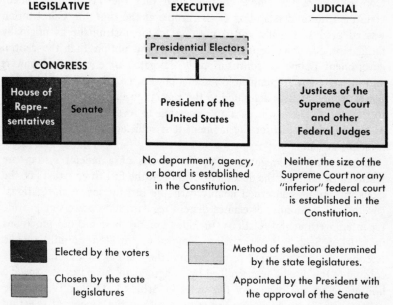

The Three Branches of the National Government as Established in the Constitution

to regulate the relations among the states themselves as well as the relations between the states and the central government. The problems of the convention being what they were, it is too much to expect that these three distinct elements should have been fully recognized and the Constitution drafted in such a way that they stand in clear juxtaposition to one another. Too many things were going on simultaneously, too many compromises and adjustments were being effected and too much accommodation to the logical incoherence of experience was necessary to admit absolute precision into the arrangements of a complex federal structure.

Consequently the three constitutions are thoroughly intermingled within the written document. The main direct expression of the principle of federalism, however, is in the Tenth Amendment which provides that "The powers not delegated to the United States by the Constitution, nor prohibited by it to the States, are reserved to the States respectively, or to the people." Although the United States Supreme Court (which in itself is both a branch of the national government and an arbiter of the Constitution of the whole) has declared that the Tenth Amendment confirmed the understanding of the people at the time the Constitution was adopted and really added nothing to the instrument as originally ratified, it does give explicit expression to the notion that the central government is one of constitutionally delegated or enumerated powers and the state governments hold residual powers, i.e., those inherent police powers which are not delegated to the central government nor prohibited to the states. There will be ample occasion to revert to the complexities of this formula later; for the moment it is sufficient to have the general principle at hand.

Other provisions regulating specific aspects of a federal system are scattered throughout the document. Although the first three articles of the Constitution are concerned mainly with the institutions of the national government, a number of clauses therein regulate state powers or provide for intergovernmental relations. Included among these are the provisions in Article I, Section 8, authorizing Congress to provide for a militia while reserving the appointment of officers and the training of the militia (according to the discipline prescribed by Congress) to the states; the specific limitations on the powers of the states in Article I, Section 10; and the various provisions which give the states a role in the process of selecting national officials, e.g., the provision in Article II, Section 1, for the selection of presidential electors in such manner as each state legislature may direct, and the original provision in Article I, Section 3, providing for the choosing of United States Senators by the various state legislatures (changed in 1913 by the Seventeenth Amendment to provide for popular election). Article IV regulates the relations among the states; provides for Congress to admit new states to the Union; prohibits the partition or merger of states without the consent of the legislatures of the states concerned and of Congress; and provides that the United States shall guarantee to each state a republican form of government, protection against invasion and, upon application of the state legislature or executive, against domestic violence. Article V, on the method of amendment of the constitution, establishes a role in the amending process for the states as component units of the federation. Article VI contains the Supreme Law of the Land Clause, binds the judges in every state to abide by it, and further provides that the state legislatures and all state executive and judicial officers shall be bound by oath or affirmation to support the Constitution. Several of the amendments (in addition to the Tenth) directly affect the federal relation. The Fourteenth, Fifteenth, and Nineteenth Amendments, for example, placed limitations on the power of the states in the effort to protect individual liberties and avoid discrimination in the area of suffrage qualifications on the grounds of race, color, previous condition of servitude, and sex.

Federalism, in the sense of preserving for the states a considerable area of governmental power to be held independently of the national government, was a *sine qua non* of securing an effective national government organization and powers in 1787. Each of the original 13 states was for practical purposes a legally sovereign national state although they were united by their colonial history, language, custom, the use of the common law, mutual participation in the American Revolution and, after 1781, by a loose governmental association under the Articles of Confederation. Experience showed the impossibility of attempting to erect a unitary system in the face of these circumstances. Caution further compelled the founding fathers to be evasive on the question of the "sovereign people" who stood behind the legalistic dual governmental sovereignty provided by the Constitution. Was the Convention, as the Preamble suggested, representative of "the people of the United States" as a national collectivity, or was it a body of delegates representing the "peoples" of the several sovereign states in their separate capacities as the method of adoption and certain internal features of the Constitution perhaps implied? In Article XXXIX of the *Federalist* Madison was equivocal in dealing with the question, holding that the Constitution was really "mixed" in its republican basis, being neither wholly federal (his usage here would conform to the notion of a confederation of sovereign states) nor wholly national (that is, approximating a unitary system in its popular basis). "In its foundation," he said, "it is federal, not national; in the sources from which the ordinary powers of the government are drawn, it is partly federal and partly national; in the operation of these powers, it is national, not federal; in the extent of them again, it is federal, not national; and, finally, in the authoritative mode of introducing amendments, it is neither wholly federal nor wholly national."

The ingenuity of the new system (and of Madison's argument on its behalf) may be granted, but the fundamental issues remained unsettled. One of these was the problem of who decided cases in which the states and the national government maintained conflicting claims to power under the Constitution when each rested its case on a popular mandate from its own constituency. Over and above this question hovered the ultimate issue of whether a state might use its claim to sovereignty to defy a national decision, even when that decision met all of the constitutional requirements for legitimacy. American constitutional history has, of course, resolved these issues although their ghosts still haunt the American scene from time to time. The United States Supreme Court acquired the role of ultimate arbiter of the meaning of the Constitution, and for more than a century it wavered politically between the poles of national and state powers in its interpretations. The second issue was settled by force in the American Civil War.

Above and beyond these particular issues and the struggles that they precipitated, however, is the gradual movement throughout American history toward national consolidation. Many factors have influenced this trend, including the tremendous geographical expansion, the assimilation of a vast immigrant population, the nationalizing of governmental problems as a result of industrialism, and the awakening of a national patriotism in response, among other things, to foreign wars. These developments are reflected in the diminution of sectional hostilities, local jealousies and postures of independence, and in the growth of national governmental power backed by a nationwide constituency. And the Constitution, drafted under conditions of extreme decentralization and unreasoning suspicion of national power, has not only survived this trend but has presided over it. The founding fathers wrought better than they knew in making the language of the document sufficiently broad to provide real flexibility and in casting national powers in general rather than narrowly defined terms. This does not mean, as some take it to mean, that federalism is a dead issue in America. It is still reflected in many institutional practices, not the least of which are the national representative system and the structure of party politics; in the marked geographical and political identity of the states; in a strong sense of personal affiliation with the constituent units on the part of citizens; and even in the continued execution by the states of important governmental functions. Some of these effects are useful; others create serious problems. Some measure of decentralization is necessary to a political unit that sprawls over a continent and contains so many diversities of geography, population, and local custom. American federalism offers a built-in response to this need. By the same token, however, it still offers opportunities for obstruction of national majorities, for the frustration of policies designed to fulfill the libertarian and egalitarian promises of the American experiment in democracy, and for considerable embarrassment of the attempt to create a cohesive national foreign policy. Some of these conflicting features of the system will be specified later, but even as generalities they point to the accuracy of the observer who said that the nature of federalism has to be sought in the diversities of economic, social, political, and cultural forces which necessitated the adoption of a federal system rather than in the abstraction of a fixed legal arrangement. From this standpoint, American federalism was and continues to be an essential and often uneasy accommodation to social and historical conditions precedent to the United States itself; in effect, it is a price exacted for a more perfect union.

The main organizational feature of the central government in the United States is the separation of powers among the three branches. The theoretical source from which the concept was drawn was Montesquieu's *Spirit of the Laws.* Montesquieu held that governmental activities were naturally separated into the three distinctive functions of law-making, execution of the law, and deciding cases arising under the law. He also thought that the success of the British Constitution was due to the assignment of these functions to three separate and distinct institutions of government—the legislature (parliament), the executive (crown), and the judiciary (courts). There is irony in the fact that Montesquieu failed to recognize the distance that Britain had already traveled along the road to parliamentary supremacy and thereby inadvertently contributed to the great organizational dichotomy between parliamentary and presidential governments in modern constitutional democracies.

Without depreciating Montesquieu's influence, it should be noted that the American experience with colonial government and with the state governments which followed gave considerable impetus to the idea of the separation of powers. The colonial governments ordinarily consisted of a popularly elected representative assembly, an appointive governor (except in the charter colonies, where he was elected), a governor's council which later evolved into an upper chamber, and a system of courts which culminated in the British Privy Council. In taking over this organization and embodying it in their new constitutions, the states accepted in practice the main outlines of the separation of powers system. The founding fathers then incorporated the device into the United States Constitution by construction rather than by a direct expression of the principle (as many of the states now do). Each of the first three articles creates a separate branch of the central government and assigns to it distinctive functions and powers. The initial words in the first section of these three articles, respectively, are as follows "All legislative powers herein granted shall be vested in a Congress of the United States . . . "; "The executive power shall be vested in a President of the United States . . . "; and "The judicial power of the United States shall be vested in one Supreme Court, and in such inferior courts as the Congress may from time to time ordain and establish."

The concomitant of the separation of powers is the system of checks and balances. In accordance with the separation principle no person may serve in more than one branch at a given time and no one of the branches may properly exercise powers belonging to either of the other two. To assist in preserving this distinction the branches are counterpoised against one another in various ways, and each is given certain specific checks on the organization and powers of the other two. In its details the checks and balances system is complicated, but a few examples will show roughly how the plan works. In the first place, the officials of the three branches are chosen in different ways and for varying terms of office. The President is able to check Congress by his veto power and Congress in turn checks the President by being able to override his veto by a two-thirds vote in each house. Furthermore the Senate acts as a check on the President by the requirements that his major appointments must have its approval and that it shares the treaty power with him. The President holds a check on the courts by his power to appoint judges, but in being appointed during good behavior (i.e., for life) the judges are given a tenure that insures judicial independence. And, whether the power was implied by the nature of the Constitution or was arrogated to itself by the Supreme Court, the function of the Court in construing the constitutional powers of all the branches gives it a substantial check on both the legislature and the executive. The Congress, in turn, has constitutional authority to reorganize the court system and the Senate may approve or reject nominees to the federal bench. The Congress also holds the power of impeachment which can be applied against executive and judicial officers alike, and this branch also retains a time-honored check on executive usurpation in the form of control of the purse. Although they belong to the same branch, each house of Congress acts as a check and balance against the other, most conspicuously in terms of the stipulation that no bill can become law unless it passes both houses in identical form.

The separation of powers system was designed to prevent a consolidation of political power; it was thought to be a mechanical arrangement for maintaining responsibility. There is considerable validity, however, in the frequently expressed charge that in attempting to limit the abuse of governmental power in this way the draftsmen of the Constitution actually devised a means for minority obstruction of legitimate exercises of governmental authority. Certainly the separation of powers has been used, at various periods of American history, to check and balance government so effectively that nothing could be accomplished even when the need for governmental action was most apparent. In this respect, the separation principle has not been an adequate substitute for the type of responsibility that the smoother working parliamentary system—with its merger of legislative and executive—has achieved in England. The American party system, the role of the President as popular and congressional leader, and the accommodation of the courts to the notion of popular sovereignty have all had their influence in narrowing the possibilities that the separation of power offers for small power blocs to frustrate majority action. But it is undeniable that some such possibilities still exist. On the other hand, certain facets of the party system, the increasingly important function of the President as legislative leader, and other aspects of the American political process owe their existence to adjustments necessitated by the separation of powers. The system as a whole is a going one despite a certain cumbersomeness in its general operation; to attempt to shift to some form of parliamentary government, as a great many critics have urged, would seem to be as impractical as it is unlikely in terms of political feasibility.

A final organizational characteristic of the Constitution that deserves some consideration is its provision for a "mixed" form of national government. In its classical origin the theory of the mixed constitution was fully developed by Polybius, who thought that the source of Roman political stability could be attributed to its mixed government. Polybius accepted the Aristotelian categorization of governments into the three main forms of monarchy, aristocracy, and democracy, each of which tended in time to deteriorate into a corresponding bad form and was in turn succeeded by one of the alternative forms. The result was a continuous movement of governments through a cycle of alternating good and bad types of monarchy, aristocracy, democracy, and back to monarchy again. In the Roman system, by contrast, all three forms were represented in balanced fashion, thus checking the cyclical displacement of single systems.

Here again, the theoretical sources were sustained by experience. During the arguments over colonial rights in the prerevolutionary period, both the American Tories and the American Whigs frequently pointed to the advantages accruing to British subjects from the stabilizing effects of the mixture of powers in the British Constitution. Since the Whig mind predominated in the Convention of 1787 it is not surprising that the issue was revived there. Some of the more conservative delegates such as John Dickinson openly expressed admiration for monarchy and aristocracy; and although persons of this persuasion realized the impossibility of writing these institutions into a popularly based constitution, they thought it advisable to incorporate as many of their *principles* as possible into the new Constitution.

In point of fact the Convention did pay a measure of homage to the idea of the mixed constitution in the institutions of the national government. The House of Representatives, a numerous body apportioned on the basis of population and directly elected for a short term, was clearly a democratic element. The Senate, on the other hand, was designed as a small body; its representative basis was territorial, its selection was in the hands of the legislatures of the various states, senatorial terms were long and, since these terms overlapped, the Senate was a continuing body. Definitely established as an upper house for purposes of restraining precipitate democratic action, the Senate was vested with about as many attributes of aristocracy as a republican-minded country would countenance. Nor was the Presidency devoid of all the characteristics of monarchy; the office was filled indirectly for a moderately long term, it combined certain attributes of head of state with those of a chief executive, and the incumbent was eligible to succeed himself indefinitely.

In keeping with the general trend of the Convention, the framers sought, through the adoption of some elements of a mixed government, to moderate the influences of unrestrained democracy without violating the doctrine of popular sovereignty. In adapting the Constitution to the life of the country, however, the latter doctrine has tended to prevail. Both the Senate and the office of President have been democratized by a combination of usage and constitutional amendment. The Seventeenth Amendment provided for the popular election of Senators and the rise of the party system turned the presidential election into a popular affair. At the same time, political institutions develop special characters of their own which are in various degrees affected by their initial conceptions. Thus it is that the ethos of the United States Senate has always possessed some of the elitist qualities of an aristocratic body, and the dignitary functions of the presidential office retain some of the flavor of constitutional monarchy.

THE RESERVATION OF RIGHTS

The reception of the Bill of Rights into the Constitution was explained earlier. The tenacity of the idea of a bill of rights as a fundamental part of American constitutionalism has been so strong that no state convention today would think of omitting one from the draft of a proposed new constitution. And the nature of the American commonwealth has been such that a sizable portion of its constitutional law—i.e., the vast body of cases in which the United States Supreme Court has interpreted the powers and limits established in the Constitution—is concerned with problems involving liberties guaranteed by the Bill of Rights.

The Bill of Rights provides for three broad categories of guarantees. The first consists of those seemingly abstract personal freedoms that protect the integrity and independence of the individual; the First Amendment freedoms of religion, press, speech, assembly, and petition form the core of these rights. A second class of guarantees relates to the protection of the individual against governmental arbitrariness when under investigation or on trial for an alleged criminal offense. This category includes a provision to protect persons and property against unreasonable searches and seizures, as well as a considerable number of specific procedural guarantees respecting forms of indictment, fair trial, and forms of punishment. In addition to the provisions of this type in the Fourth through the Eighth Amendments, the body of the Constitution contains limitations on the suspension of *habeas corpus* and prohibitions against the passage of bills of attainder and *ex post facto laws*. The final type of limitations on governmental action in the Bill of Rights are those provisions designed to protect property. Although guarantees preventing unreasonable searches and seizures and quartering of troops may be included under this heading, the most important clauses affecting rights to property are the two which prohibit the confiscation of property without due process of law and guarantee against private property being appropriated for public use without just compensation. It may readily be seen that the framers of the Constitution and the draftsmen of the first ten Amendments drew heavily upon the English Bill of Rights, certain long-standing common-law procedures and, in a few instances (such as the prohibition of an established religion and the limitation on quartering of troops), upon their immediate colonial experiences in framing restrictions on government.

Two great problems have dominated the litigation arising under the constitutional guarantees of individual liberty in America. The first involves the attempt to give specific meaning to the abstract pronouncements of the Constitution. Every society is faced with balancing its responsibilities for self-preservation and the maintenance of order against the claims of individuals for immunity against state interference. The exercise of rights cannot, of course, be purely arbitrary or capricious; some corresponding obligations are implied. At the very least there is a limit on the extent to which rights may be claimed when they are used for the eventual abolition of these same rights. Furthermore, a person may be held responsibile for the abuse of rights when he uses them to injure society or to deny equal rights to others. In most areas of civil liberties the Court has produced doctrines that furnish some guidance when a particular case of alleged violation of a constitutional right is submitted for judicial decision. The Court, for example, has applied more than one test in determining what constitutes legitimate curbs on freedom of expression. At one time it used the "bad tendency" doctrine as a measure of the conditions under which free speech could be limited; at others the more stringent "clear and present danger" doctrine as developed by Justice Holmes has furnished the standard for the exercise of the police power to limit free expression. In its contemporary concern about internal subversion the Court has wavered in the attempt to develop a standard for deciding the point at which free speech sufficiently threatens the safety of the society to allow a measure of public control. The Court's attempt to provide consistency in the face of the tremendous diversity of civil liberties cases compels dogma to yield to common sense. In the longer run, however, certain general trends do establish themselves. As we shall have occasion to see later, for 70 years after the Civil War the courts were seemingly more concerned with the use of such doctrines as due process to deny government attempts to regulate the economy than with individual human rights; during the past 25 years they have tended to leave economic decisions to the political branches and to focus their attention on questions involving substantive and procedural personal rights.

The second problem which has repeatedly charged the perpetual debate on civil liberties is the extent to which the federal government (especially the courts) can protect individual rights against interference by the state governments. Although not of exclusive concern, the main issues in this connection have arisen in the field of race relations. The problem is complicated, of course, by the fact that the Constitution's Bill of Rights was designed to apply against the central government, and most of the state constitutions contain corresponding guarantees which the individual states are responsible for upholding. However, the body of the United States Constitution contains certain prohibitions against state action that run on behalf of individuals, and the Civil War amendments added civil rights clauses that have vitally affected public policy in this area. The Fourteenth Amendment, for example, includes a "due process" clause in relation to state action which parallels the due process restraint on the central government in the Fifth Amendment. In a long series of cases, the United States Supreme Court has applied the due process clause of the Fourteenth Amendment in such a way as to incorporate at least the First Amendment freedoms into the protections against state action. The same Amendment contains the "equal protection of the laws" clause which restrains a state from denying equal protection to any person within its jurisdiction. And the Fifteenth Amendment prohibits the denial or abridgement of the right of United States citizens to vote on the grounds of race, color, or previous condition of servitude. Under these provisions the federal courts have undertaken the scrutiny of many areas of action in which appellants have charged the states with deprivations of rights.

One by one the barriers erected by southern state governments to prevent Negroes from voting were struck down under these provisions. More recently the federal courts have abandoned the formula developed in

Plessy v. *Ferguson* (1896) under which the states might maintain legally enforced segregation if "equal facilities" were provided for both races. Although the *Plessy* case was concerned with transportation, the doctrine was used to validate segregation as an exercise of state police powers in the fields of education, the use of recreation facilities, and other functions. Latterly the courts have returned to a stricter interpretation of the Fourteenth Amendment in which it appears that attempts at legal segregation in itself constitute a substantive denial of equation protection of the law. The monumental case was the United States Supreme Court decision in *Brown* v. *Board of Education of Topeka* (1954), which denied the local authorities the right to enforce segregation in public education. The *Brown* case has been followed by an elaborate line of decisions striking at racial segregation in all of the areas in which it had previously been publicly enforced. Although these decisions clearly indicate that the states do not have legal power to enforce segregation, the practice has by no means been wiped out in the states. Until quite recently Congress had passed only limited legislation in the civil liberties field (mainly in relation to voting) which the executive could enforce uniformly, and the nature of the judicial process makes court enforcement a somewhat sporadic affair since it depends on overruling specific violations brought forward in litigation. Despite these disadvantages and despite the fact that a program of "massive resistance" to nationally enforced desegregation has been put up by most of the southern states, the legal sanction for the practice has been disallowed and this in itself has wrought a great change in national attitudes and a more limited alteration in local performance. Both national political parties are committed to the support of a policy of ending racial discrimination, and even without positive congressional action the President, acting through the Department of Justice, has been increasingly active in investigating and bringing legal action to halt the use of state powers to preserve segregation. In this, as in all other fields of civil rights, there is no such thing as a complete realization of ideals; the gains have been substantial, but each gradual step forward is still likely to raise new problems.

THE NECESSITY FOR CHANGE

The final item among the essential elements of the Constitution is a provision for piecemeal amendment. In keeping with the idea of its

superior legal position, the formal amendment of the Constitution requires a procedure that is much more difficult than the process of framing
ordinary law. And in conformity with the federal structure of the Constitution, the amending process depends on specific action at the level of
the states. Amendment consists of two steps, proposal and ratification,
and each of these steps may be carried out by two different methods. An
amendment may be proposed by a two-thirds vote in each house of
Congress or it may be proposed by a convention called on application
of the legislatures of two-thirds of the states. The latter method has never
been used, and inasmuch as the Constitution is silent on the detailed
arrangements of such a convention, nothing authoritative can be said
about its possibilities. Once an amendment has been proposed it may be
ratified by a favorable vote of the legislatures of three-fourths of the
states or by conventions in three-fourths of the states. All of the amendments except the Twentieth have been ratified by legislative action.

Although thousands of suggested amendments have been introduced
in Congress, only 29 have actually been proposed to the states for ratification. Of this number, 24 have been ratified during the entire course
of America's history. The amendments fall into definite categories of
their own. The first twelve were passed in the early period under the
Constitution; these might be said to be the "adjusting" amendments.
The first ten are the Bill of Rights, the Eleventh was designed to protect
the states against suits in federal courts by citizens of other states or
foreign subjects, and the Twelfth changed the manner of casting the
electoral votes for President and Vice-President. The next three were
not passed until after the Civil War, and they are usually designated as
Civil War amendments because they prohibited involuntary servitude
and extended certain civic rights to the freed slaves (discussed above)
and placed certain disabilities on those who had engaged in rebellion.
Then a period of more than 40 years ensued before the passage of the
Sixteenth Amendment in 1913, which allowed the federal government
to levy an income tax. With this alteration there began a series of
"Twentieth Century" amendments: the Seventeenth Amendment (also
ratified in 1913) provided for the popular election of United States
Senators; the Eighteenth (1919) later repealed by the Twenty-first
(1933), prohibited the manufacture, sale, or transportation of intoxi-
cating liquors in the United States; the Nineteenth (1920) extended
suffrage rights to women; the Twentieth (1933) altered the inaugura-

tion dates of the President and Vice-President and the time for convening Congress; the Twenty-second (1951) limited the time that a person might serve as President; the Twenty-third (1961) made provisions for the inhabitants of the District of Columbia (which is the geographic site of Washington and is not incorporated in any state) to vote in presidential elections, and the Twenty-fourth (1964) prohibited the states from requiring the payment of poll taxes as a qualification for voting in the election of national officials.

As integral parts of the Constitution, the amendments have had an influence on American public life equivalent to that of any other part of the document. Perhaps the most striking feature of the amendments considered as a bloc has been their effect in democratizing political practice. Leaving aside such items as the great social experiment of prohibition (a conspicuous failure) and one or two other amendments which were neutral in this respect, all of the amendments except the Twenty-second seem to have had a direct or indirect democratizing tendency. The expansions of suffrage, the direct election of Senators, the protection of individual rights, the social and economic implications of the graduated income tax, and even the adjustments in presidential elections and the dates of assuming office have all made some contribution to the conception of a government resting on as broad a basis of popular responsibility as possible.

Of course, after nearly 175 years of national experience the Constitution is infinitely more than the original written body and its 24 formal amendments. The Constitution consists of the vast body of practice which has grown up in connection with the attempted application of its sweeping contents. The small number of amendments which have been appended to it is in itself a testimony to its flexibility as an instrument. Each branch of the national government has made some contribution to the expansion of the Constitution's meaning as it has been applied to successive ranges of problems confronting the nation. Custom and usage have brought about other practices, such as the political parties system which, even though unmentioned in the document itself, is no less a constitutional instrument than other institutions which owe their existence to the words of the document. Up to this point an attempt has been made to present the Constitution in a general way by outlining the conditions under which it came into existence, suggesting the complexities of its sources and influences, and briefly relating the interplay of its essential parts. The succeeding chapters consider in detail the basic law's various institutions, their functions, their limits, and something of their relations to one another. And both logic and experience indicate that the appropriate place to begin is with the legal guardian of the Constitution.

QUESTIONS FOR FURTHER DISCUSSION

1. To what extent are the political ideas behind the Declaration of Independence and the Articles of Confederation antithetical to those embodied in the Constitution, and to what extent are they complementary?
2. How well has the Beard thesis on the economic basis of the Constitution stood up to contemporary historical criticism?
3. At one time it was fashionable to refer to the unwritten British Constitution as "flexible" and to the written American Constitution as "rigid." Is this distinction valid?
4. What are the major ways in which the Constitution has become increasingly democratized since its inception?
5. Some of the recommendations for revising the Constitution have stressed the need for unifying the branches of government in a manner characteristic of the British Cabinet system. Is this feasible?

II

The Supreme Court and the Constitution

THE AMBIVALENCE OF JUDICIAL POWER

Immediately across the plaza behind the Capitol in Washington, D.C. there stands, in ponderous classical architecture, the building which houses the United States Supreme Court. The physical relation of the two buildings is altogether appropriate because in an almost literal sense the Court stands behind the government as guardian of the Constitution or, as one writer has put it, as the keeper of the Covenant. Although the draftsmen of the constitutions of other modern national states have used the Court's organization and function as models for their own supreme constitutional courts, the combined juridical and political role of the Supreme Court has never been successfully duplicated. Like the other institutions of American government, the Court's political influence has waxed and waned in relation to the other two branches; its conception of its own responsibilities has altered from time to time, and its interpretation of constitutional powers and limitations has fluctuated within widely separated extremes. Despite these seeming inconsistencies the Court has at all times served as surrogate for the ancient governmental principle of the "rex" in American life. The "rex" was a permanent representative of the moral order who acted as an intercessor and counselor for the "dux" or authoritative ruler. Withdrawn from the tumult of public affairs and dedicated to contemplation, the "rex" was able to provide guidance and stability to the ruler beset by necessities for action. The Court does much the same thing; it does not initiate action (at least in the direct sense in which the Congress and the President do), it always frames its pronouncements in terms of the Constitution as Covenant, it exerts its main force through its superior grasp of the mysteries of the Constitution, and its decisions are reached in the solitude of monastic confinement rather than in the public halls of state or in the market place. Although the Court has often been accused of violating its trust by enunciating a false morality or by conferring legitimacy on actions that threaten to destroy blessings conferred on the righteous, its prestige has been maintained remarkably well and its place in American political life has been so firmly fixed that it is difficult to imagine the system at work without it.

The Court's role is often treated as dominant in American political life; and if the notion of an institutionalized "legal sovereign" (as a supplement to popular sovereignty) is not obsolete, the Court can plausibly lay claim to this position. As the late Chief Justice Charles Evans Hughes said, "We live under a Constitution, but the Constitution is what the Supreme Court says it is." A great many people inside the United States and most outside observers are puzzled by the enigma of apparent judicial supremacy in a government widely regarded as a prototype of democracy. Even though the extent of the Court's capacity to forestall popular action is frequently overemphasized, its power is formidable. Shortly after the turn of the twentieth century Justice John Marshall Harlan, a judicial figure whose notoriety was less than that of several of his fellow justices who were his inferiors in legal talent, said that ". . . the power of the Court, for good or evil, can scarcely be exaggerated. If it cannot actually shape the destiny of our country, it can exert a commanding influence in that direction. It can by its judgments strengthen our institutions in the confidence and affections of the people, or, more easily than any other department, it can undermine the foundations of our governmental system."

An explanation of the Court's evolution to the place ascribed to it by Justice Harlan cannot be made on the basis of the initial reception of the institution into American government or in terms of the Constitutional provisions for it. In the late eighteenth century eminent figures could decline to serve on the Court or resign from it out of concern for the presumed inconsequence of the post or the loss of status entailed by incumbency. Thus Robert Hanson Harrison was appointed by Washington and confirmed by the Senate, but preferred instead to retain his position as Chancellor of the Maryland state court system; and John Rutledge resigned after two years as Associate Justice to become Chief Justice of the Supreme Court of South Carolina, although he returned to the United States Supreme Court in 1795 as Chief Justice. Despite the fact that other figures of distinction were willing to serve on the Court, even to the point of seeking appointment, the judicial quiescence of the early period seemed calculated to bear out Montesquieu's definition of the position of this branch when he said, "The national judges are no more than the mouth that pronounces the words of the law, mere passive beings, incapable of moderating either its force or rigour." Hamilton underscored this view in the *Federalist*, even while he was arguing for judicial review, by insisting that the ". . . judiciary has neither force nor will, merely judgment." And he was confirmed in the argument by Chief Justice John Marshall, who of all the Supreme Court Justices in American history did most to refute in practice these supposedly inherent limits on the power of the courts. Marshall pointed out that the "Courts are the mere instruments of the law and can will nothing. . . . Judicial power is never exercised for the purpose of giving effect to the will of the Judge; always for the purpose of giving effect to the will of the Legislature; or in other words, to the will of the law." About the only adventurous move by the Supreme Court during its first decade was taken in *Chisholm* v. *Georgia* (1793), in which the Court (in compliance with the language of the Constitution) accepted jurisdiction in a suit brought against a state by an individual from another state. The reaction was swift; the Eleventh Amendment was adopted to prohibit extension of the judicial power of the United States to suits brought against a state by citizens of another state or subjects of a foreign state. The assumption of the Court's full role as constitutional arbiter did not occur until the political situation and personalities combined in a manner that enabled the Court to expand its own powers while simultaneously broadening the meaning of the Constitution.

If the view of the function and powers of the judicial branch that prevailed in the late eighteenth century did little to enhance the Court's powers, neither does the content of the judiciary article of the Constitution. The article is attenuated; although it establishes a "judicial power of the United States," the Supreme Court is the only federal court specifically provided for and even its detailed organization is left to Congress. According to the Constitution, judges of the Supreme Court and inferior federal courts hold office during good behavior; and although the jurisdiction of federal courts is broadly defined, it is not made exclusive. Thus the organization of the entire system of inferior courts, the regulation of most of the jurisdiction of the federal courts, and even the number and qualifications of the justices on the Supreme Court are subject to congressional enactment. Although the life tenure of judges may act as a restraining factor, Congress could conceivably abolish the entire system of lower federal courts; and in other ways might act to limit the role of these courts or enhance the functions of state courts at their expense. Even today a cursory appraisal of the appropriate provisions of the Constitution and the legislation affecting the federal court system will yield little insight into the place of the courts—and especially the Supreme Court—in American political life.

ORGANIZATION AND JURISDICTION OF THE FEDERAL COURTS

The contemporary federal court system varies in its details from the original establishment in the Judiciary Act of 1789, but the essential outlines remain the same. It consists of three tiers of courts: the lower courts of original jurisdiction known as the federal district courts; the middle-level Courts of Appeal which have only appellate jurisdiction; and, at the apex of the entire structure, the Supreme Court of the United States. In addition there are certain federal "Legislative Courts" whose specialized jurisdiction is not pertinent to this discussion. Altogether there are 91 United States District Courts (including those in federal territories other than the states) with the number of judges varying from district to district in terms of case loads and other factors. In most cases these courts sit in divisions with a single judge presiding, but in some cases—notably when the constitutionality of a state or federal law has been challenged—a three-judge panel is mandatory. Only recently the pressure of litigation caused Congress to apportion a sizeable number of new judgeships among the districts, bringing the total to more than 300. There are 11 Courts of Appeal in the United States; 10 cover circuits (geographical divisions) in the states and territories and 1 handles appellate work in the District of Columbia. The Courts of Appeal also vary in numerical composition; in some types of appeals a single judge hears the case, most cases require three judges, and in a few instances all of the judges in the circuit sit *en banc*. A Supreme Court Justice is still formally assigned to each circuit, although this is largely a vestige of the period prior to 1891 when the Justices actually rode circuit as members of the old Circuit Courts. Since 1869 the Supreme Court has been composed of a Chief Justice and eight Associate Justices, although prior to that time the number of justices had varied from as few as five (the original number was six) to as many as ten in accordance with the original congressional act.

As outlined in the Constitution the jurisdiction of federal courts falls into two broad classes. One class relates to the character of the cause—that is to say, the law to be enforced—and the other class depends on the nature of the parties to the case. The first embraces cases involving so-called "federal questions"; specifically these are suits arising over issues affected by the Constitution, laws of Congress, treaties entered into by the United States, and admiralty and maritime jurisdiction. The second or "parties" class extends to cases involving ambassadors, other public ministers and consuls; controversies in which the United States is a party; and certain "diversity" cases such as those between states, and between citizens of different states. Cases involving a federal question (as well as the smaller number of "parties" cases), whether of a civil or criminal nature, may originate in a United States District Court. Congress has not, however, drawn a complete line between the jurisdiction of federal courts and that of the state courts in regard to matters of federal concern, so many cases involving federal issues are still heard in state courts. Congress has provided, for example, that diversity of citizenship cases (including corporations as "citizens") involving less than $10,000 shall be tried in state courts. Furthermore, while Congress has established exclusive jurisdiction of federal courts over cases involving federal criminal law, suits in which the federal or state government is a party (except for suits between state governments and their own citizens), admiralty and maritime cases, and suits under patent, copyright, and bankruptcy statutes, other types of federal cases may be tried either in federal or state courts. In cases in which a federal issue is raised during the course of a hearing in a state court it is usually possible to "remove" the litigation from the state court to the federal district court in the area.

The United States Courts of Appeal have no original jurisdiction; the cases that they hear are mainly appeals from the District Courts within their respective circuits. They also handle appeals from certain administrative tribunals, especially those that fall into the category of independent regulatory commissions (e.g., the Interstate Commerce Commission) which have quasi-judicial competence in exercising their powers of administrative regulation. Technically speaking, a Court of Appeals is supposed to review only the legal aspects of a case and not the findings of fact made by the District Court or the administrative tribunal. The distinction is a difficult if not impossible one to maintain, so in practice a broad power of adjudicatory supervision over the lower federal courts and administrative agencies rests with the Courts of Appeal.

Almost all federal cases are finally disposed of in the District Courts; of the remainder the overwhelming proportion are brought to a conclusion in the appropriate Court of Appeals. The remaining cases, however, reach the United States Supreme Court; and, although these represent a small part of the total litigation in the United States, they are by all odds the most important in determining the general configuration of the public law (and thus the public policy) of the United States. The Supreme Court has a narrow area of original jurisdiction marked out for it by the Constitution. Today that jurisdiction is largely restricted to suits between states and suits between the United States and a state, and these types of cases are comparatively few. The overwhelming proportion of Supreme Court cases are appellate. Depending on the nature of the issue, appeals to the Supreme Court may come from the highest court in a state, from a United States District Court, from a United States Court of Appeals, or from a specialized "legislative" court. At one time the Supreme Court had very little control over the types of appeals it would hear; gradually, however, the right of appeal was restricted so that the Court now has a considerable discretion in choosing the cases it will accept on appeal. The types of appeals in which Supreme Court jurisdiction is mandatory by act of Congress are: (1) cases in which a Court of Appeals holds a state statute to be in violation of the United States Constitution, laws, or treaties; (2) cases in which a federal District Court or Court of Appeals holds an act of Congress to be unconstitutional; (3) cases in which the highest court of a state declares a federal law or treaty unconstitutional or sustains a state law which has been substantially challenged as being in conflict with the United States Constitution, laws, or treaties (allowable *appeals* from state supreme courts never go to the other federal courts, but always directly to the Supreme Court); and (4) cases in which a Court of Appeals "certifies" a question of law to the Supreme Court, usually concerning an issue which has been ruled on differently in two circuits and on which there is no definite Supreme Court holding. Even in some of these appeals the Court has a measure of discretion which is based on the concept that a "substantial" federal question must be involved for the appeal to be compulsory. In other suits, it is possible for a litigant who has received an adverse decision in the lower court to petition the Supreme Court to review the case on the grounds that a federal question of substance is involved. If the Court decides that there is a valid reason for intervening (for example, if the case is one of considerable import on which there is no authoritative doctrine) it may grant a writ of *certiorari,* which has the effect of calling the case up to the Supreme Court for hearing and decision. Rarely are more than 10 to 15 percent of the requests for *certiorari* accepted by the Supreme Court, and the Court cannot order a case to be placed on its list of cases to be heard on its own motion.

The Supreme Court sits each year from October through the following June; occasionally the session will be extended, and in rarer instances a special session may be held. For two weeks of each month about four hours a day are given to hearing oral arguments in the cases on the Court's docket (the printed briefs are filed long before the suit is scheduled for hearing). Oral arguments are normally limited to one hour for each side, and the counsel for the litigants must be prepared to undergo stringent questioning by the Justices, who face them across the bench where they sit in black-robed dignity on their high-backed leather chairs. After two weeks of argument, which may involve some 15 to 20 cases, the Court recesses for two weeks to deliberate on the accumulated issues and to write opinions. Beyond some formal aspects of the procedure little is known about what transpires in the closed meetings of the Court. The Court holds a conference to discuss the cases before it at the end of every week. After each Justice has expressed his views, or "recited," a poll is taken with the Justices voting in reverse order of seniority. From the scanty evidence available it seems reasonable to conjecture that the discussions in these conferences reach a higher level of debate on fundamental questions than is achieved in any other institution of American government.

Following the ascertainment of the majority position on the issues before it, the Chief Justice assumes responsibility for writing the opinion of the Court on the case, or assigns this duty to another Justice. Since unanimous decisions are the exception rather than the rule, dissenting opinions may also be written. Dissent performs a variety of functions in the judicial process; it may herald a future doctrinal position of the Court, open new vistas of the law, or simply indicate the breadth of the issues that have to be taken into consideration in dealing with the problems of a viable political system. Paradoxical as it may seem, dissenting opinions do not detract from the force of the Court's decisions. Instead they seem to have infused a substantial measure of vitality into the whole judicial process by indicating that even though a positive and binding affirmation has been made, the work of shaping the public law is never completed. In some cases Justices may agree with the majority decision but differ with the grounds of that decision as expressed in the opinion; in such instances a separate concurring opinion may be forthcoming. The opinions are delivered orally (Monday is "opinion day") and later published in the *United States Reports*. The pronouncements of the majority of the Court on basic legal issues are controlling throughout the entire American court system.

Above all else, the currently prevailing decisions reported by the Supreme Court are the source of the law of the American Constitution. Professor Corwin, in the introduction to the most recent edition of the annotated *Constitution of the United States* (1953), has expressed this principle as follows:

> As employed in this country, Constitutional Law signifies a body of rules resulting from the interpretation by a high court of a written constitutional instrument, in the course of disposing of cases in which the validity, in relation to the constitutional instrument, of some act of governmental power, State or National, has been challenged. This function, conveniently labelled "Judicial Review," involves the power and duty on the part of the Court of pronouncing void any such act which does not square with its own reading of the constitutional instrument.

It is conceivable, of course, that the United States might have allowed the Constitution to be adapted through a combination of usage and congressional interpretations in a manner paralleling the development of the Conventions of the Constitution and statutory enactments that have constitutional status in Britain. In point of fact the American Constitution has evolved much of its contemporary meaning in precisely these ways, but any expansion by usage or by ordinary law remains subject to the power of the Court to grant or withhold its sanction where the exercise of the resulting authority is challenged in a case before it. An understanding of American constitutional practice depends on a grasp of the underlying factors which have given rise to the Court's function in constitutional interpretation and of the uses which have been made of it.

DISTRICT COURTS

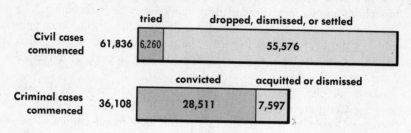

	tried	dropped, dismissed, or settled
Civil cases commenced	61,836	6,260	55,576

	convicted	acquitted or dismissed
Criminal cases commenced	36,108	28,511	7,597

COURTS OF APPEALS

Appeals from lower courts   3,692

Appeals from administrative boards   1,024

Original proceedings   107

SUPREME COURT

Cases disposed   2,142

     1,922   By dismissal or denial

     220   By adjudication

Numbers of Cases in the Federal Courts in 1962. *Source: Statistical Abstract of the U.S., 1963, pp. 157–160.*

AMERICAN POLITICS AND THE COURTS

At least four distinctive features of the American political heritage have influenced the position of the Court in relation to the Constitution. These are the reception of the common law, the production of a written Constitution, federalism, and accession to the Supreme Court of certain great figures who created for it a dynamic role in the life of the nation through the enunciation of doctrines such as judicial review. The effects of these influences are cumulative rather than independent, although it seems certain that the first three are ancillary to the final one.

The early emigrants took the English common law with them to the American colonies and adapted it to their local needs. For a time it appeared that there might be a move in the direction of a codified law, but the strong appeal to common-law rights by James Otis in the arguments against the Writs of Assistance in 1761 and the other evocations of common-law doctrines in the struggle against the King and Parliament which led to independence greatly strengthened the tradition in America. Furthermore, since the Americans lacked a direct voice in Parliament, they could appeal to the famous *dictum* enunciated in 1610 by Coke in Bonham's case: ". . . when an act of Parliament is against common right and reason . . . the common law will control it and adjudge such act to be void." This doctrine had been vigorously repudiated by the British Parliament because, as one commentator put it, the British were not prepared to surrender the supremacy of Parliament (in 1610 merely an incipient supremacy) to the supremacy of lawyers. But in colonial America judicial review was on the side of *vox populi* and thus attained a status as a defense against tyranny that was not possible in a society in which parliamentary representation was evolving as the ultimate answer to the problem of responsible government. In this connection it is interesting to note that in the early nineteenth century the democratically inclined Jeffersonians (or at least some of them) demanded alteration of the legal system when a conservative Supreme Court appeared to them to be reading common-law doctrines of property and commercial contract into the Constitution for the benefit of supporters of the defeated Federalist party.

In the enhanced form given it by the adoption of Coke's position on judicial review, the common law survived and made its own contribution to the placing of "Court over Constitution." As heavily judge-influenced, if not entirely judge-made, law operating in a society that is highly legalistic in its political practice, the common law has played a considerable part in enlarging the prestige of the judiciary as a conservator of the law. In addition, the concept of a law broadening down from precedent to precedent lays stress on the experimental as the life of the law and thus provides a useful balance between tradition (which an emerging national state badly needed) and the dynamism through which new law could be made to fit the needs of a "new" and self-consciously progressive society. The availability of such a legal tradition and the extension of its method to the area of constitutional interpretation has helped to make a seemingly rigid Constitution flexible; the Constitution could be, as it is, innured as a traditional symbol and at the same time adaptable as an instrument.

The existence of a fixed legal document—a written Constitution—as the basic or superior law was also destined to enlarge the judicial role. Instead of attempting to regulate politics through a hallowed traditional practice, the rules were established in a precise legal form. What, then, could be more fitting than that lawyers (and in the common-law tradition, the highest rank of lawyers—judges) should interpret and apply the rules? The judges have benefited, too, from the sanctification of the Constitution as a symbol. Since the oracle speaks through them and since their calling requires both a mastery of legal technique and special admission to the professional cult, their investiture of office is an impressive one. The legalistic character of so much of American government derives in no small part from this experience. Americans are accustomed when confronted with political problems, whether great or small, to ask first not "What should we do?" but rather "What can we do?" Response to practical questions in terms of what is inside and what is outside the law is pronounced in America. Such an attitude undoubtedly has had a stabilizing effect in disseminating the notion of the rule of law and in establishing an implicit consensus. But justification through law is no substitute for the assumption of moral responsibility in either individual or nation, for the law can be bent to many purposes. Because the Supreme Court exercises a policy influence that has no equivalent in other judicial bodies, its findings are subject to much the same type of attacks that the disgruntled constantly level against the so-called "political branches." It therefore needs all the prestige generated by the legal tradition to maintain a position which has implications far beyond the strictly legal functions of the normal court.

Federalism further complicates the interrelation between law and politics in the United States. Federalism represents the quintessence of constitutional legalism because the formulation of the principle rests on the attempt to divide (by precise definition) the sum of legitimate governmental powers into approximately equal shares and to apportion these shares of potential authority geographically. An abstractly contrived federal constitution (even one with a considerable base in experience) demands a final arbiter on the practical questions arising from rival claims to power by state and nation. The framers of the Constitution recognized this problem and discussed judicial review as a means of securing the conformity of state constitutions and laws to the Constitution of the United States as "the supreme law of the land." The first Congress, in fact, proceeded to write into the Judiciary Act of 1789 a specific provision conferring power on the Supreme Court of the United States to review and invalidate state actions conflicting with legitimate exercises of powers under the United States Constitution. That power has never been effectively challenged, although from time to time state legislatures have passed resolutions which purport to "interpose" state sovereignty between the Court and the state legislation which it has voided. The most recent examples of interposition are those passed in various southern states against the Court's holdings in the school desegregation cases. The utility of interposition lies entirely in its function as a catharsis for the frustrations of local politicians; its legal standing is nonexistent. While some students of constitutional law might take exception to the broad language of Mr. Justice Holmes when he said that he did not ". . . think the United States would come to an end if we [the Supreme Court] lost . . . power to declare an Act of Congress void," few would fail to concur in his judgment that ". . . the Union would be imperiled if . . . [the Court] could not make that declaration as to the laws of the several States." Given the nature and condition of the federal union, however, could anyone doubt that the clear case for judicial review of state legislation would be used as an example in support of judicial review of congressional acts?

The foregoing elements of the American system lend support to the abstract idea that the courts have a policy as well as a juridical function; in the struggle for partisan advantage the adversaries have turned this potential into actuality. And in this context the human element becomes dominant in shaping the political institutions to the service of particular ends. In the absence of great figures on the bench the political branches might have been accepted as the interpreters of their own powers under the Constitution, guided, of course, by the type of party instrumentalities created for public control of these agencies. Given the divisive forces in American life, the absence of the Court's influence in helping to create a sacerdotal function for the Constitution might have led to the fulfillment of Jefferson's desire for a new Constitution in each generation. Paradoxically, the type of partisanship in which the Court has indulged from time to time has increased the tenacious hold that the Constitution as symbol has had on the minds of the American people.

Although many illustrious names appear on the list of Justices who have occupied places on the highest bench, Chief Justice John Marshall deserves special recognition for his achievement in inaugurating the Court as at least a partner, if not in some ways the "legal" superior of the other branches. Marshall served as Chief Justice from 1801 to 1835, during which time he was responsible for many doctrines that enhanced the Court's position. Above all else, however, looms his opinion in *Marbury* v. *Madison* (1803), the most famous case in American jurisprudence. In that case the Court undertook to apply the principle of judicial review to an act of Congress. The facts behind the suit were disarmingly simple: William Marbury was one of a number of "midnight appointments" (Marshall's own appointment as Chief Justice was another) made by retiring President John Adams, literally on the eve of Jefferson's inauguration in March, 1801. In the haste of evacuation of offices some of the commissions appointing 42 new Justices of the Peace for the District of Columbia were not delivered. Acting under Jefferson's orders, the new Secretary of State, James Madison, refused to deliver the commissions. As one of the disappointed nominees, Marbury brought suit in the Supreme Court in the form of an application for a writ of mandamus against Madison to force delivery of the commission. In his wide-ranging opinion Marshall was forceful in proclaiming Marbury's right to his commission and in supporting the legal remedy of mandamus as the proper corrective for the failure of an administrative official to perform his duty. But he went on to point out that the Supreme Court was given original jurisdiction by the Constitution only in enumerated types of cases and that Congress had no discretionary power to extend this original jurisdiction. The Court therefore had no power to issue the requested writ and section 13 of the Judiciary Act of 1789 (which authorized the Supreme Court to issue writs of mandamus in an original proceeding) was declared unconstitutional.

To say that this was a political decision is grossly to understate the case. Marshall went out of his way to chastize the executive and to assert the power of the Court over Congress in the area of constitutional interpretation. From the standpoint of avoiding devastating political repercussions, however, Marshall had one great strategic advantage on his side: the provision declared unconstitutional was one in which Congress had attempted to bestow a power upon the judiciary itself rather than one which conferred additional power upon the executive or asserted a new power on behalf of Congress. This apparent act of self-immolation served to divert attention from the larger act of constitutional self-aggrandizement implied in the assumption by the Court of the power of judicial review. The logical alternative would have been to dispose of the case simply on the grounds that the Court lacked jurisdiction in the suit at hand because it was empowered to issue writs of mandamus only in cases which were brought before it on proper appeal or in conformity with the Constitution's authorization of original jurisdiction. In point of fact, one of the cardinal principles that the Court later came to apply as part of its practice of judicial restraint is that an act will not be voided if it can possibly be construed to conform to the Constitution. Congress itself later cured the Judiciary Act by stipulating that the writ could be issued by the Court in cases arising under its specified original jurisdiction. To have taken a course that led to the preservation of the Act, however, would have been to miss a golden opportunity to strike a blow from the stronghold of the Federalist party—the judiciary—at the executive and legislative branches, which since 1800 had been in the hands of what to the Federalists were the dangerously radical Jeffersonian Republicans. Marshall could at once instruct the lower courts in their future duty (mandamus *was* pronounced to be the appropriate legal remedy), in effect accuse the executive of nonfeasance (it was clearly asserted that Jefferson and Madison were wrong to withhold the commissions), and put Congress on notice that the Court stood as constitutional guarantor against any popularly radical uses of its power. All this could be done, too, in a decision on an issue which was unlikely to produce an all-out political offensive against the judicial branch. Nothing dear to the cause of the Federalists was sacrificed except Marbury's interest in a minor judicial post.

The Court's action in Marbury, then was part of a larger struggle that was taking place in the national political arena. The antagonists had arranged themselves into two great opposing factions or parties; the ultimate prize was the right to determine the nature of the Union, and the immediate object was to establish control over the reading of the rules of the competition as laid down by the Constitution. The Jeffersonians had won a great popular victory in 1800. In terms of a policy mandate they were committed to a strict construction of the Constitution (i.e., to placing a severe limitation on the exercise of national power), to decentralization (with a primary emphasis on states' rights), to an economy basically agrarian, and to localized democracy. The Federalists had a substantially different vision of the Union; their view was nationalist and therefore depended for its fulfillment on a broad construction of the Constitution in order that national power and commercial and industrial wealth might be erected into mutual supports. For the first 12 years of the Constitution's history the Federalists were in power, and during most of that time the administrative genius of Alexander Hamilton was applied toward what he regarded as the complementary objectives of national power and governmentally assisted economic self-sufficiency. When the Federalists were deposed they were still able to retain some measure of influence through control of the demonstrably weak judicial branch in a checked and balanced government. As Jefferson put it, "The Federalists have retired into the Judiciary as a stronghold, and from that battery all the works of republicanism are to be beaten down and erased." John Marshall, whose opinions so fully reflected the fiscal and governmental doctrines of Hamilton (his justification of judicial review in Marbury is nearly a verbatim repetition of Hamilton's argument in the *Federalist*), was to strengthen the position of the Court to the precise degree necessary to prevent a radical reversal of the national direction set by the Federalists.

The assumption of the power of judicial review was the most dramatic move of the Court in the expansion of its own influence, and indeed its political effects were so pronounced that no other act of Congress was invalidated until the *Dred Scott* decision of 1857. But the interpretative possibilities of the Court were far from exhausted by a single act of self-aggrandizement. Marshall found ample opportunity to dogmatize

Hamiltonian principle in his exegesis of the Constitution. Hamilton had scoffed at laissez-faire as an economic policy (laissez-faire was closely associated with physiocratic localism and democracy in eighteenth- and early nineteenth-century America), and relied on his special version of mercantilism for the erection of a great national power. Only a strong and active central government could provide the conditions and the direct support necessary for the development of a balanced, self-sufficient economy; nor could a great state be brought into being without commercial and industrial superiority. Marshall systematized this doctrine in a series of decisions which expanded national powers, sustained specific aspects of Hamiltonian mercantilism, and severely limited the power of the states to regulate commercial activities in the public interest.

Although they do not exhaust the sources used by Marshall, the clause giving Congress power to make all the laws "necessary and proper" to the execution of its specified powers, the extension to Congress of the authority to regulate interstate and foreign commerce, and the provision denying the states the power to pass laws impairing the obligation of contracts provided the principal constitutional foundations for Hamiltonian concepts. In *McCulloch* v. *Maryland* (1819), the National Bank (a joint venture in the creation and control of credit on the part of government and private investors which was one of the essential elements in Hamilton's program) was held to be a valid function of the national government as part of its "implied powers" under the "necessary and proper" clause. As such the notes issued by the Bank were immune from state taxation. In *Gibbons* v. *Ogden* (1824), the Court broadened the meaning of the interstate commerce clause to the point of allowing Congress to govern all intercourse that concerned more than one state. The immediate result of the decision was to confer a right on shippers (under the National Coasting License Act) to use all internal navigable waters free of state regulation. In the *Dartmouth College Case* (1819), Marshall applied the limitation of the contract clause with such rigidity as to deny the state of New Hampshire the power to alter the terms of a royal charter antedating independence. And such was his concern for protection of "vested interests" against the depredations of state government that in *Fletcher* v. *Peck* (1810), Marshall prevented the state of Georgia from rescinding the sale of 35 million acres of public land even though the transaction had been fraudulently perpetrated.

The Marshall Court made a permanent impression on the American governmental system. Some of its effects seem quite clear and others may only be conjectured, but it is difficult to pass judgment on any of them except through the perspective of the observer's predisposition toward certain governmental forms, practices, and policies. At their best, the visions of hindsight are ambiguous because so many features of the system are products of contingencies whose full implications could not have been foreseen while under development.

In creating a more influential political role for the Court, Marshall certainly contributed to the legalistic bent of American government and thereby narrowed the possibility that the exercise of political power might become entirely dependent on the operation of the party system. However, there are other constitutional obstacles in the way of a full growth of party responsibility in America, so it does not appear any more accurate to say that the Supreme Court holds its special position because of the weaknesses of the national party structures than it does to say that party organization and influence continue to be incoherent and diffused because the Court can ultimately turn any political decision into a legal one.

Similarly, in its expansion of the Constitution's meaning to extend broad powers to the national government, the Marshall Court certainly was perpetuating Federalist policy when popular support had shifted to the opposition and its policies. In doing so there is no denying that the Court was presiding over the merger of the Constitution, nationalism (as opposed to states-rights localism), and mercantilist (i.e., government supported) capitalism, without much regard to popular political processes. Yet in historical perspective it is easy to see that the establishment of extensive national powers—in contrast to the strict construction and narrow localism of the Jeffersonians—was essential to the evolution of the great national state that America has become. Furthermore, the broadening of the meaning of interstate commerce, the development of the doctrine of implied congressional powers, and the flexible reading of other parts of the Constitution have opened the way to popularly based governmental action to control the abuses of private economic power. They have also led to a conception of the general welfare that is not based solely on the increase of wealth without regard to its distribution and use. Most of the programs that are now subsumed by the term "welfare state," such as the social security system, the social welfare program, public housing, legislation regulating conditions of employment and wages and hours of labor, and public health measures, owe their constitutional justification to the principle of broad construction. The fact that the Court was slow to apply the principle in a manner conducive to the realization of these programs does not impair its utility for adapting an eighteenth-century constitutional order to twentieth-century demands.

Even in its early ventures in restricting state powers in order that vested economic interests might be free of local regulation while enjoying the benefits of national assistance, the Court was creating a precedent for constitutional restraints on state action that could later be used for different—and some would argue, more valid—purposes. If national powers and direct constitutional restraints could be used to stay the hands of the local units when they were the only agencies that could muster the will and machinery to regulate economic power, a later set of judges could undertake to enforce restraints on state police powers when they were used to deprive individuals of fundamental human rights guaranteed by the Constitution.

In 1835 Marshall was succeeded as Chief Justice by Roger B. Taney, a thoroughgoing Jacksonian Democrat. Although neither the political role which Marshall had done so much to develop for the Court nor the trend toward nationalizing the Constitution could be radically reversed, the policy orientation of the Court was at long last compatible with the political trend of the country, and the thrust of its decisions reveals this situation clearly. The tortuous process of judicial accretion gradually brought to view three complementary tendencies of the Taney Court that bear on this point. One was the development of the notion of judicial self-restraint. In a number of decisions the Court found that the questions raised were nonjusticiable; that is, they were not controversies of a nature to permit settlement by the courts. The best known of these cases was *Luther* v. *Borden* (1849), in which certain types of issues (in this instance a controversy over the legitimate government of Rhode Island arising from the Dorr Rebellion) were declared to be "political decisions" properly belonging to Congress and therefore outside the sphere of the courts. A second doctrinal position of the Taney Court was the stress on the authority of the states in areas which under Marshall might have been held to intrude on federal power. And finally, a severe limit was placed on the claim to constitutional protection of vested property rights when they conflicted with a decision reached by popular processes.

The two latter positions are so closely related in their practical effects that they tend to merge in particular decisions of the Court. The main policy effect of this line of decisions was to open the way for local democratic action by removing some of the impediments that Marshall had erected against state action and to limit the possibility of special privilege in the interest of a real (rather than presumptive) laissez-faire competition. Taney was not a states-righter in order to prevent the exercise of national power, but one who recognized that in his era the scope of governmental responsibility, and therefore the possibility for popular action, was broader at the level of the states than it was in the national sphere. Although he did hold some national powers to be exclusive, he was not prepared to deny the states the power to regulate on the grounds that a specific national power (especially control of interstate commerce) constituted a barrier to such action, even in areas in which the power was not exercised by the central government. The classic example of the direction of the Taney Court is the *Charles River Bridge* case (1837), in which the Court upheld the power of the state of Massachusetts to permit the construction of a second, competing (and badly needed) toll bridge across the Charles River despite claims of the original company that its rights under the contract clause were being violated.

Just as the decisions of the Marshall Court had political ramifications that extended far beyond the immediate concern of those who made them, so did those of the Taney Court. If, for example, the judicial restraint imposed by the notion of a "political question" could be used to recuse the Court in the face of a popularly based decision in some cases, it was also applied (until overturned in the case of *Baker* v. *Carr* in March, 1962) to stay action by petitioners for judicial remedy against state legislative bodies which had wilfully refused to reapportion congressional and state legislative representation despite clear constitutional requirements that they do so. In a slightly different context, it might be pointed out that the Taney Court tended to uphold a laissez-faire economic policy against mercantilist tendencies when the former agreed with popular opinion in a predominantly agrarian economy. Later, however, the doctrine of noninterference furnished the basis for pejorative appeals against any attempt to control the social effects of industrialism, without much attention to the limitations imposed on free competition by business itself through the corporate device, market manipulation, and related practices. Finally, if states' rights was the major support of individual liberties and popularly based politics prior to the Civil War, changing circumstances and attitudes made it possible for this conception to be evoked as a barrier both to the full realization of civil liberties and to the effectuation of policies popularly endorsed by a national constituency.

Like the Marshall Court during the first third of the nineteenth century, the Supreme Court in the period following the Civil War was slow to adapt to the change in the political atmosphere. Until the death of Chief Justice Waite in 1888, the Taney position of judicial restraint may be said to have prevailed generally, although it was under attack from a substantial minority on the bench. The Court continued to allow broad scope for regulatory action and even acted to invigorate constitutional protections of individual rights, including those recently added by the Fourteenth and Fifteenth Amendments. But when the composition of the Court had changed sufficiently, its power was evoked to provide the final sanction against any political effort to interfere with the operation of the "natural order" of an industrial economy. Social Darwinism was read into the Constitution by the skillful readjustment of the recently added due process clause of the Fourteenth Amendment. The exercise of state police powers was narrowly restricted through the rigid application of the due process clause to the protection of property and by the doctrine of presumptive federal exclusiveness in the transitional zone of inter- and intrastate commerce. And when the corporations reached the point where their geographic and economic expansion placed them beyond the effective control of the state governments (even if the states had been allowed the scope to regulate) most national regulatory efforts were struck down or rendered nugatory. The principle of dual federalism (under which the reserved powers of the state governments were erected as barriers to otherwise constitutional federal legislation), strict construction of delegated federal powers, and the narrowest possible construal of congressional statutes were all brought into play. The use of these interpretative concepts, either singly or in combination, resulted in such actions as the invalidation of the federal income tax law; the emasculation of the Sherman Anti-Trust Act as a possible means for controlling corporation activities that restrained freedom of commerce while opening the way for the effective use of the Act against strikes and boycotts by labor organizations; and the mutilation of the powers of the Interstate Commerce Commission to regulate railroad rates. The application of rigid and mutually sustaining curbs on national and state powers produced the so-called "twilight zone" in which neither level of government could take effective political action involving substantial regulation of the private economy.

THE SHIFTING ROLE OF THE COURT

It is possible to argue that the Supreme Court was really in line with the controlling popular sentiment during this era of unimpeded capitalism. But it is more plausible to suggest that the Court was in the vanguard of the forces which determined the political character of the times. The period between Reconstruction (*circa* 1865 to 1876) and World War I was one of extremely close presidential elections and narrow party margins in Congress. It was also the age of reform, of locally-based radicalism and of the emergence of the Republican bargain with the southern Bourbon Democrats. Without the corrosive effects of the Court on the policy produced intermittently by various reform coalitions, both national and state, the popular basis of American politics might have been realigned well before Franklin Roosevelt managed the task in the 1930's.

With the collapse of the economy in 1929, followed by the sweeping victory of the New Deal Democrats in 1932, the differences between the political branches and the Court were unequivocally revealed. Not only had the economy broken down, but many of the myths which had reinforced the politics of "normalcy" were severely damaged in the process. The old politics of extreme sectionalism, judicial supremacy, and governmental quiescence were deluged in the demand for national action. The industrial order which pre-New Deal politics fostered so assiduously had produced an alteration in the social composition of the nation which was largely ignored by the Republican party. The country had become industrial, urban, and economically "nationalized." Franklin Roosevelt revitalized the popular support of the Democratic party on the basis of this change; many of the vestiges of sectionalism were submerged by the national coalition that he managed to effect among urban labor, the small farmer, and a sizeable segment of the white-collar class. Roosevelt's facility at popular, party, and congressional leadership enabled him to utilize this mass popular basis to secure a policy mandate for his experimental program to deal with both the short- and long-range social and economic problems that had been so dramatically revealed and intensified by the depression.

If Jefferson had reason to rail against the use of the judiciary to strike down the works of his administration, Roosevelt had far greater cause to do so. Prior to 1933 the Court had had 50 years of experience in the development of doctrines of governmental negativism, and it proceeded systematically to apply this experience in striking down New Deal legislation. Within a period of less than 18 months in 1935 and 1936 the Supreme Court ruled at least a dozen major statutes unconstitutional. This action is all the more striking when it is considered that in less than 100 cases have congressional acts been invalidated during the entire history of the Court, with nearly all of them occurring between 1887 and 1937. The opinions in the New Deal cases were based on the familiar grounds of dual federalism (intrusion of the federal government on the reserved powers of the states), a narrow interpretation of the commerce clause, and the resurrected doctrine of unconstitutional delegation of legislative powers to the executive. The latter two doctrines, for example, were applied in the *Schechter*, or so-called "sick chicken" case (1935) to invalidate the National Industrial Recovery Act, a statute which aimed at economic recovery of the entire industrial structure through a governmentally supervised program of "self-regulation" of business. In another basic area, Mr. Justice Roberts' complex opinion in *U. S.* v. *Butler* (1936) voided the Agricultural Adjustment Act, which attempted to regulate agricultural production through benefit payments for acreage reduction and to finance the payments with a tax on the processing of agricultural commodities. The grounds on which the decision was based were the federal invasion of the reserved powers of the states and the illegal regulation of agriculture under the guise of a tax. Other more narrowly based regulatory legislation, such as the Bituminous Coal Act, was struck down, and the line of decisions threatened to obliterate general social legislation such as the Social Security Act, the National Labor Relations Act, the Fair Labor Standards Act, and the Public Utilities Holding Company Act.

Following one of the most sweeping presidential and congressional election victories in American history in 1936, President Roosevelt decided to wage a head-on battle with the Court in order to ". . . save the Constitution from the Court and the Court from itself." In February, 1937, he provided for introduction of a bill reorganizing the judiciary.

The striking feature of the proposal was the "court-packing" provision which permitted a temporary enlargement of the Supreme Court to a maximum of 15 members by adding a Justice for each incumbent over the age of 70 who refused to retire. The bill produced one of the monumental struggles of American politics. Under the skillful direction of Mr. Justice Hughes, operating largely through the decimated Republican congressional delegation and a group of dissident Democrats, the Court managed to stave off the attack when the Senate Judiciary Committee reported the bill unfavorably in a document that took the President severely to task for his attack on constitutional instrumentalities. The outcome is an excellent illustration of the tenacity of the hold exerted by traditional political practices on the imagination of the American public. Despite one of his famous "fireside chats" on the subject and despite his unquestioned personal popularity and the undeniable public endorsement of his policies, Roosevelt was unable to convince the American public that the character of the contemporary Court was deliberately political and effectively directed against another major premise of the American political system—the doctrine of popular sovereignty.

But if the Court's victory over Roosevelt was a revealing one in terms of constitutional mythos, there was a pyrrhic quality about it. While the battle over the court bill was at its hottest the Court in a sense began its retreat on the judicial review front by sustaining the type of social legislation that it had earlier overruled. The closest approximation to a complete reversal was in *West Coast Hotel* v. *Parrish* (1937), in which a state minimum wage act was upheld despite the fact that less than a year earlier a similar statute had been voided. The change was not a temporary one. Following the defeat of the judiciary bill a chastened Supreme Court proceeded to reverse numerous earlier precedents in sustaining New Deal measures. The trend was so obvious and so far-reaching that Mr. Justice Roberts was led to note that the decisions of the Court were moving ". . . into the same class as a restricted railroad ticket, good for this day and train only." A short while after the defeat of the court-packing plan the "nine old men," or at least the majority group that had clung tenaciously to the economic tenets of the Gilded Age, were gone from the Court. The Court had won the engagement over judicial reorganization but it lost the war; or at best it managed a negotiated truce on the basis of heavy concessions.

Since 1937 the Court has continued to exercise a constraining power in relation to the policy institutions, but the power has been applied mainly to check these institutions when they threatened the constitutional guarantees of individual civil liberties rather than as a protection of property rights through a judicially-evolved economic policy. The Court has bowed to the popular will in not interfering unduly with the policy role of the Congress, the President, and the states in relation to the social and economic questions confronting them. At the same time the Court has concentrated on the prevention of arbitrary governmental intrusion on the fundamental freedoms of the First Amendment. The clearest development in defense of these rights has been made in relation to the power of the states. Well before the Court fight, as early as 1925 in *Gitlow* v. *New York*, the Court had begun (in a somewhat casual way) to incorporate the First Amendment freedoms into the due process clause of the Fourteenth Amendment in order to protect freedom of speech and press against impairment by the states. During the past two decades this incorporation has been greatly extended and the Court has broadened the "equal protection of the laws" clause, in the manner illustrated in the preceding chapter, as an important further support.

The Constitution is still one of limited and balanced powers, even to the extent of temporarily restraining local or national majorities under certain circumstances. And the Supreme Court is still an important balance wheel. Brilliant as it is both in phraseology and as a superficial explanation of the Court's ultimate susceptibility to the massive influence of the popular will, Mr. Dooley's well-known aphorism about the Supreme Court following the election returns is still exaggerated. Much to be preferred as an interpretation of the Court's position vis-a-vis the Constitution and American democracy is the inelegant proposition that the Court's true function is to allow time to appeal from the people drunk to the people sober. As the foregoing description indicates, the political branches and the American people have a variety of recourses against arbitrary powers of the Court; but the Court has its reciprocal checks, in the exercise of which Congress, the executive, and the public generally concur. In most respects the Court, in Mr. Justice Jackson's words, retains its position as "the keeper of the nation's conscience."

QUESTIONS FOR FURTHER DISCUSSION

1. The United States Supreme Court has been severely criticized by various segments of the society from time to time. How do you explain this situation in terms of the role of the Court?
2. How has the system of dual Courts (federal and state) complicated the process of adjudication in the United States?
3. What are the political implications of judicial review in America?
4. How does one justify the contemporary activism of the Court in the field of civil liberties and civil rights, and its self-restraint in the area of regulation of the economy?

III

The Role of the President

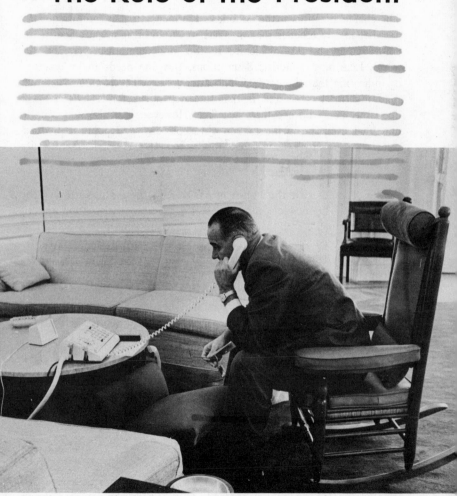

ORIGINS AND CONDITIONS
OF THE OFFICE

The characterization of the American Presidency that is more frequently heard than any other is that it is the most powerful single office in the contemporary world—at least in the noncommunist part of the world. Like most aphorisic descriptions, this one needs to be qualified by indicating that the power which attends the office is potential rather than institutionalized and is therefore dependent for its effective use upon the man who occupies the office. However, it is also pertinent to note that even for an incumbent whose personal and political predilections tend toward a constricted application of the potential authority of the Presidency, the office is still as exacting as any in modern constitutional government.

The demands that the Presidency makes on the man who holds the office and the tremendous potential that is latent in the position are not due simply to the fact that the President is the administrative head of one of the two overwhelmingly great powers in contemporary world politics, although this fact alone would have a considerable bearing on the question. It is rather that the general structure and mode of operation of American politics have thrust upon the presidential office a combination of functions and responsibilities that has no parallel in other constitutional democracies. And here is another contradiction similar to that presented by the United States Supreme Court, for the Presidency was not originally contemplated to be of such moment. The evolution of the office once more illustrates the adaptability of the Constitution to political experience; an apparently legally fixed institutional arrangement has been moulded to the exigencies of a changing society without doing violence to a persisting political tradition.

The American Presidency was brought into being under an ominous cloud of suspicion of executive power. Every suggestion favoring the creation of a vigorous executive power in the Convention was met by a counterargument against the dangers of incipient monarchy and the unwillingness of the public to accede to the establishment of a strong chief executive vested with independent powers. On five separate occasions the Convention voted for congressional appointment of the executive and there was a strong sentiment in favor of making the office a plural one. However, delegates such as James Wilson, Gouverneur Morris, Alexander Hamilton (who wanted an even stronger position than was established), and eventually James Madison maintained an unrelenting pressure on behalf of an independent, single-head agency which could operate, as Wilson put it, with "energy, dispatch and responsibility." On their side these advocates had the separation of powers principle as a bulwark against the subserviency of the institution to Congress. In addition, there were examples of effective offices of governor in states such as New York and Massachusetts. Furthermore, a certain disillusionment with popular legislative assemblies—reflecting the diffusion of their local constituencies and their lack of responsibility—was already setting in; the need for a focal point of national leadership was discerned. In fact, one of the main reasons for the Convention (although not always expressed as such) was the deficiency of administration both in the executory and the policy sense. It is not enough that a government be endowed with formal powers and that a system of public law reflecting these powers exists; the capacity to mould public policy from grants of authority and put the policy into effect must also be present.

The result of the Convention struggle was a settlement on certain basic features of the Presidency that have favored the development of the office to its contemporary position. At the same time, the establishment of most of the attributes of the office which favor a strong President had to be compensated by concessions to adamant opponents of executive power, and some of these compromises have profoundly affected the manner in which the position must be managed.

The first such feature of the office is that it is occupied by a single person. Many delegates wanted a plural executive as a protection against a possible trend in the direction of monarchy, but the issue was finally resolved in favor of a concentration of authority and responsibility, thus obviating any tendency towards a dispersal of the functions of the office or the differentiation of a multi-member administrative head into a cabinet-type executive. The qualifications set for the office are not stringent; in order to be President one must be a natural-born citizen of the United States, have attained a minimum age of 35 years, and have been a resident of the United States for 14 years. Although the qualifications of various presidential candidates have been quibbled over from time to time, no serious constitutional problems have been raised regarding the precise meaning of "natural-born" citizen or residence within the United States.

A second major characteristic of the Presidency that emerges from the constitutional arrangement is the manner of selection. This process, too, was a compromise. Although most Convention delegates opposed popular election, there was controversy over the form of indirect election to be used. Delegates who generally feared excessive power were anxious to maintain legislative control over the Presidency. Before the issue was finally settled the Convention voted on it some 30 times. As has been indicated the major objection to selection by Congress was the violation of the separation of powers principle, and the proponents of a strong executive did not believe that a President thus dependent on the Congress would be able to act with initiative and vigor. The method of selection that was settled upon was calculated to overcome objections from both sides. Electors equal in number to the state's Representatives and Senators in Congress were chosen in each state in a manner prescribed by the state legislature. These electors then met in their respective states, where each one voted for two candidates. The candidate who received the highest number of votes, provided it were a majority, was declared President; the candidate who was second in the electoral balloting would then become Vice-President. If no single person had a majority of the electoral ballots, but two or more candidates had a majority *and an equal number of votes* the United States House of Representatives would choose from among such candidates. If neither of these conditions for election were met, the House could choose the President from among the five candidates whose electoral votes were highest on the list. This complicated method afforded initial independence from Congress, in accordance with the demands of some delegates; at the same time it was indirect, decentralized, and provided for a secondary resort to congressional selection (which many who argued for a weak executive apparently felt would become the normal practice).

The system did not work as intended because the party system soon intruded. By the election of 1800 the Congress and the country as a whole were fairly sharply divided between the Federalists and the Jeffersonian Republicans. Through congressional caucuses operating under recognized party leadership, the Jeffersonians nominated their candidates for President and Vice-President and the Federalists did the same, with the result that the electors were chosen in each state on the basis of their adherence to one or the other of the party slates. Since all of the Republican electors voted for both Jefferson and Burr (nominated as Jefferson's Vice-President), these two candidates were tied and the tie had to be broken by the House of Representatives. The Federalists in the House attempted to thwart the aims of the Republicans by voting Burr into the Presidency instead of Jefferson. Largely through the good offices of Hamilton this maneuver was frustrated, and Jefferson was elected President. Shortly thereafter, the Twelfth Amendment was adopted to prevent a recurrence of this situation; it provided for electors to vote separately for the candidates for President and Vice-President. Under this Amendment the stipulation that a winning candidate must receive a majority of electoral ballots continues, and the House of Representatives still makes the selection from the three leading candidates if there is no electoral vote majority. The only presidential election in which the House has had to intervene since 1800 was in 1824, when it elected John Quincy Adams over Andrew Jackson, despite Jackson's electoral vote plurality and his clear popular victory in the states (about half of them) in which the electorate rather than the legislature chose presidential electors. In a number of other elections in which a strong third party was in contention the possibility has existed that the final decision might be thrown into the House of Representatives.

Although the effects of the method of electing the President will be considered more fully in the chapter on political parties, the procedure is such an enigma to casual outside observers that some of its main implications may be mentioned here. The most striking feature is the extent to which the operation of the party system has made the electoral college redundant and turned the Presidency into a national popularly based office. It was originally intended that the electors should be indirectly elected and that they should exercise independent judgment; moreover, it was expected that the decentralization of the electoral discussions would result in the choice of a President who would be free from local or national "factionalism" in a manner which comported with the ideal of national nonpartisanship. However, politics was not to be so easily detached from government as this mechanical arrangement implied. As indicated above, party nomination became the established order in 1800, and with the rise of the national nominating convention in the 1830s the basis of the nomination was broadened to include delegates from various local party constituencies. At the same time the election process gradually expanded until all of the states provided for popular choice of the electoral slate. Today each state party organization provides for the nomination of electors pledged to support its presidential and vice-presidential nominees, in practice the voters then vote for these electors as a bloc (in some states only the names of the nominees for President and Vice-President appear on the ballot, so the public is not even aware of the identity of the persons being chosen for the electoral college), and the total electoral vote of the state thus goes to the candidate of the party which receives a plurality of the popular votes. There is no doubt in the minds of the voters that they are participating directly in the election of a President and a Vice-President when they cast a party vote in this manner.

Despite the fact that certain refinements have been made in both the convention system and in the election process, and regardless of the fact that the presidential election has evolved from an indirect, highly dispersed method to a virtually direct popular decision that is national in scope, vestiges of the original intent are clearly present and exert important influences. The most conspicuous of these is the decentralized nature of the process, which plays an important role in both nomination and election of a President. The national party conventions are composed of delegations roughly equal in number to twice that of the electoral college (now consisting of 535 votes). Control of the approximately 1200 votes at the party convention is diffused among the party leaderships of the various states and territories from which the delegations are drawn. The delegates are selected in a variety of ways, depending usually on the state laws regulating the parties. In most instances, candidates for the delegation will be pledged to the support of a particular candidate for the party's presidential nomination, and in others, they will be unpledged.

In view of this situation, a prospective presidential candidate must make his bid for convention support to leaders of the state and local party organizations, to chairmen of state party committees, congressional district party committees, and municipal party committees in the larger cities. It is helpful, of course, if the candidate has a substantial national reputation, and it may benefit him to be a recognized leader among his colleagues if he is a Senator, but the success of his nomination campaign will ultimately depend less on these factors than on the impact that he makes on the cross section of localized political powers-that-be. That impact will depend on a variety of factors. Party leaders must be convinced, first of all, that the candidate can win and, secondly, that support of his candidacy will directly strengthen themselves and their organizations through future local elections and in terms of patronage. Out of these disparate elements a prospective presidential nominee must be able to form a coalition that will be large enough and will be sufficiently committed to make an impressive showing in the early convention balloting. It is preferable, of course, to amalgamate enough state delegations (or portions of them) to secure a majority, and therefore the nomination, on the first ballot. Since this is a rare feat, the conventions are often erratic and unpredictable; they have sometimes been described as a quadrennial form of American political madness. Usually one of the "favorites" will win the nomination, but in a few instances deadlocks among the stronger candidates will lead to the nomination of a "favorite son" (a man with strong backing in a single state) or even an outsider or "dark-horse" candidate. Perhaps the most notable instance of this was the Democratic Convention in 1924, which nominated John W. Davis after 103 ballots.

Even when the nomination has been secured, the success of the campaign is heavily dependent on the capacity to secure popular pluralities within enough states to win a majority of the electoral votes. This process demands great skill in holding together certain organizational and regional groupings that are heterogeneous to say the least, and occasionally are openly hostile to one another. Some accommodations of these diversities will already have been made in the convention. The vice-presidential nomination, for example, is not conceived so much as a selection of the potential successor to the President as it is a means of balancing the ticket. Thus if the presidential candidate is an easterner, it is desirable for the vice-presidential nominee to come from another region, and it is considered important also to offset the general political outlook of the prospective President with a running mate identified with a different point of view. Furthermore, it is recognized that convention campaign platforms are generalized to the point of meaninglessness in order to accommodate the spectroscopic makeup of American political parties, and that it will be necessary for the candidates to develop the pertinent issues during the course of the campaign. But such concessions to the appearance of party unity will not overcome the real differences within a party's ranks. Calculation of the forces that need to be appeased and persuaded in order to effect a winning coalition is a major part of a shrewdly managed campaign. This is an important factor in producing the apparently unfocused and highly flexible treatment of issues that characterize some presidential campaigns.

With the increasing industrialization and urbanization of America, the urban vote and the distribution of various ethnic and socio-economic groups within the metropolitan areas have tended to play a larger and larger role in these calculations and have correspondingly diminished the regional alliances that formerly predominated in national elections. The successful presidential candidate today must aim first of all at capturing certain key states with large electoral votes, such as New York, Pennsylvania, Ohio, Illinois, California, Michigan, and Texas. President Franklin Roosevelt's success in mobilizing majority blocs within the great urban centers (without, at the same time, losing certain traditional areas of Democratic party strength, especially in the so-called solid South), for example, did much to change the structure of American presidential elections by elevating his party to at least a semipermanent dominance in terms of popular adherence.

One other feature of the electoral college system that produces recurring periods of doubt is the proportional difference between the popular and the electoral vote. Since the entire electoral vote of a state goes to the nominee receiving a plurality of its popular vote, there is always a heavy distortion of the popular vote as it is translated into electoral college votes. It is, for example, possible for a candidate to carry key states by small margins and win the electoral college vote by a landslide, yet lose so heavily in the other states that he has only a narrow plurality or perhaps even a minority of popular votes. The possibility that a "minority" President might be elected has been an increasingly disturbing one as the office has emerged as a nationally democratic institution. Numerous proposals have been advanced as means of coping with the contingencies inherent in the present electoral system. The most frequent and seriously considered proposals have pressed the idea of securing a closer correspondence between the popular and the electoral vote. The Lodge-Gossett resolution of 1948, for example, provided for abolishing the electoral college as such, while retaining the present allocation of electoral votes in each state, with these votes being disrtibuted in strict proportion to the popular votes for presidential and vice-presidential candidates. Under this plan a plurality, rather than a majority, of the electoral votes would be sufficient for election, and in the event of a tie in the electoral vote a nationwide plurality of popular votes would determine the winner. Although proposals of this type have had sporadic support, the state party organizations have resisted change because the winner-take-all principle enhances the statewide party's power in relation to the local organizations.

In addition to the principle of the single-head executive and the indirect method of election, a third constitutional characteristic affecting the office's potential was the establishment of a fixed term of office in conjunction with the possibility of indefinite self-succession. Numerous proposals were advanced for a chief executive subordinated to the Congress, for a very short term of office, and for limitations on re-eligibility. In settling for an independent executive who was to be selected for a four-year term with no limits on the number of terms that a man could seek, the Convention strengthened the hand of the President by placing the office in a position in which the national constituency could be used in a variety of ways to permit the executive to influence public policy on major issues and to enhance presidential powers in conflicts between Congress and the President. Of course there is ambivalence in this feature of the Presidency because independence undoubtedly has hardened the effects of the separation of powers and therefore tended to stimulate legislative-executive conflict and to weaken the possibility of internal responsibility. However, given the factors in American politics which work toward diffusion and localization of popularly based power, it is at least doubtful that a parliamentary executive would have encouraged the development of responsible party government. A strong case can be made for the independent American Presidency as a generator of such national political cohesion as the country exhibits; a parliamentary executive might very well have led to a multi-party (or multi-factional) arrangement that would have been much closer to continental than to British practice. In a sense the adoption of the Twenty-second Amendment (limiting self-succession essentially to two full terms) bears out this judgment. It seems to have been produced by political forces which favored diffusion of influence against Franklin Roosevelt's use of indefinite tenure to mold an effective constituency on a national basis and to use this force as a strong support for a party program. In this context it may be argued that the Twenty-second Amendment is the single major constitutional change in the United States history that obstructed rather than promoted the trend toward nationalizing the American democracy. And the full effects of the addition of this lame-duck element to the constitutional basis of the office have yet to be realized.

The fourth and final constitutional characteristic of the Presidency that has promoted the growth and development of the office is the assignment to the President of certain powers which he exercises in his own right; the creation, as it were, of a presidential prerogative. The specific powers are few, of course, and broadly framed, but Article II of the Constitution does state at the outset that "The executive Powers shall be vested in a President of the United States . . ." and then proceeds to outline certain basic areas of presidential competence. The great charge on the office—to take care that the laws be faithfully executed—is all but buried in a host of lesser grants of authority. The President is Commander in Chief of the armed forces, he appoints (with the advice and consent of the Senate) major officials, including ambassadors, other public ministers and consuls, and federal judges; he commissions officers of the United States; he makes interim appointments during recesses of the Senate, and he may require reports in writing from heads of executive departments relating to their duties. In the field of foreign affairs he has the power to make treaties (if two-thirds of the Senators concur), and he receives ambassadors and other public ministers. In the judicial area he has power to reprieve and to pardon, except in cases of impeachment. And in relation to Congress, he has the responsibility for providing information on the state of the Union, he has the authority to recommend measures that he deems expedient, he may convene one or both houses in special session, he may adjourn Congress if there is disagreement between the two houses on a time for adjournment, and he has a suspensive veto over acts of Congress. Out of these prosaic specifications have evolved the vast responsibility and authority of the President for the development of foreign and domestic policy, the implementation of these policies, and control of the civil and military establishment which is engaged in their execution.

The enhancement of these powers through usage has depended primarily on three factors to which some reference has already been made. The first of these is the fact that the Presidency is the only American representative institution based on a national constituency. In consequence the incumbent has had to assume—under the pressures of a party system that has democratized the Presidency nationally—new representative functions that Congress could not undertake because it is an eclectic body whose members are drawn from constituencies so heterogeneous that party considerations have had almost no unifying impact on them. In its relation to the President (as one coordinate branch to another), Congress has been somewhat victimized by federalism and notions of grass-roots representation. Closely related to this difference in the constituency basis of the President and Congress is a second factor—the direction of society's evolution, which since the Civil War has been steadily toward large-scale industrialism, with all that this implies in the way of centralization of government in order to cope with problems arising from a broadened geographic scope of economic activities and larger concentrations of people. Finally, and most recent, is the increasing part played by America in international affairs. The framing and conduct of foreign policy has long and properly been conceived as essentially executive in nature, so the new American role in this field has intensified executive duties and heightened the ceremonial and symbolic aspects of the presidential office.

The story of the Presidency as an institution is incomplete without a further understanding of the way in which the powers of the office, stimulated by the movements of history, have been adapted to the life of the nation. In this context the best approach is to try to see the President in his various roles and to appraise the uses to which these roles have been put. The three great functions of the office (which embrace a formidable array of subordinate responsibilities) are: (1) the President's position as head of state or chief ceremonial dignitary; (2) his position as chief executive, which includes the crucial authority for directing the conduct of foreign affairs; and (3) his position as political leader. This last involves a complicated process of party and popular leadership—a function which eventually requires the President to furnish a type of congressional leadership that makes him in a sense the chief legislator of the country. To assay a brief analysis of these three roles in combination soon brings one to the realization that any one of them considered separately imposes burdens of responsibility sufficient to stagger the imagination.

THE CHIEF OF STATE

The President is not merely a chief executive or head of the administrative branch of the government; he is Chief of State. As such he combines certain functions of constitutional monarchy with the responsibilities of a Prime Minister, or in a republican sense he combines the functions of President and Chancellor. As President Taft said, the President is "the personal embodiment of their [the American people's] dignity and majesty." Some of the duties connected with this function are solemn, almost priestly in character; these would include the great ceremonial speeches, proclamations of thanksgiving and commemoration, conferring the highest military awards, presiding over state dinners, and reception of diplomats. Others are symbolic of commonplace features of American life or are representative of a national addiction to some more or less ordinary activity, such as throwing out the first ball on the opening day of the major league baseball season or receiving hordes of visiting boy scouts and representatives of commercial, benevolent, or recreational organizations. In this capacity the President is a one-man distillation of the American people. However, the public appears to be ambiguous in its demands on this function of the Presidency, for it somehow seems to want an admixture of the idealized heroic figure and the homely qualities of the common man. Americans take almost as much interest in every detail of the President's life—his shirts, his dogs, his golf, his church attendance, his reading habits, his hobbies, and his social activities —as the British do in the life of the royal family. And the President's family is naturally included in this vicarious personal relation of the head of state with his people.

Perhaps Lincoln best fitted the national image that the Americans vaguely seek in the President, insofar as he "walked with God but kept the common touch." Certainly Washington set an almost inimitable tone of dignity in an age of considerable formality, yet in the twentieth century many objected to Woodrow Wilson because of a presumed coldness in his austere dignity. To many, Franklin Roosevelt combined an inspiring presence with warm informality as effectively as any man who has occupied the office; and although the Republicans in 1952 made much of restoring "dignity to the White House" through the accession of Dwight D. Eisenhower, some felt a retrospective warmth for Harry Truman's somewhat rustic candor.

Apart from the symbolic aspects of the function, the President's role as head of state carries with it considerable utilitarian political value. Not only is it a factor in the public's acquiescence in the outcome of national elections (the victor is, after all, President of the entire United States, as the post-election statements following the extremely close

1960 election amply illustrate), but the powers of the office itself are in no small sense animated and its authority enlarged by the charismatic quality conferred by its ceremonial requirements. The brevity of the form of introduction of the incumbent—"Ladies and Gentlemen, The President of the United States"—speaks volumes on this score. The unequaled status of the office gives the person who occupies it an initial edge over political friends as well as opponents in his capacity to influence and direct; when a Senator or a Representative, for example, is asked to the White House to confer on legislation or even when a General of the Army is rebuked, there can be no doubt that the confrontation has been with no ordinary person. On occasion the dignitary character of the Presidency may reshape a major political career or affect the broadest movements of national politics. It is alleged that Theodore Roosevelt's shift from an anti-labor position supported by a dogmatic affirmation of classical economics to a moderately pro-labor attitude backed by a willingness to promote governmental intervention in the economy occurred during the anthracite coal strike of 1902 and was motivated by what Roosevelt regarded as an affront to his office. The report was that the chief negotiator for the mine operators, George F. Baer, wanted to settle the strike by using federal troops to starve the miners into submission—while the eastern part of the country froze. Baer was so haughty in his manner toward everybody concerned, including Roosevelt, that the President declared later: "If it wasn't for the high office I hold I would have taken him by the seat of his breeches and the nape of the neck and chucked him out the window." Literally from that time forward Roosevelt became a "liberal" President, and he attempted to carry his party with him; as some observers have said, he dragged the Republicans kicking and screaming into the twentieth century.

THE ADMINISTRATIVE FUNCTION

The classic function of the presidential office, however, is that of chief administrator; the President as a dignitary may reign, but it is of equal if not more importance that he rules. In this capacity the President is responsible for the work of an incredibly complicated administrative structure in which approximately two and one-third million civilian employees are engaged, and for the preparation and execution of a federal budget currently amounting to almost $100 billion dollars a year. There is not much consistency in the way in which the various departments, agencies, authorities, boards, and commissions are organized. Most of the 3000 operative units of the administration, however, are grouped into hierarchical arrangements, so that some 40-odd major departments, branches, authorities, commissions, and agencies constitute the central units covering this complex arrangement.

The most notable form of central administrative organization is the department, which is usually broken down into bureaus (the major functional, or line, units) and then further subdivided into divisions. Each of the executive departments has a single administrative head, whose title, except for the heads of the Justice Department (Attorney-General) and the Post Office (Postmaster General), is secretary; and collectively these ten department heads constitute the President's Cabinet. In addition to the Attorney-General and the Postmaster General, these include the Secretaries of State, Treasury, Defense, Interior, Agriculture, Commerce, Labor, and Health, Education, and Welfare. To persons accustomed to thinking of the collective responsibility of a cabinet in the parliamentary system, the American Cabinet may seem an anomaly. No collective responsibility is vested in the Cabinet; executive responsibility remains with the President. Even the functions of the Cabinet are somewhat hazy and tend to depend on the use to which a particular President wishes to put the institution. Although the Cabinets of most administrations meet fairly regularly, it is primarily a sounding board and a source of collective advice for the President. And President Eisenhower's efforts to improve administrative coordination through an expanded Cabinet secretariat does not appear to have changed conditions appreciably. In some cases even these purposes may be more effectively served by presidential advisors from outside the Cabinet, which since Jackson's time have been referred to as the "kitchen" cabinet. Recently the Vice-President has been invited to attend Cabinet meetings and from time to time the President may ask other officials to attend these sessions. Cabinet votes on issues before the body are the exception rather than the rule, and the "sense" of the meeting imposes no formal obligation on the President. On one occasion when Lincoln found his entire Cabinet against him he remarked forthrightly, "Seven nays, one aye—the ayes have it." On the whole it must be concluded that the heads of the executive departments are more influential in their individual positions than in their unified capacity as Cabinet, although one factor in the desirability of these positions as compared to others of seemingly equal functional importance undoubtedly derives from the prestige of being a member of the Cabinet. The Cabinet is one of the oldest of the executive institutions and, although it is unlikely that a Cabinet officer will succeed to the Presidency under the current presidential succession act, the members of the Cabinet are included in the line of succession.

Several other line agencies of great importance remain directly under the President but outside the Cabinet. Included among these are units such as the National Aeronautics and Space Administration. From time to time consideration is given to the possibility of moving some of these agencies "up" to Cabinet status, as was done with the Department of Health, Education, and Welfare (a move which also involved grouping formerly separately administered functions). The most recent attempt in this direction was the effort to create a Department of Urban Affairs. The President has a general legislative grant of authority to reorganize component parts of the administration unless his proposed changes are specifically disallowed by either the House or the Senate. Acting under this authority President Kennedy submitted a plan to elevate the Housing and Home Finance Agency to the Cabinet rank of Department of Urban Affairs, and he further expressed his intention of appointing the incumbent Director of the Housing Agency, Robert Weaver, as Secretary of the new Department. This action would have resulted in Weaver's becoming the first Negro Cabinet member in American history. Although the proposal was badly defeated in the House of Representatives, President Kennedy's action was widely regarded as a shrewd political move both for its popular appeal to groups who felt slighted by lack of attention to mounting problems of urbanization and for its effect on proponents of increased executive action in the field of civil liberties.

Two other forms of administrative organization also play an important role in the American system. One of these is the so-called independent regulatory commission and the other is the public authority or public corporation. The first was developed as a unique American solution to the problems of the great industrial state. Essentially it is a technique for regulating business, especially businesses affected with a public interest and which tend to be natural monopolies. The regulatory device seeks to ensure effective service to the public through governmental intervention without going to the length of public ownership. The first of these agencies to be established was the Interstate Commerce Commission

(1887), which was originally designed to regulate railroads, but has since expanded into the other areas of surface transportation. The form was later extended to the control of trade practices (Federal Trade Commission), Communications (Federal Communications Commission), power (Federal Power Commission), securities (Securities and Exchange Commission), and other activities. Although the President appoints the multi-member heads of these agencies, they are designed to be independent of his authority in the exercise of their functions because their activities involve quasi-judicial (decisions on cases brought before them) and quasi-legislative (rule-making) powers in addition to executive functions. The appointments to this type of unit are for fixed, overlapping terms and are bipartisan; in consequence, the President's power to remove members is limited, as is his power to direct their activities. It has been suggested (especially by the President's Committee on Administrative Management, often referred to as the Brownlow Committee, 1937) that the existence of these organizations outside the line authority of the President tends to create policy conflicts and that their function should be departmentalized. A long-standing criticism of the "headless fourth branch" of the government has been that the regulatory agencies often tend to identify with the interests of the industries they are supposed to regulate, sometimes to the point of losing sight of the public interest. The efforts that have been made to bring these agencies under tighter executive control have thus far been successfully resisted, with the regulated industries themselves playing a major pressure role in maintaining the status quo.

On the other hand, public corporations, of which the Tennessee Valley Authority is perhaps best known, are organized along the lines of private corporations, with a board and a general manager. This type of organization is designed to allow the proprietary activity to be conducted with a broader fiscal autonomy than is permitted in other governmental agencies. The power of the President to remove board members from public corporations is less restricted than it is in relation to members of regulatory commissions, and experience indicates less difficulty in integrating their activities into the general administrative program.

The tremendous growth of the administrative function in recent years has resulted in a gradual enlargement of the staff function in the Executive Office of the President. Staff agencies provide the President with the tools for carrying out his administrative responsibilities; they collect information, they furnish technical assistance on organizational and procedural problems, they perform functions of control and co-ordination, and they render essential advice from the vantage point of their experience with line agencies. They are especially valuable to the President not only because he has a freer hand in choosing and organiz-ing them than he has in the case of many other administrative organiza-tions, but also because they are not directly involved in specific government programs—instead they are promotive of the entire admin-istrative function. Closest to the President in this connection is the White House Office, which is made up of his major legislative, admin-istrative, political, and diplomatic assistants, as well as his legal counsel, corps of executive secretaries, and military aides. Those who followed the career of Sherman Adams as Assistant to President Eisenhower will realize the potential influence that may accrue from close association with the President; it was widely accepted that Eisenhower would not act on some proposals that came to him unless the pertinent documents were marked "O.K.—S.A."

Also included in the Executive Office, but outside the immediate circle of the White House Office are certain key staff agencies for co-ordinating and controlling the administrative structure. The Bureau of the Budget (with the Director of the Budget as its head) is perhaps the most important of these units for control purposes. Not only is it the agency concerned with the preparation of the executive budget and the execution of the congressionally approved budget, but it also serves as a clearing house for legislation proposed by the various administrative units and (through its operations and methods branch) as the major instru-ment for dealing with problems of administrative organization and procedures. The three-man Council of Economic Advisers is responsible for the preparation of the annual report on the national economy and for advising the President on matters of economic policy. The National Security Council, consisting of the major figures in the field of national defense and foreign policy, serves as a coordinating device in these two increasingly important and interrelated areas, somewhat after the fashion of an inner cabinet. Other agencies in this category include the National Aeronautics and Space Council, the Office of Emergency Planning, the Office of Science and Technology, and the Office of the Special Repre-sentative for Trade Negotiations.

No small part in the growth of the executive function of the President

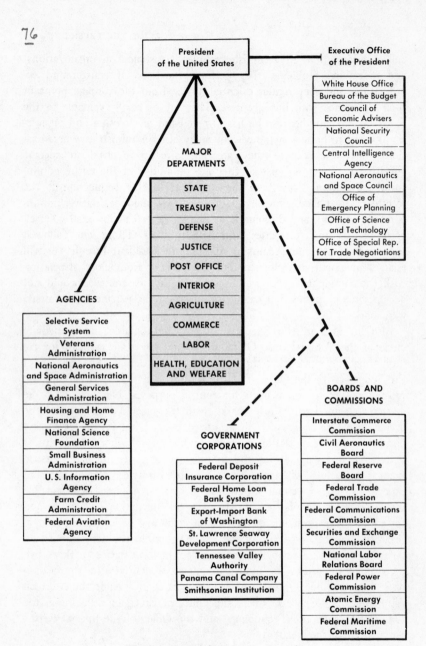

Organization of the Executive Branch

has been played by his position in foreign affairs. In this area the President's constitutional powers are shared with the Senate, inasmuch as nearly all major appointments are affirmed by that body and two-thirds of its members must concur in treaties made by the President. However, the Constitution itself, various acts of Congress, court decisions, custom, and the diplomatic practice of other national states have all joined, both by way of logic and of experience, to make the executive clearly dominant in this field. This development is a striking example of the pragmatic alternation of practice and attitudes, since as late as two weeks prior to the end of the 1787 Convention the draft resolutions still conferred exclusive power on the Senate to make treaties and appoint ambassadors.

In diplomatic relations the President's power to appoint and remove the principal officers in the State Department and other pertinent agencies, his power to receive envoys from other countries, and the latitude he has in treaties and executive agreements form the major instruments of control. The choice of a Secretary of State, like the appointment of the other Cabinet officers, is generally accepted as a presidential prerogative and strong opposition within the Senate is rare. This is not always the case, however, with the appointment of ambassadors; ideological objections are sometimes raised against nominees, which suggests the tenuous nature of executive-legislative relations and a reluctance to yield entirely to the President in foreign affairs, especially where some domestic political advantage may be at stake. The full impact of the President's place in foreign affairs is best illustrated by the highest level negotiations, such as the treaties ending major wars or the "summit" conferences, which he conducts personally on behalf of his country. The power of recognizing foreign governments is almost entirely at the discretion of the President, although there are circumstances (e.g., the case of Red China) in which internal political pressures obviously impinge so heavily that his decision may not be an entirely free one. However, throughout American history—for example, in the revolt of Spain's American colonies in the 1820s and in the Panama Canal dispute in the early twentieth century—rapid diplomatic recognition on the part of the President has helped to stabilize new regimes and thereby contributed to the fulfillment of existing foreign policy or to the development of new policy.

Treaties, of course, occasionally provide the ground for major conflict between President and Congress. The outstanding example is the Treaty of Versailles (with the League of Nations "riveted in"), the defeat of which by the Senate broke Woodrow Wilson's heart, as the fight to save America's place in the League had broken his body, and had incalculable consequences for the future of world peace. Increasingly, however, Presidents have turned to the executive agreement as a flexible substitute for foreign treaties. Although they have been used throughout American history, the proportion of executive agreements in relation to treaties has increased enormously over the past 25 years, a period which roughly parallels America's active re-entry into international politics under strong executive guidance. Executive agreements have full legal standing in the courts despite the fact that they are not subject to Senate ratification. Many are made solely on the basis of the President's constitutional authority, while others have the prior sanction of acts of Congress. Examples of the former include the Atlantic Charter and the "destroyer deal" in 1940 under which the President provided Britain with 50 over-age American destroyers in exchange for the use of bases in the Western Hemisphere. Although the latter action was without precedent and was legally questionable, both Congress and the public accepted the decision with some enthusiasm, and in the later passage of the Lend-Lease Act Congress gave it a form of retrospective sanction. A different order of things is demonstrated by the Reciprocal Trade Agreements Act, first passed under the *aegis* of Secretary of State Cordell Hull in the 1930s and continuously renewed since that time; here the President is given specific authority by Congress to enter into trade agreements under which stringent reductions may be made in American tariff rates in exchange for similar concessions from abroad.

If war is diplomacy carried on by other means, the President's war powers certainly enter into the discussion at this point. As Commander in Chief the President may take far-reaching action with respect to the armed forces. Although Congress controls the purse, the President may use his independent powers effectively to force the legislative hand, as Theodore Roosevelt did when he sent a naval fleet on a "good-will" mission around the world despite some serious doubts over the question of supply. Roosevelt ordered the ships halfway around the globe, which was as far as available funds would take them, and left it for Congress to provide the means for getting them home. A somewhat similar situation exists with respect to a declaration of war; although Congress alone can declare war, it is possible for the President to utilize his executive powers in a manner which commits the country beyond the possibility of revocation. Thus, although it did not eventuate in a formal declaration of war, President Truman's action in ordering American troops into Korea in 1950 (albeit as a fulfillment of the United States' obligation under the UN Charter and with the sanction of the Security Council) presented Congress with a *fait accompli* of such magnitude that it could only sustain his action completely if a disastrous national situation was to be avoided.

During the course of an actual war, the combination of the constitutional powers of the President, the delegation of extraordinary authority by the Congress in certain fields, and the tacit acceptance of the idea that national survival demands a wide latitude for presidential discretion heightens executive power to the point characterized by some observers as "constitutional dictatorship." Modern warfare may become total war, with the result that, from the American Civil War through the Korean conflict, American Presidents such as Lincoln, Wilson, Franklin Roosevelt and Truman have had power pressed upon them or assumed the initiative for mobilizing economic and human resources to meet the demands of all-out effort. It is sufficient to mention such measures as conscription, rationing, price controls, the establishment of priority usages in raw materials, manpower, and transportation to indicate something of the range of authority and arbitrary discretion that a President must assume in time of national peril. Even though this great accretion of powers diminishes after a war as a result of repeal of emergency legislation and a natural revulsion against the harshness of wartime discipline, an almost indefinable residue of Presidential power has been the heritage of each major war of the past century. Despite the fact that the powers may become dormant, as they were between the Civil War and World War I, the experience of his wartime predecessors has provided each successive war President with precedents for the use of extraordinary powers in extraordinary times. Nor are these lessons entirely lost in time of peace; we never go all the way back to the situation which preceded the crisis, and the solutions to economic problems, for example, which have been developed in time of war are looked to for application when peacetime problems are confronted. It was not the Great Depression alone which placed the main burden of responsibility on the President for foreseeing and applying policy correctives to serious imbalances in the national economy; the experience with rapid adjustment through broad executive discretion under war conditions had a great deal to do with the matter. The powers of the President are by no means compartmentalized; the enhancement of one area of his complex office, whether by accident or design, will be diffused into all the other areas of responsibility.

THE PRESIDENT AS POLITICAL LEADER

The final great role of the President is that of political leader. The President does not just set administrative policy designed to carry out the will of Congress and preside with dignity over the affairs of state; he is a towering figure on the political scene. His potential as political leader extends to at least three areas, each of which interacts with the other two as well as with the other basic functions of the office. The President is a national popular leader, the leader of his party, and the leader of Congress, or as has been differently expressed, he is the chief legislator of the country. Behind each of these functions there is an effective cause: The President is a popular leader because he combines selection from a national constituency with his symbolic function as Chief of State; in this capacity he has the dual sanction and the dual responsibility that derive from popular selection and investiture of great office. The President is party leader because he is the choice of his Party (except for the Vice-President he is its *only* choice at the national level) and its most important unifying symbol; regardless of which party controls Congress, the party that elects a presidential candidate is really considered the party in power because this is the party that constitutes *the administration*. The President is a congressional leader because someone—and someone with precisely the President's other political qualifications—must attempt to unite the complex constituencies which elect a Congress (and a bicameral Congress, at that) into the semblance of a majority (even if the basis of the majority shifts with every issue), and because the complexities of modern government demand that an executive program drawn from experience in administration be placed before Congress. The political capital accruing to the office in the form of popular support, patronage, party influence, and weight of position must be carefully expended in persuading, cajoling, and pressuring Congress into passing the administration's program. Although lacking both the final sanction of dissolution and an effective disciplinary control over members of his party, the President is expected to get a majority of his legislative proposals made into law and failure to do so will naturally weigh more heavily against him than against Congress or the political system as a whole. And this necessity for legislative implementation of his program by no means ceases, as former President Eisenhower came to know, when the President and the congressional majority are from different parties. As a political leader the President is both the formulator of a cohesive national political opinion and the interpreter of the meaning of that opinion as it is translated into public policy. No mean talent for political leadership is required for holding the complex forces with which the President must work in the sort of balance that is required to meet these demands.

As the functions of government have expanded and become vastly more complex, the President's political leadership role has resulted in an enlargement of the responsibilities of the office to the point at which its exactions may exceed what is possible. The President is looked to today as the primary guardian of the internal prosperity of the country; over the past 30 years, in particular, an elaborate administrative apparatus has been developed for maintaining surveillance over the nation's economic health and for the immediate application of therapy at the slightest sign of abnormality. At the same time the task of preserving domestic peace and tranquility through the maintenance of day-to-day, routine (but indispensable) services of government has become infinitely more complicated as a result of a developing technology and changing patterns of society. And the presidential office has not been able to divest itself of any substantial share of this burden, either by delegation or decentralization. At best some organizational and procedural innovations have been developed to enable the President to supervise these activities more effectively. Finally, the tremendous task of maintaining a maximum defense effort under the hazardous conditions imposed by a bipolar world has been added to the other primary demands on the Presidency.

THE CONDITIONS OF GREATNESS

If the story of the Presidency as an institution is best told in terms of the emergence of the foregoing powers, functions, and responsibilities out of the interplay of the potential of the office and historical events, the standards for assessing the qualities of individual Presidents may not be as nebulous as they sometimes appear to be. A given President may be appraised in terms of the skill he displays in the exercise of each of the great functions, both as separate activities and in combination with one another, and all within the framework of the problems of his times. In the broadest sense Machiavelli's concept of the interplay of *virtú* and *fortuna* is applicable to the Presidency. In order to establish presidential greatness, the conditions for heroic action must be present and the tangible and intangible personal attributes necessary to meet these conditions effectively must be forthcoming. Even in times that do not call for heroic virtues, a President with great talent can still make a considerable impact on the office and on the affairs of state. And no matter what crises impend, a mediocre President will somehow allow his opportunities to elude him.

Practically every commentator plays the game of ranking or categorizing various occupants of the office. Since this is a form of self-indulgence that may have some value in establishing the nature of American political institutions, there is no reason to bypass the opportunity here. George Washington, Abraham Lincoln, and Franklin Roosevelt seem to me to have clearly marked themselves as Presidents of the first order of greatness, and it is possible that Thomas Jefferson, Andrew Jackson, and Woodrow Wilson should be ranked alongside them.

Washington's place is not established solely because he was the first person to occupy the office and therefore was bound to set some of its precedents. It is rather the kind of precedents he set that make him outstanding. Washington was not a brilliant man; the compelling ideas of his administration were those of Hamilton. But he was a man of great strength of character who had enormous prestige, so his mere presence in the office strengthened national unity during the crucial early days of the Union. Furthermore, he pursued a definite and consistent policy which, even though popularly repudiated in 1800, has strongly influenced all subsequent political periods. His (or Hamilton's) administrative conceptions—especially those of strong executive leadership, professional quality and integrity among public servants, and scalar organizations with strict lines of command and responsibility—have never been completely submerged as ideals of American public administration.

Lincoln's greatness has to be measured alongside the tragedy of his times. It is also difficult, as has so often been pointed out, to disentangle Lincoln as man and President from Lincoln as surrogate in legend. Although dead less than 100 years, Lincoln seems to be beyond the limits of time and far less real than his contemporaries either at home or abroad. Lincoln came to office as the President of a republic already hopelessly divided, but he never lost his vision of unity. Although he took charge of the Union's war effort with a vigor and initiative unmatched by any predecessor in a national crisis, he personally suffered not merely for and with the section he governed, but with the country as a whole, and his clarity of mind was never overcome by the emotional pressures of revenge or desire to humiliate. He became a great popular leader under the most inauspicious conditions possible, and he used virtually dictatorial powers with restraint, wisdom, and humility. He pointed the way to the waging of total warfare without permanently impairing the standards of popular rule.

Franklin Roosevelt's claim to greatness rests on the multifold uses he made of the resources of the office. As a popular leader he was unexcelled. His early achievement in rallying a nation on the verge of economic and social disintegration is matched only by the skill with which he later persuaded the country of the perils of totalitarian aggression and guided American policy away from isolationism and toward active intervention in international affairs. His willingness to experiment boldly and broadly has often been criticized as indicating lack of understanding of economics and failure to develop consistent views on public policy. Yet it is surprising how many of his experiments have persisted and been accepted as established means of promoting the general welfare. In retrospect Roosevelt's tendency to avoid ideological commitments and to work pragmatically within the framework of a going political system seems far more compatible with American political experience than the more dogmatic persuasions of his critics from both the right and the left. Roosevelt was able to translate his skill at popular leadership into effective party leadership and thence into legislation; he remade the national Democratic party and vastly expanded the President's role as congressional leader. Finally, though not definitively, Roosevelt has sometimes been scored as a poor administrator, and there is considerable evidence of looseness of organization and lack of procedural consistency in his administration. But at the same time, it was during his term of office (particularly by putting into effect the recommendations of the previously mentioned Brownlow Committee), that the President was given the staff tools to make the authority of the office commensurate with its responsibilities. In taking the initiative for transferring the Bureau of the Budget to the

Executive Office of the President, providing high-level advisors within the White House Office, and creating an executive planning organization, Roosevelt made it possible for a President to come closer to fulfilling the charges of the office than would have been conceivable before these steps were taken.

Jefferson's place in presidential history rests to a large degree on his effectiveness as a party and congressional leader, on his statesmanship in acting against long held concepts where the result, as in the Louisiana Purchase, was clearly in the national interest, and in changing and democratizing public policy without disrupting the standards of integrity of public service set in the Washington administration. Jackson's greatest achievements were in the areas of popular leadership and the assumption of presidential prerogative. Although he left a legacy of spoils that still lingers in some areas of American government, the office of the President was both a greater office and a more democratic one when he left it than it had been before. Although Wilson's idealism cost him dearly in a period characterized about equally by cynicism and shortsighted complacency, he was a forerunner of Franklin Roosevelt both in domestic economic reform designed to cope with an industrial economy and in the establishment of a definite concept of America's role in foreign affairs. No small part of Wilson's positive achievements were made in the face of serious political obstacles and his great failure in foreign affairs had a noble quality about it, especially in terms of the superiority of his foresight.

Presidents such as Theodore Roosevelt and Harry Truman probably belong to a different, but still high, order of presidential merit when compared to the Presidents discussed immediately above. Roosevelt's aggressiveness in foreign and domestic policy, his great popular appeal, and his willingness and ability to stand up to and assert his dominance over Republican party leaders reflect the sort of strength that might have made him an outstanding President if the times in which he served had made greater demands on him. Truman, on the other hand, started with many handicaps, not the least of which was the fact that he was serving in the shadow of Franklin Roosevelt. He was beset by lack of reputation which he never quite overcame either with the public or his party. He gave a somewhat false impression of being a pedestrian officeholder and he was frequently in trouble over personal trivialities. Nevertheless he had a dogged courage, a capacity for growth, and a deep sense of understanding and respect for the presidential office. His major decisions, such as the atomic attack on Japan, the Truman Doctrine, Marshall Plan aid, the Berlin air lift, the Korean intervention, and others, place him far above the level of mediocrity in assessing and fulfilling the requirements of the office.

Although only a few examples of traits and contributions could be cited for each President included in this listing, in every case in which a particular President's conduct of office has singled him out for the stamp of greatness or near-greatness, the three great functions of the institution have been combined with a considerable degree of perspicacity. Furthermore, each of these Presidents has been able to make some ineradicable mark on one or more of these functions, usually by expanding their scope in order to meet some persistent national demand. The full measure of the office, then, is the use made of it, and as its potential uses have expanded it has become increasingly necessary for successive Presidents to utilize every resource of the office that has been inherited from their predecessors. To be seriously deficient in any one of the important roles or in their subtle interplay deprives an incumbent of presidential distinction. Of greater consequence, however, is the fact that neglect of any one of the three functions in the contemporary setting of perpetual crisis imperils the incumbent's career, the presidential office itself, the party in power, and even the welfare and security of the country and the entire free world.

QUESTIONS FOR FURTHER DISCUSSION

1. What are the principal arguments for and against changing the electoral college method of electing the President?
2. In what ways are the President's powers of appointment limited?
3. What are the weaknesses of the present method of succession to the Presidency in the event of death, resignation, or disability?
4. Discuss the main theoretical concepts behind the efforts at reorganizing the federal administrative structure over the past 30 years.
5. How has the President's role as a popular leader been altered by the changes in American participation in foreign affairs since World War II?

IV

Congress: A House Divided?

THE "FIRST" BRANCH OF GOVERNMENT

If both the United States Supreme Court and the Presidency have exceeded original expectations in the use of the powers and functions of their respective offices, in some respects the Congress may be said to have fallen short of the institutional role that the founding fathers projected for it. To be sure, the separation of powers principle decreed that the three branches should be coordinate, but the prevailing winds of doctrine whispered *"primus inter pares"* insofar as the legislative branch was concerned. Not only was executive power suspect and the possibility of judicial activism minimized, but the very nature of the emerging union lent special popular favor to the legislative assembly in its competition with other institutions.

The legislature is the "law-making" branch, and the legal powers vested in the central government are specified in the First (or congressional) Article of the Constitution. The Congress was thus conceived to be the initiator and formulator of the public policy within the framework of which the President and the courts were to act. In a legalistically-oriented society the branch which formally enunciates the law already has an increment of prestige not attaching to other instrumentalities of government. More than this, however, the structure of Congress was particularly suited to the idea of representation, both generically and as a response to domestic conditions, in a way that was not open to the Presidency or the Court. Not only was it a large body which could be conceived as a surrogate for the people themselves, but the manner of apportionment and selection of Congress could yield a true sense of agency which fully reflected the decentralized and pluralistic ethos of the new country. Furthermore the constitutional compromise on representative form produced a bicameral system that gave tangible support to the dualism of the federal system: collectively, the House of Representatives was able to represent the population on a national basis, while the geographic basis of representation in the Senate sustained the identity of a separate and independent unity of peoples at the level of the states. All of the rational, sentimental, and symbolic reasons for the early American preference for the legislative over other governmental institutions are effectively summed up by T. V. Smith's remark that "America is the one country which was legislative-minded from its birth as a nation."

However, some of the features of Congress which appeal most strongly to the American's sense of governmental propriety have been instrumental in reducing its efficient role in American government at least to a position of comity with the other branches. The expansion and marked centralization of governmental functions which accompanied the process of industrialization have everywhere resulted in new functions and new leadership roles for the executive. The simultaneous maturation of the system of national political parties has further tended to support this trend by merging party leadership into the executive. Such a tendency may display itself less openly in a parliamentary system because, even though the election may serve primarily as a determinant of who governs the country (i.e., which political party will form a cabinet or executive composed of previously designated party leaders), the route to executive office and the higher levels of party leadership is still through the representative assembly. Thus even if the parliament is conceived as a mere ratifier of executive decisions which have the prior endorsement of the party and (through the party) of the electorate, parliament continues to be the field of governmental action in which the cabinet executive operates.

This is not, however, the case in a presidential system. The congressional route to the Presidency is by no means the only or necessarily the easiest way; the choice of an American presidential candidate is very much an open one in terms of the candidate's political background. Although the Senate has been one important stepping stone to the Presidency in recent times, a Cabinet post, the governorship of a key state, the military, and even certain business or professional positions may make a man as readily available for the presidential nomination as a substantial senatorial career (which is the usual source of a congressionally-based claim to nomination). The popular expectation that a member of Congress will directly represent the interests of his constituency and that a Senator will serve his state in the same manner acts as a definite restraint on the attempt to project a legislator as a national leader through the congressional field of action. Nor can the Senator or Congressman expect either the congressional or the external political party organization to sustain him in a national leadership role. Party power is too decentralized to act as a buffer between the special demands of constituency and a record of consistent adherence to a program (party-based or otherwise) conceived as a response to the idea of a "national interest." Furthermore, internal congressional leadership, as will be emphasized later, is in most cases less closely related to the party function and to general policy considerations than it is to seniority and to specialization in particular legislative areas through committee assignments. The factors which generally, though not always, prevent Congress from generating effective internal leadership for a unified national program whose composite parts embrace a wide variety of legislative subjects are essentially the same ones which handicap the individual legislator's efforts to achieve national executive and party stature.

When a Senator or, more remotely, a member of the House of Representatives overcomes these handicaps and becomes President (as he may do, particularly if his congressional constituency faithfully reflects the *national* basis of support for his party), his field of action shifts from the legislative body to the independent executive branch. The result is that even though his rise to executive authority may have been given an initial impetus by his performance in Congress, neither his direct accession to power not his continuation in office is dependent on the legislative body. Readers of Allen Drury's novel *Advise and Consent* will be aware that, even though congressional-executive relationships are a crucial factor in American politics, the two branches are effectively separated, not only by legal barriers, but by vastly different customs, habits, expectations of behavior, conceptions of responsibility, and permissible means of influence open to them. And there is little discernible residue of identification with the House or the Senate to help a former member of Congress bridge the gap between his new role as President and his erstwhile function in Congress. There are, of course, means of persuasion and sources of influences by which a President exercises congressional leadership, some of which were discussed in the preceding chapter, but these arise almost exclusively from sources other than his former status as a legislator. Congress cannot claim the responsibility for placing or maintaining the executive (the administration or "the government") in power.

By the same token the mantle of national party leadership is passed on to the potential President at the time of his nomination; individual members of Congress may help to place it there in their capacity as local party leaders, but the unified function of either house or of Congress as a whole is negligible in this respect. Witness, for example, the late Senator

Robert Taft of Ohio who, though designated "Mr. Republican" in token of a peerless reflection of ideal Republican principles in his capacity as a Senator, could not translate this outstanding attribute into effective national party leadership because he lost the nomination to a popular general who was not even identified with certainty as a Republican until the campaign for 1952 convention delegates was under way.

The fact that much of the initiative in developing a national policy has passed from the legislative branch to a separately constituted executive does not mean that Congress supinely yields to the President on all important issues. Congress still possesses its constitutional authority to pass or withhold its assent to legislation, to grant or refuse supply (i.e., to control the purse), and to serve as a check on the administration, both through controls on the organization of the executive branch and surveillance over the way in which the laws are enforced. Thus Congress can obstruct or promote the program of the administration, and is a force with which a President must contend. And because Congress is an amalgamation of elements representing the regional, cultural, economic, and political diversities of the country, its potentialities for negation of the administration's program are as substantial as its lack of capacity to generate its own unified political leadership and policy. To be sure the Congress has been the dominant force in national politics in certain eras of American history, even in comparatively recent ones; but by and large these have been periods characterized by weak Presidents and, more often than not, either by single-issue politics of a semi-hysterical variety or by a notable absence of positive governmental achievement. Typical periods of legislative predominance occurred in the latter part of the nineteenth century (except possibly for Cleveland's administrations, and especially the first, from 1884 to 1888) and in the "return to normalcy" of the 1920s, both of which were prime examples of governmental quiescence. It is noteworthy that these were also times in which capitulation to private interests was pronounced. The post-Civil War Reconstruction Period, on the other hand, is the best case in point of a legislative seizure of initiative in a frenetic attempt to subsume all issues in one emotive cause; in this case, the demand for punitive action against the rebellious South. A somewhat comparable situation developed at the end of Woodrow Wilson's presidential tenure (1919–1920) with the recurrence of isolationsm and a (partly legislative induced) national anti-ideologial hysteria which itself was highly charged with compulsive ideology. The brief and unlamented period to which Senator McCarthy's name has become attached is the most recent instance of a development that displayed similar tendencies, although the extent of direct congressional culpability in this case is more doubtful than it was during Reconstruction and the aftermath of World War I.

To say that Congress seems unable to produce an internal leadership capable of developing a unified national policy and that certain periods of congressional predominance have produced unhappy consequences is not to belittle the important functional role that the representative assembly plays in American government. It is rather to be aware that there are certain organizational and operational features of the system that continue to work their effect and that some of these limit the extent to which Congress can do certain things. That these usages have produced modifications in the practice of American politics is unquestionable, but this by no means relegates Congress to an insignificant or inactive status. Despite the enlargement of executive influence and its apparently greater adaptability to the function of policy initiation, constitutional democracy is still heavily dependent on legislative assemblies to represent the pluralistic features of national life as only a sizeable multi-member body can; to grant the executive the means—largely in the forms of authority and money—to carry out the functions of government; to check on the executive's performance; and to criticize, debate, restrain, and moderate the proposed solutions to public issues which come before it. The special conditions under which Congress performs these functions and its manner of conducting legislative business should furnish a fuller understanding of the complex forces that enter into American politics as a whole.

THE REPRESENTATIVE FUNCTION

The first of the conditioning factors is the representative character and composition of Congress, which for present purposes may be partly established by an examination of the distribution of seats throughout the country, the method of selection, and the qualifications and general characteristics of the members. Attention has already been drawn to the fact that the bases of apportionment of the House of Representatives and the Senate differ, the House seats being distributed according to population and those of the Senate according to the geography of federalism, with each state having two Senators. House membership is set by a congressional act (the Reapportionment Act of 1929, as amended) at 435. Prior to the establishment of this permanent reapportionment scheme Congress (through the year 1910) met the situation by enlarging the size of the House after each new census. Each state is guaranteed at least one representative and the remainder of the seats are allotted to the states on the basis of a mathematical formula known as the "equal proportions" method. Following each decennial census the Bureau of the Census in the Department of Commerce prepares for the President a table showing the number of seats to which each state is entitled according to the formula. The President then submits this table to Congress, and the new apportionment becomes effective 15 days later unless Congress approves a different distribution in the meantime. The 1961 reapportionment, which followed the 1960 census and for practical purposes took effect at the 1962 congressional elections, involved shifting a total of 21 seats. Sixteen states lost from one to three seats each and ten states gained from one to eight seats each (these include the new states of Hawaii and Alaska whose representation was accommodated until the 1963 session by temporarily raising the House membership to 437). Stronger pressures were brought to bear in 1961 than in any previous reapportionment under the plan to pass legislation increasing the House membership in order to avoid cutting the number of seats in some of the states, but all efforts failed and the 435 maximum was retained.

Although the allotment of seats to the states is a function of Congress, the districting within the states is in the hands of the state legislatures. Since 1842 Congress has required all states entitled to more than one member of the House to select representatives from single-member districts. There is, however, an exception under the present act which provides that failure of a state to redistrict after a reapportionment in which it has gained or lost seats shall result in the election at large (i.e., on a statewide basis) of any additional representatives to which the state is entitled, or of the entire delegation if the state's representation has been reduced. Prior to the 1929 Reapportionment Act, Congress also required that congressional districts be composed of compact and contiguous territory, but this requirement was omitted from the existing statute.

The method of allocating seats is indicative of the federated nature of American political processes even in relation to central governmental

institutions; and the effects of the practice further emphasize and rein-
force the federal influence. The very fact that Congress distributes the
representation to the *states* and that each state is guaranteed at least
one representative regardless of population has a directly restrictive effect
—albeit a minor one—on the populational basis of apportionment. Four
states fall below the population figure that would entitle them to representation in terms of strict ratios, which on the basis of a 1960 United
States population of slightly less than 180 million would amount to an
average of approximately 410,000 persons for each representative.

More serious consequences arise from redistricting practices of state
legislatures. One of the more conspicuous of these practices is the gerrymander. Gerrymandering is the name given to the deliberate arrangement of the geography of electoral districts in order to maximize the
political strength of the party or faction in power. In laying out districts
the controlling party or faction within the apportioning agency distributes its support so that the number of seats in the legislative assembly
yielded by its popular votes is as large as possible. Conversely, this process
involves grouping the opposition's support in such a manner as to reduce
its effectiveness in translating voting strength into legislative seats.
Effective use of the gerrymander has a multiplier effect on American
politics. It perpetuates the ruling power of what would normally be
ephemerally dominant groups in the legislatures of the states, and by
so doing it prevents the translation of changes in the sociological
composition or party adherence of the states into changes in the
representative structure. Since gerrymandered state legislatures determine
the congressional districts, a further consequence is a Congress which
mirrors the representative distortions of the states.

Closely related to the deliberate process of utilizing the gerrymander
to secure partisan advantage is the failure to reapportion state legislatures
at all (usually referred to as the "silent gerrymander"), and to redistrict
congressional seats only when a change in the number of seats assigned
to a state necessitates such action. In the latter cases the shifts in
boundaries of districts will usually be made with a view to disturbing the
electoral geography as little as possible.

Perhaps the most notable result of failure to reapportion has been the
retention of an excessive rural influence in state legislatures and in
Congress, despite a rapid trend toward urbanization in the American
population as a whole. In almost all states with a sizeable representa-

tive delegation, the representatives of urban districts in Congress represent far larger populations than do their colleagues from the rural areas. A two-to-one differential is not at all unusual and there are some instances in which states have at least one district containing a population of 250,000 or less and another with 700,000 or more residents. Several states have had no congressional reapportionment for 30 years or more.

Although the American population is 70 percent urban, nearly 60 percent of the United States House of Representatives is elected from predominantly rural districts. Furthermore, the Democratic party has its main strength concentrated in the urban areas, so the rural disproportion seems generally to favor the Republican party. Even in places such as the one-party Democratic South, the tendency toward rural overrepresentation appears to have a considerable effect on the type of Democrats returned to Congress, although this is one section of the country in which rural dominance is undoubtedly of considerable effect in curtailing the possible growth of the Republican party. A further indication of the way in which malapportionment affects the party balance is the fact that there are presently more states in which a Democratic governor faces a legislature with a Republican majority in one or both houses than the reverse. Since the Democrats are, broadly speaking, the national majority party at the present time, this tends to confirm previous suggestions about the ways in which the executives—elected on a statewide or nationwide basis—tend to be more representative of the various American bodies-politic as a whole than are the legislative assemblies.

The broad question of reapportionment has recently been dramatically confronted as a major legal and political problem in America. Until 1962 the courts held the apportionment of legislative bodies to be a "political question" which was not subject to judicial review except in very narrowly circumscribed instances. The leading case was *Colegrove* v. *Green* (1946), involving an appeal against an outrageously distorted congressional districting pattern in the state of Illinois. Since the Supreme Court holding in the case was based on a four to three vote, in which one member of the majority concurred in the decision without committing himself to the "political question" dictum on which the majority opinion turned, many political and reform organizations continued to entertain hopes of an eventual reversal. It was somewhat absurd, as more than one observer noted, to suggest to citizens that their only recourse against an inequitable apportionment is to the polls, where they are counted out in advance. In March, 1962, the United State Supreme Court held, in *Baker* v. *Carr*, that the federal courts were competent to review cases of alleged inequities in the apportionment of seats in the Tennessee legislature. This decision generated a massive volume of litigation. Within a year citizen suits had been filed challenging the constitutionality of arrangements for state legislative apportionment in 34 states. A number of legislatures enacted or tried to enact reapportionment measures. In several states reapportionment plans became embroiled in partisan deadlock.

The promise of judicial relief for malapportioned state legislatures, made in the *Baker* decision, produced a number of suits challenging the validity of congressional districting. In February, 1964, in *Wesberry* v. *Sanders*, a case involving the state of Georgia, the United States Supreme Court held that substantial numerical discrimination in populations of congressional districts violates Article I of the Constitution. And in June, 1964, in a notable series of decisions involving a total of fifteen states, with *Reynolds* v. *Sims* (arising in Alabama) serving as the leading case, the Supreme Court held that the equal protection clause of the fourteenth amendment requires that seats in both houses of state legislatures be apportioned on a population basis. The court has thus moved swiftly and irrevocably into the "political thicket" of reapportionment. In the *Wesberry* and *Reynolds* cases the court used forceful language in setting the one man-one vote basis as the virtually exclusive general standard for apportioning both houses of state legislatures, as well as each state's contingent in the federal House of Representatives. The full practical ramifications of this line of decisions have not as yet been felt because litigation is a ponderous method of reorganizing the distribution of legislative representation. Even though the boldness of the Supreme Court's decisions in the reapportionment cases may have surpassed the most sanguine expectations of the proponents of equal representation in preparing the way for the extinction of the silent gerrymander, most observers will concur in the judgment that the death throes may still be long and complicated.

The United States Senate, of course, was never intended to be a popularly based chamber, and the disproportion of populations represented there is tremendously exaggerated. The two smallest states, which have populations of approximately a quarter of a million, each elects two senators, as does the state of California with a population of seventeen millions. The 26 smallest states, which contain only about twenty percent of the nation's population, elect a majority of the Senate. Although complaints have been made about this situation throughout American history, mostly on the grounds that the arrangement deliberately frustrates the strict majoritarian propensities of democracy, the fact that the representative structure of the Senate was the product of a deliberate constitutional decision and that it makes the federal idea specific insofar as national institutions are concerned is sufficient to satisfy most Americans of its utility. Furthermore, Article V of the Constitution, guaranteeing each state equal representation in the Senate, is practically speaking an unamendable part of the Constitution. There is a certain irony in the fact that although the Senate's general style and deliberative processes are more leisurely, more restrained, and are more clearly the products of tradition than those of the House, the Senate today is probably less conservative than the House in terms of supporting programs involving social and economic change. This apparent contradiction of the intention of the framers seems in itself to be related to the process of social change. Although the Senate was long regarded as the bastion of agrarianism because a majority of states were dominated by rural interests, the recent urbanization of the country has produced a considerable alteration in this respect. Since the House districts are so much the products of the gerrymander, they tend generally to be far less diversified internally than are most of the states. This condition (together with the short term of the House which makes its members politically vulnerable practically all of the time) has led to an intensification of the Congressman's ties to locally dominant issues, whereas the Senator appears to be freer to take a broader perspective. Furthermore, the larger size of the House reduces the possibilities for a member to make his presence felt as an individual and encourages the development of collectivities (or blocs) of like-minded Congressmen. The multiplication of these competing forces enhances the opportunities for opposing proposed courses of action and diminishes the chances for majority cohesion directed to a positive purpose. The Senate, on the other hand, is less volatile than the House and is able to offer a broad scope for influence on the part of the individual Senator (even to the point of fostering an occasional display of eccentricity), while at the same time achieving a degree of internal coherence that is apparently impossible to reach in the House.

SELECTION AND MEMBERSHIP

The methods of nominating and electing the members of Congress vary somewhat, since the election laws are established and administered by the states. There are, however, certain regularities which the Constitution itself establishes or permits Congress to impose. The Constitution, for example, requires that the states extend the right to vote in congressional elections to all persons who are qualified to vote for the most numerous house of the state legislature; and it prohibits the denial of the right to vote on grounds of race, color, previous condition of servitude, or of sex. The Constitution also prescribes a reduction in a state's representation if arbitrary exclusion from suffrage is practiced, but this provision has never been used. In addition to these requirements Congress has provided that members of the United States House of Representatives shall be elected from single-member districts (except in certain previously noted cases), that the secret ballot be used in congressional elections, and that the date of congressional elections be uniform throughout the United States.

Congressional general elections are accordingly held every two years (in the even-numbered ones) on the Tuesday after the first Monday in November. At each of these elections all 435 members of the House are selected and, since the Constitution was amended in 1913 to provide for the direct election of Senators, one-third of the Senate is elected at each congressional election. Senators thus serve six years, and the two from a given state are never chosen for full terms at the same election. In most states the political parties nominate their candidates for Congress in primary elections conducted in accordance with the state laws in the late summer or early fall prior to the November election. In states in which a strong party system is operative, the official party organization (the state central committee or the appropriate congressional district committee or corresponding party conventions) may endorse congressional candidates, in which case any opponent who chooses to challenge the party oligarchy's decision is likely to have an uphill fight in the primary. In many states, however, the party organization is either not strong enough consistently to fight off its own insurgent groups, or it makes little or no effort to influence the outcome of the primaries. The displacement of the convention system of nomination by the primary (which took place around the turn of this century) has had a pronounced effect in weakening party controls. If a central party organization cannot exert strong influence on the choice of candidates who run under the party label, it cannot hope to have much effect on development of issues or the maintenance of party discipline. The constituency organizations of the individual candidates thus tend to become the most influential factors in the nomination of congressional candidates, and the dominant social or political characteristics of the constituency tend to be the most affective force in determining the congressman's issue orientation. In American politics one looks in vain for the type of party mechanism that is capable of refining the main campaign issues, choosing candidates who will rise or fall with the tide of the party, and binding the legislative party into a united force for purposes of governing or of maintaining a loyal opposition.

Constitutional qualifications for membership in Congress are not overly stringent. A member of the House must be 25 years of age, have been a citizen of the United States for at least 7 years, and be an inhabitant of the state from which he is chosen. Custom sustains the localization of American politics by obliging Congressmen to be residents of the districts from which they are elected. Senators are constitutionally required to have attained a minimum age of 30 years, to have been United States citizens for at least 9 years, and be inhabitants of the states from which they are elected. The respective houses of Congress are judges of the election returns and qualifications of their own members. Although many persons feel that Congress should not go beyond constitutionally prescribed requirements in determining whether or not to seat a member, especially since each house has general power to expel its own members by two-thirds vote, there are a few cases in which the House of Representatives, particularly, has assumed a broad discretion in refusing seats.

The general characteristics of the members of Congress indicate that Americans, in common with electorates in most places, do not follow the "mirror" principle of electing representatives who reflect all of the attributes of the body politic in true proportions. Instead, the statistically typical Congressman or Senator tends to be possessed of qualities that are generally associated with a high degree of prestige in America. Although the range of ages of Congressmen may be from the low thirties to the late eighties (or more rarely, even the nineties), the average age is somewhat above the average of the adult population, with the House members falling in the early fifties and the Senators in the late fifties. Members of the Congress are substantially above the level of the population as a whole in formal education and tend to be drawn from occupations with a preferred status and a fairly high income. Law being the accepted route to political prominence, it is hardly surprising that almost two-thirds of the Senate and well over half of the House in the Eighty-seventh Congress (which was elected in November, 1960, and served in the sessions of 1961 and 1962) had been lawyers. Businessmen and bankers made up the next highest occupational groups, and they were followed by farmers, teachers, and journalists in descending order. Although a smattering of members indicated that they were in professions other than those listed, it is noticeable that none of the members lists himself as having a primary occupation falling in the skilled or unskilled labor class, or as having come to Congress from a position of leadership in the trade union movement. The preponderance of Congress is male; the Eighty-seventh Congress listed 15 women in the House and two in the Senate. The religious affiliations of Congressmen are ordinarily roughly proportionate to the distribution of church membership throughout the population as a whole. By and large the Congress is made up of people descended from northern European stock, with several generations of American residents comprising their ancestry. However, in a constituency with a dominant bloc drawn from a different ethnic group, the representative probably will derive from that group, a fact which largely accounts for the presence of a few Negro members and of persons of eastern and southern European ethnic backgrounds. A very high proportion of members will have had substantial political experience, usually in state or local government, prior to election to Congress. A Congressman is thus likely to be well-rooted in the area from which he is elected; and since politicians ordinarily are not introverts by nature and must be practicing extroverts if they wish to continue in office, he probably is an active participant in civic affairs, service clubs, and veterans' organizations in his home community. Although representatives of the radicalism of both the right and left are present in varying proportions in most Congresses, the dominating tendency is toward a middle-class moderation, a tendency which is associated not only with the personal characteristics of the membership but also with the factors which led to their selection.

CONGRESSIONAL ORGANIZATION

Congresses last for two years and are numbered consecutively from the first Congress of 1789. The Eighty-eighth Congress, for example, was elected in November, 1962. A new Congress, having been elected in the November election of an even-numbered year, is convened in the following January, usually on the third day of the month. This new Congress will sit for its first session until late summer or the fall of that year, and will reconvene for its second session in the following January. The second session of a Congress may be somewhat shorter than the first because of the necessity for campaigning for the summer primaries.

On the opening day of its first session each Congress organizes itself, or rather the House of Representatives organizes itself since the Senate is considered a continuing body which has only to fill in the gaps in its membership and organization instead of reconstituting itself. The main components of the official organization are the presiding officers and the committee system; in addition, the congressional parties have developed an institutional machinery which, though lacking the capacity to maintain party discipline, plays a secondary role of considerable importance. In point of fact, the party organization and the official organization are intertwined in several ways and the one issue on which a given Congress almost invariably divides along strict party lines is internal organization.

The presiding officer of the House of Representatives—the Speaker of the House—holds the most important position of leadership in Congress, and many observers rate this position as second only to the Presidency in terms of potential political effectiveness. Although the Speaker is ostensibly elected by the House, he is actually the designated leader of the majority party in that chamber. Both parties go through the formality of nominating a Speaker, but the outcome is assured. Normally, once an individual has been chosen for this position by his party he will continue to maintain his pre-eminence until his death, or until he voluntarily relinquishes his claim. However, in a recent congressional party shuffle, the Republicans displaced their former House leader, Joseph Martin, who had served as Speaker during the last two Congresses in which the Republicans had House majorities.

As presiding officer, the Speaker preserves order, recognizes members who wish to speak, interprets and applies the rules, puts questions to a vote, refers bills to committees, and appoints select and conference committees. Some of these formal duties, of course, are handled in an established manner which leave the Speaker little discretion, while others are subject to the possibility of his being overruled by the House. In interpreting and applying the rules, for example, the Speaker usually relies on precedent and may be overruled by the House, but not all circumstances are covered by precedents and it is rare that a Speaker is not sustained in his decisions. Similarly, although the Speaker's power of recognition is limited by many rules and customs, he does have discretion in matters of recognition in some instances, most notably on days when motions to suspend the rules are in order. Perhaps most important of all are the facts that the Speaker is at the center of all consultations regarding House affairs and that he represents the House to the public and to other governmental institutions in a variety of ways. These powers, together with the great prestige of the office and the man who occupies it, offer a considerable opportunity for the Speaker to affect both the substance of legislative business and its method of transaction. In contrast to the Speaker of the British House of Commons, the United States Speaker is expected to be politically partisan. He may vote on all matters and he can descend from the rostrum to take part in debate, although the latter step is sufficiently rare to point up the extreme importance of the issue at stake when it happens. The Speaker, in fact, derives part of his total influence from his partisanship; he is expected to be, and almost invariably is, a good party man who is willing to exhaust his personal ambitions in the control he exerts over House affairs, and for this he is respected. The assumption of this role makes it possible for him to work closely with the President on behalf of the party's program if he and the President are of the same party, and to try to arrive at a *modus vivendi* if they are from different parties. It should be noted, however, that his partisanship must remain within the bounds of what is considered "fairness" to the opposition (and for that matter, to insurgent members of his own party) as measured by the mores through which the House as a whole maintains its distinctiveness and sense of internal integrity. The late Sam Rayburn, who served longer as Speaker than any other person, combined the personal characteristics for successfully fulfilling these diverse functions as well as any Speaker in recent history.

The presiding officer of the Senate is, of course, the Vice-President of the United States. In keeping with staunch senatorial independence which is an important source of the *esprit de corps* of that body, the Vice-President has neither the formal powers nor the support of Senate expectations which would permit as much influence as the Speaker has in the House. The Vice-President can vote only to break a tie and may not participate in debate. The Senate elects a president *pro tempore* from the majority party to preside in the absence of the Vice-President.

The committee system is in many ways the key to the complex operations of the American Congress. Although Congress uses special or select (temporary) committees for particular purposes at times, and employs conference committees to settle differences between the two houses over the final version of bills, reference to the "committee system" is nearly always in terms of the standing (or permanent) committees in each house. The standing committee system is a product of custom and usage; in its earliest sessions Congress began to make use of special committees for breaking down the legislative task, and gradually some of these evolved into permanent committees specializing in various legislative subjects. The procedures and prerogatives of the committees were developed in much the same way, although many of these are now included in the rules or in statutes. From time to time Congress has made an attempt to overhaul the structure and clarify the responsibilities of the committees. The most comprehensive of these efforts was the Legislative Reorganization Act of 1946. At that time the number of House committees was reduced from 48 to 19 and the Senate committees from 33 to 15. Furthermore, the Act provided (with certain minor exceptions) that individual House members would serve on only one standing committee and Senators on no more than two each. The Act went into considerable detail in defining the jurisdictional area of each committee, despite the fact that the complexity of contemporary legislation makes it almost impossible to avoid some overlapping of committee functions in relation to actual bills. The 1946 statute remains the controlling instrument for the general structure and operation of the committees, but older habits continue to make their impact felt in the interplay of political power both within the individual committees and among the committees considered as a system.

In the Eighty-seventh Congress there were 16 standing committees in the Senate and 20 in the House. Apart from minor changes, each house had added to the 1946 list a committee primarily concerned with problems of space aeronautics. In addition to these, there has been a standing joint committee on atomic energy since the passage of the Atomic Energy Act in 1946. Membership on committees varies in the House of Representatives from nine on the Un-American Activities Committee to 50 on the Appropriations Committee; the smallest committee in the Senate is the one on the District of Columbia with seven members and the largest is the Appropriations Committee with 27 members.

Technically, the standing committees are elected by the houses of Congress. Under this system it would be conceivable for the majority party to ride roughshod over the minority party. However, in practice the number of seats to be assigned to each party is worked out in advance by the majority party leadership; and the minority party leaders are consulted (or at least informed) in advance of the places their party will fill on each committee. It is customary to divide committee assignments between the parties approximately in proportion to the size of the party delegations in the house concerned. In limiting the number of committees on which a Congressman may serve the 1946 Act provided something of a sanction for this usage. A majority party will not usually allow its control of certain committees to be placed in jeopardy by adhering rigidly to this percentage division, so in closely balanced divisions (and especially in the case of key committees) the majority may claim a disproportionate share of the seats, usually in the face of strong protests from the opposition. Under any circumstances, the minority party will be represented on all of the standing committees.

The actual committee lists are prepared by the committee on committees of each of the parties in the respective houses. Among the Democrats in the House of Representatives, the Democratic members of the Ways and Means (taxation) Committee serve as that party's committee on committees; otherwise these selection committees are separately chosen by the party conferences or caucuses. The actual committee lists prepared by the committees on committees are made up practically exclusively on the basis of the well-known seniority system. Under this system, the members of each committee are ranked (by party) in the order of their respective lengths of service on the particular committee, and are entitled to move up in rankings when persons above them no longer serve. The chairman of a committee, therefore, is the member of the majority party who has the longest period of service on the committee, and the ranking minority member is a sort of "shadow" chairman who will assume the chairmanship when his party regains the majority.

There is, furthermore, a second general rule of the seniority system which decrees that length of service in the house be used as a basis for determining the claim of an individual to a place on a committee of his choice. This means that a new member of Congress will be unlikely to obtain a seat on one of the committees regarded as highly desirable, such as Appropriations, Taxation or Foreign Affairs (although when he was majority leader in the Senate President Lyndon Johnson worked to deny Democratic Senators a second major committee post until every Democratic Senator had at least one top assignment). The interplay of these two seniority practices also means that a considerable amount of haggling and legislative infighting may be involved in sorting out claims when individuals move from one committee to another. Length of service in the house cannot be used, however, to claim committee precedence (or ranking) over another member who has longer service on the particular committee, and once on a committee a member is entitled to stay there.

The merits and demerits of the seniority system have been gone over endlessly by observers in and out of Congress. One of the more common arguments against the procedure is that seniority bears no relation to any attribute of leadership or to any other criterion by which the adequacy of legislative performance is properly measured. By placing emphasis on mere survival, the system insures that committees will be dominated by Representatives and Senators from safe constituencies—which normally means members from one-party areas or from constituencies with a high degree of social, economic, or ideological cohesion. Thus the committees will tend to remain under control of congressmen who are out of touch with the controversial issues on which campaigns in diversified (and strongly contested) constituencies turn. Yet it is the latter areas in which public opinion and the party struggle are active in bringing forth issues, and it is the shifting of opinion and party power in these same areas that determines the outcome of national elections. The specific example most often cited is the dominance of committee chairmanships by the southern bloc when the Democrats are in power.

Although the ties that bind organized southern politics to the national Democratic party are loose indeed, mere adherence to the party label and a vote with the party on organizational matters is sufficient to establish an absolute claim on these seats of power by the most disaffected, stand-pat element in what is accepted as the party of change. In general, it is the rule rather than the exception for committee chairmen to be out of accord with majority opinion in their own party, and this situation is merely exaggerated by the relation that southern members bear to the Democratic party.

Other charges may be leveled at the system. The longevity principle encourages specialization to such an extent that leadership is almost totally disintegrated. And since members choose membership in committees which reflect interests that predominate in their constituencies, this dispersal of power enlarges the effectiveness of pressure politics to the point at which members may become primarily the representatives of particular interests. On the other hand, the frequently expressed opinion that committee chairmanships are largely occupied by members approaching senility is not altogether accurate. Although the average age of committee chairmen is somewhat higher than the average age of members of the respective houses, the differential is less than might be expected. A recent study showed the age of committee chairmen in the House to exceed the average age of House members by 11 years; in the Senate the difference was only six years. By far the largest groupings of chairmen fell in the age intervals 50–59 and 60–69.

Given the structure of Congress, as a whole, it seems doubtful that the seniority system will soon be displaced. Even if the supporting argument that the process guarantees experienced leaders who attain their positions by an objective determination of priority seems weak, the seniority system so influences the total operation of Congress as to be virtually unassailable in practice. Too many Congressmen have too much investment of time and too many other commitments to the system to permit any general agreement on a different method, even if a positive need for change should be admitted. The dispersal of power represented by the committee system as such is a product of weak and diffused national party structures, of locally instructed delegations, and highly subjective appraisals of the politically relevant; the seniority system is less the cause of these elements in the constitution of Congress than one among several functions of them.

Attention is properly focused on the causes and effects of the seniority system because the chairmanship of a congressional standing committee is a position of great power. Woodrow Wilson long ago likened the dispersal of power in Congress to so many seignories, with the standing committee serving in the capacity of court baron and the chairman as lord-proprietor. As such he has many privileges; by skillful use of them he can go a long way toward controlling the legislative subject area defined by the committee's title. The chairman has, for example, extensive control over the agenda of committee meetings, choice of the members of subcommittees, and reference of bills to subcommittees. Through the first of these powers the chairman can drag out the action of a bill or hasten its consideration. By fixing the membership of subcommittees—which have tended to proliferate in direct proportion to the reduction in the number of standing committees since 1946—he can effectively bury a bill, attach subcommittee amendments to it, or secure a favorable recommendation from the subcommittee to the committee. Any of these things can be accomplished, too, with almost no regard for the wishes of the party leadership in Congress or in the executive. The chairman further has an active voice in the choice of the participants in the floor debate from the majority side, and his influence in the selection of conference committees is pronounced. Occasionally a chairman will find himself confronted with an obstreperous majority or a coalition of the committee which will override his broad discretionary power and, more rarely, a committee chairman will be bested by administration leaders in the Congress if they wage an all-out fight. But with so many opportunities for manipulation and with such compulsive attachment to the system on the part of most Congressmen the pre-eminence of the chairman is assured in nine cases out of ten.

The party leadership in Congress may lack extensive power, but the organization of the parties is comprehensive. The broadest instrument through which cohesion is attempted is the conference or caucus, which is the American counterpart of a meeting of the Parliamentary party. Only the House Democrats continue to refer to meetings of the legislative party in that chamber as a caucus; House Republicans and Senate Republicans and Democrats apply the term "conference" to this institution. Prior to the convening of a new Congress, caucuses or conferences are held by the parties in each house in order to select nominees for positions to be filled on opening day. Although caucuses may be held at other times, party leaders are reluctant to try to use them either as a means of control or for ascertaining party views, and when such moves are made they are usually vigorously resisted by the rank and file. Since there is no effective way of binding members to sustain caucus decisions, many Congressmen feel that it is better for the leadership to apply its efforts to producing a majority where it finds it in the Congress than to attempt the impossible task of securing total party unity in a general meeting.

The next instrumentality in the organizational structure of the congressional parties is an agency known in the Senate as the Policy Committee and in the House as the Steering Committee. Although the size of these committees varies somewhat, they are usually large enough to include representation from the major geographical areas of the country as well as the major components of party leadership. They thus tend to be made up of seasoned members who have considerable prestige in the House or Senate. Although these committees are not expected to formulate a comprehensive legislative policy for their parties, and do not attempt to do so, they do try to adopt a position on specific legislative proposals and to secure support for this stand from the other members in the congressional party. To this end they may select the measures on which party cohesion is most desired and adopt a strategy (in terms of timing, debate planning, etc.) designed to implement passage. On the whole the Senate Policy Committees seem to be more active and more effective than their counterparts in the House.

The party conferences or caucuses also designate floor leaders for their parties in each house. The majority floor leaders have sizeable responsibilities and considerable opportunity to influence the actions of Congress. It is their function to oversee the majority party's program in the respective houses. Since a heavy portion of the program will be framed in the executive branch, the majority leader will be expected to work closely with the President, although not to the extent of compromising his position as a legislator; if he represents the administration's views to his fellow party members (and to cooperative members of the opposing party), he is also supposed to inform and warn the President of the sentiments and disposition of the House or Senate. He is a key figure in planning legislative action and in maintaining the relations with committee chairmen and other individuals and groups necessary to effect party purposes. He informs the House or Senate of the courses proposed, puts the motions to keep the legislative program going, and often participates in debate. The arts of persuasion and compromise, the ability to command virtually universal respect, and the virtues of patience, tolerance, and a certain sympathy with the other person's point of view are important attributes of the man who aspires to these positions. In the

Democratic party in the Senate, the majority leader combines this function with the chairmanship of both the party conference and the Policy Committee. Former Democratic Senate leader President Lyndon Johnson is often cited as a prime example of a successful Senate leader despite the fact that he served during a period of division in party control of Congress and the Presidency. In fact, some commentators insist that Johnson's pragmatism and ability to compromise made him effective precisely *because* of party-divided government. The minority floor leaders have similar, although usually more negative, responsibilities in directing the opposition. They choose the legislative areas in which they will do battle with the majority, plan the strategy of the opposition forces, and try to make sure (through contact with the majority leaders) that they know what to expect and have ample opportunity to present their case.

The party conferences or caucuses also select chief whips to assist the floor leader in each house, and these party whips in turn choose a varying number of assistant whips, drawing them usually from the major sections of the country which have party representation in the House or Senate. It is the duty of the whips to ascertain the views of party members on present and pending legislative business, and to maintain as much party discipline as possible by persuading members to vote in accordance with the party's stand and by making certain that party members are out in full strength on crucial votes.

CONGRESS AT WORK

Much of the process by which legislation is enacted is implicit in the foregoing discussion of congressional organization, but a brief description of the procedure may help to pull some disparate parts of the discussion together. The passage of legislation is, after all, the essential function of Congress, and all of its other powers and activities are in some way related to this primary responsibility. As a preliminary it might be well to lay out certain fairly obvious but important facts. First of all, for general purposes of legislation the two houses of Congress are equal. Except for revenue bills, which must originate in the House but may be amended by the Senate, bills may originate in either house, but they must be passed in identical form through both houses before they can be enacted into law. All bills therefore go through the same general procedure in each house, although the details differ since each house operates under its own set of rules. Bills are given three readings in each chamber (perfunctory though some of these may be) and go through the committee stage in both House and Senate before they are enacted into law.

One of the first items of congressional procedure that catches the attention of the observer who is unacquainted with the process is the sheer volume of legislation. This work load is mainly the product of the unrestricted introduction of bills. Any member is free to introduce as many bills on as many different subjects as he may desire. There is no agency to perform the function carried on by the Cabinet in England of determining the number, the subjects and the contents of "public bills," and in assuring that these bills have a virtual monopoly of legislative time. In a sense all bills in Congress are "private member" bills, since they are all introduced (including the administration bills) by members in their individual capacities or by the committees. In recent sessions each Congress has had from 12,000 to 15,000 or more bills and resolutions introduced, and it is not unusual for more than 2000 bills to make their appearance on the clerk's desk on opening day in the House of Representatives. Once a bill is introduced, it remains alive throughout the remainder of that Congress unless it is actually passed, defeated, or withdrawn.

Although bills bear the name or names of the persons introducing them, this sponsorship is no indication of the actual origin of the measures. A steadily increasing number of important bills are administration bills, many of which are drafted in executive departments or agencies and then passed on to administration leaders, sympathizers, or appropriate committees for introduction. Other bills come from private sources; some of these originate with major economic or political interests, while others are introduced as a form of courtesy to a Representative's constituents. Bills in the latter category are often labeled "by request" in order to indicate that the sponsor has no substantial commitment to the proposal. The fate of most of these bills—burial in committee—is predetermined by this label. A sizeable number of bills are initiated almost entirely in the committees as a result of the experience of working in a specialized area of legislation. Some bills, of course, are products of individual legislators or small groups of Congressmen working on their own initiative. Most of the technical work in drafting legislation for Congress is handled by a staff of lawyers organized into the Office of the Legislative Counsel; this office is divided into sections under separate directors for furnishing bill-drafting services to the Senate and House respectively.

Once a bill is introduced it is given a number and assigned to a committee. Most assignments are virtually automatic; but the presiding officer is responsible, and may influence action on a marginal bill by assigning it to a sympathetic or to a hostile committee. The Speaker has broader discretion than the Vice-President in assigning bills; some Vice-Presidents simply make it a practice to assign bills to the committee desired by the sponsoring Senator. The presiding officer can be overruled in this respect by majority vote of the chamber, but this is a rare occurrence.

Woodrow Wilson said, "Congress in session is Congress on public exhibition, whilst Congress in its committee room is Congress at work." Largely because of the immense amount of legislation introduced and because of the lack of central direction such as that afforded in cabinet government, committees must perform the major function of sorting out the bills and selecting the ones which will be allowed to proceed further in the highly competitive process by which a bill becomes an Act. Committee chairmen, especially, but occasionally the committee as a whole, have virtually life or death control over bills. The overwhelming proportion of bills—three-fourths or more of those introduced—never get beyond the committee stage and most of these are pigeonholed after a cursory examination by the chairman of a committee or a subcommittee. The ease with which a committee may end the life of a bill by not reporting it has provoked much criticism. There is, to be sure, a "discharge rule" in the House, but it requires a petition with 218 signatures followed by a seven-day delay before it can be made effective. These stringent requirements, together with the accepted notion of the "integrity of the committee system" severely limit the usefulness of this procedure.

The intensity of committee activity is indicated to some extent by the fact that a tabulation showed an average of 30 committee or subcommittee meetings each day of a recent congressional session. This volume of work in itself suggests that committees perform functions other than those of selection agencies. Their second great responsibility is to consider bills in detail, section by section, provision by provision, for the purposes of evaluating the need for the legislation, the extent to which the bills at hand fit these needs, and the possible effects of the measures in all of their relevant connections. In accordance with its findings a committee may decide to amend a bill or to draft a substitute for the one introduced. On most bills of general interest the chairman will hold a public hearing in which interested parties such as lobbyists, administrative agencies, or other groups are given a chance to present information and to express their views. In some cases the committee or a subcommittee may invite expert testimony at public or other hearings, and the committee staff or the Legislative Reference Service of the Library of Congress may furnish data in the form of reports or answers to specific inquiries. A committee may deliberate in public at times, but most of its own arguments and its actual decisions take place in "executive" or closed sessions. However, the votes of the committee members and the general record of the committee's actions appear in the report on a bill.

Once a committee completes its considerations and decides to report a bill favorably, as amended, or in the form of a substitute, the bill goes on one of the calendars used in each house. It is then ready to be brought up for debate before the entire membership of that house. At this stage of proceedings the rules and practice of the two houses are somewhat divergent. The Senate being a smaller body than the House and the "upper" chamber, its members are more privileged as individuals. The result is a more leisurely and less thoroughly managed procedure. Bills are rarely taken up out of calendar order in the Senate (except occasionally by unanimous consent) and there is no effective cloture rule there. The latter hiatus leads to the often discussed tactic called the filibuster, by which a bill may literally be talked to death by an opposing minority. The most effective use of a filibuster is near the end of a session when important measures such as appropriations bills remain to be passed before adjournment and the bill against which the filibuster is directed precedes these crucial items on the calendar. A small group of men may then get the floor and hold up proceedings until their conditions are met. The filibuster has most often been used in recent years by southern Senators to prevent the passage of civil rights bills involving race relations, although this has by no means been its exclusive use. In fact some of the most avid civil libertarians and opponents of the filibuster have been known to resort to the filibuster when it suited their purposes. Senator Wayne Morse of Oregon, a strong civil rights exponent and often an outspoken advocate of tighter cloture, held the floor for 22 hours in 1953 while opposing legislation to return the oil-producing tidelands to the states. At the time this established a new record for an individual speaker; however, it was broken in 1957 by Senator Strom Thurmond of South Carolina who talked for more than 24 hours.

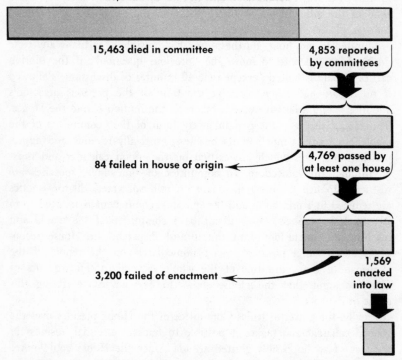

20,316 bills and resolutions introduced

15,463 died in committee

4,853 reported by committees

4,769 passed by at least one house

84 failed in house of origin

1,569 enacted into law

3,200 failed of enactment

Legislative Measures in the 87th Congress. *Source:* Adapted from Floyd M. Riddick, "Eighty-Seventh Congress; Second Session," **XVI**, Western Political Quarterly, 133–148.

Although Senate cloture is so difficult as to be virtually impossible to invoke (the final step is a two-thirds vote of the Senators present), on most legislative matters the leadership of the two parties can agree on a general time allocation for partisan debate and set a time at which a final vote will be taken without violating the principle of virtually unlimited debate. Thus the filibuster is reserved mainly for use against measures in which minority blocs of the Senate have an absolutely un-compromising commitment; if this obstructive tactic were habitually employed as an opposition weapon, the legislative process would break down entirely.

In contrast to the Senate, the House of Representatives uses several devices to expedite its business and to take up important measures other than in the order in which they appear on the calendars. The House, for example, has a continuous cloture rule under which individual speeches are limited to one hour. Furthermore, it is possible at virtually any time during House debate to move the "previous question"; if the motion carries, debate is halted (except that 40 minutes of discussion is allowed if no debate had taken place at the time of the previous question's adoption), and a decisive vote is taken on the motion before the House. The House also uses the parliamentary form of the "committee of the whole" to transact much of its business, especially revenue and appro-priations measures which are carried on the union calendar and must go through this procedure. In committee of the whole, speeches are restricted to five minutes, there are no roll call votes, dilatory tactics are reduced to a minimum and the quorum requirement is reduced from 218 to 100 members. After sitting as a committee of the whole and reaching its conclusions with the utmost dispatch, the House recon-venes and is in a position to act immediately on the report of the chairman of the committee of the whole. Several careful students of Congress argue that the House shows to best advantage during this phase of its work.

Finally, the powerful Rules Committee of the House presides over the general calendar and makes it possible to transact essential business in the face of an impossibly glutted agenda. Since the House could never get through all of its pending business it is necessary that some arrange-ment be made for establishing priorities on matters listed on the calendars. By bringing forth special orders, which are then ratified by the House, the Rules Committee can arrange the daily order of business so that measures can be taken up out of calendar sequence. The Rules Com-mittee also drafts resolutions which control the total length of debate on particular bills and divide the time between proponents and opponents of the bills. In addition, the Rules Committee may apply the "gag" or "guillotine" on a particular bill by placing special limits on debate, by precluding floor amendments and leaving only the Committee amendments for consideration, and by overriding in advance dilatory tactics in matters such as points of order.

The usefulness of the Rules Committee in expediting business is at times offset by its capacity for extending its considerable powers. By refusing to take a bill off the calendar for debate the Rules Committee can block legislation strongly advocated by the administration and/or one of the standing committees. Alternatively the Committee may demand changes or an overhauling of a measure before it will acquiesce in the demand that the bill be taken up. These powers tend to transform the Rules Committee into a supercommittee without portfolio in relation to the standing committees on substantive areas of legislation. In 1961 a coalition of southern Democrats (including the chairman) and Republicans on the Rules Committee were consistently taking action to strangle the measures advanced by the Kennedy administration, which was then newly in office. A bitter fight ensued, but Speaker Sam Rayburn's influence finally prevailed and the committee was enlarged from 12 to 15 members, so that the antiadministration majority was reversed. Chairman Howard Smith of Virginia, in a final gesture of retaliation, did not provide seats in the committee room for the three new members.

If a bill survives all of these stages and is given a favorable vote on the question of final passage in the house in which it was introduced, it crosses the Capitol to the other chamber and goes through the entire process there. If the bill should be amended in the second chamber, it is sent back to the house of origin to determine whether that body will concur in the amendments. If the latter refuses, a conference committee to settle the issues outstanding is in order when either of the two houses requests it. This procedure is necessary in a relatively small percentage of the legislation passed by Congress, but it occurs more often on major bills than on minor ones. The conference is, in fact, another "supercommittee" arrangement. Since conference reports are not subject to amendment in either house, and since the bills on which conferences are held are often crucial ones, these *ad hoc* groups are further strong links in the chain of committee power. In appointing members of conference committees the presiding officers normally follow the recommendations of the chairman of the committees which handled the bill in the two houses, and these chairmen will usually place their own names at the top of the list. Conference committees vary in total membership, but the House and Senate are equally represented, the compromise which is reached is usually subject to ratification by the separate components (i.e., House and Senate members) of the committee, and minority representation is included among the conferrees from each chamber. The conference is free to make a decision that diverges widely from the final version of the bill as approved by the two houses, and conference reports are seldom rejected. These considerable powers over the ultimate content of key bills and the scope for manipulation during the selection of a conference's membership almost inevitably produce a substantial amount of behind-the-scenes maneuvering whenever the need for a conference arises.

When a bill has cleared both houses it goes to the President for his approval. The President has ten days from the time the bill is delivered to him to sign it or veto it; otherwise the bill becomes law without his signature. However, if Congress adjourns during the ten-day interval, the President may withhold his signature and the bill does *not* become law. The latter practice is referred to as a "pocket veto" and is an absolute one. If, as is usual, Congress continues in session beyond the ten-day period and the President vetoes the bill, it is referred back to the congressional house of origin with the President's accompanying veto message. Congress is thus given an opportunity to reconsider the measure and to pass it over the President's veto if a two-thirds vote can be mustered in each house.

Some of the nonlegislative powers and functions of Congress have been discussed or at least alluded to in this and preceding chapters. For example, the role of the Congress in amending the Constitution, which is known as a "constituent" function, was discussed earlier, as were its electoral functions in relation to the offices of President and Vice-President and its shared responsibilities in the fields of executive appointment and treaty-making. The latter two powers, especially, make up substantial parts of the congressional work load. In a recent session the Senate acted on 48,000 nominations (these include military commissions as well as civil appointments) and considered a total of 28 treaties, ratifying 10 of them and carrying the remaining 18 over for further disposition.

The use of "senatorial courtesy" with regard to the confirmation of presidential nominations is worthy of note. The device is a simple one whereby appointments referred to the Senate for advice and consent are quietly checked with the Senators from the state in which the appointment is to be made. If a Senator indicates his objection to the nominee, the Senate will almost invariably accept his objection and reject the nomination. In effect the practice virtually demands that the President clear appointments within a given state with the Senators from the state, especially when one or both Senators are members of the President's political party. The political consequences of senatorial courtesy are important inasmuch as they provide some senatorial patronage and thereby improve the Senator's position, both with state political organizations and the national administration. The custom is also a factor in diffusing the sources of national party leadership and weakening party discipline.

Attention has also been called to the fact that Congress has a duty of legislative overseeing *via-à-vis* the administration's performance. The growth of administration has made this an increasingly difficult task, but Congress still attempts to carry it out mainly through its power to control the broader features of the organization of the executive branch and through budget review and hearings. Each house also has a standing committee on government operations to review programs and procedures of administration, and all of the standing committees were charged by the Legislative Reorganization Act of 1946 with responsibility for checking on the execution of laws which they handled in the bill stage. The United States Congress does not have an order of business comparable to the question period in the British House of Commons, but a steady stream of requests and inquiries go out of the offices of individual Congressmen to the executive departments and agencies, and dissatisfaction with the responses can lead to consequences ranging from mild rebuke on the floor of one of the chambers to a full-scale congressional investigation.

The investigatory power, itself, is another of the important ancillary functions of Congress, and it is not limited merely to legislative inquiries into the administration of the laws passed by Congress. In fact it is difficult to delimit the various functions to which the congressional investigation may be put. The courts have long since held that the investigatory power is an essential adjunct of the law-making authority. It seems to be generally agreed that the investigatory function may be used to secure information in areas in which Congress contemplates legislation, to ascertain the effectiveness with which laws are being executed, to uncover wrongdoing in the government, and simply to inform the

American public on problems essential to the country's welfare. More than 800 investigations have been conducted by Congress throughout its history; these range from minor and short-lived inquiries to such celebrated investigations as that which uncovered the Teapot Dome scandal of the 1920s, the Kefauver Committee investigation of crime in interstate commerce, and the celebrated McCarthy investigations culminating in the Senator's censure by his fellow members of the Senate. The scope of potential inquiry by investigation is thus extremely broad and the means by which the investigations are carried out are also quite broad. Standing committees, subcommittees, and special committees have engaged in congressional investigation, and at least one standing committee—the House Committee on Un-American Activities—conducts investigations into questions of alleged disloyalty as its main function. The committees have, or may be vested with, broad powers to enable them to carry out their inquiries, including the authority to subpoena witnesses, to compel the production of papers, and to cite witnesses for contempt.

Much criticism has been directed at the abuse of investigatory powers by congressional committees. Chief among the complaints have been the charges that some investigations seem to have been carried out less with a view to securing information than to seeking publicity for those conducting them; that the atmosphere in some cases has been less than judicial, in fact, it has been hostile, intimidating, and embarrassing to witnesses, and that there are numerous cases in which persons have been effectively denied constitutional rights by being forced to testify or by suffering serious damage to reputation (and to their economic welfare) as a result of allegations, leading questions, or insinuation. Recently both the courts and Congress have attempted to meet some of these charges by defining the purposes of investigations more carefully, by developing specific procedural standards, by extending more substantial protections to witnesses called to testify, and by reviewing both projected and completed investigations with greater care.

One other function of Congress which deserves brief explanation in this broad catalogue is the judicial-type power of impeachment. Impeachment charges may be brought against the President, Vice-President, and all civil officers of the United States for treason, bribery, or other high crimes and misdemeanors. The articles of impeachment in such a case are prepared by a committee in the House of Representatives, and if the House approves these charges the impeachment trial takes place in the Senate. The trial is conducted before the Senate by a group of house "managers" and conviction requires a vote of two-thirds of the Senate. Punishment in impeachment trial convictions is limited to removal from office and prohibition against holding any office of honor, trust, or profit under the United States in the future. This sentence, however, does not act as a bar against trial in the courts for an indictable offense. Only 12 impeachment trials have been held throughout American history, most of them involving judges; the most celebrated was that of President Andrew Johnson in 1868, in which the Senate, under the prodding of the radical reconstructionists, fell only one vote short of securing a conviction.

THE SYSTEM IN RETROSPECT

In this chapter much emphasis has been placed on what may seem a somewhat disjointed and haphazard approach to the vital problem of legislation. The congressional representative system has been described as highly localized and narrowly reflective of constituency social patterns and interests. Voting in Congress tends to follow regional or other bloc lines rather than the vague lines of national unity marked out by the party structure and emphasized by the President as a national party leader. Even a reasonably knowledgeable observer may well wonder what holds such a legislative body together and enables it to provide the legislation essential to the maintenance of political order in a great national state. Perhaps the most important unifying factor is commitment to the system itself, which is a commitment to certain not always clear constitutional ideals as well as to a pattern of expectations and mores internal to the Congress itself. The American government was deliberately framed in a manner designed to check and impede precipitous governmental action, and the founding fathers were perhaps more successful than they realized in promoting this aim. At the same time, opportunities for delay and obstruction were not intended (and for the most part have not been used) to paralyze governmental action. America is not only a very large but is an incredibly diverse country and its pluralistic features alone would cause any democratically-based consensus on policy to be slow to develop and tenuous at best; the representative and procedural features of Congress merely emphasize the tortuous nature of this process.

Perhaps one reason Congress passes so much more legislation than most parliamentary bodies is the extreme necessity for compromise and piecemeal approaches to the solution of problems that virtually everybody recognizes to be problems. If much of the legislation in so-called "normal" times is a sort of patchwork of pragmatism rather than a rationally coherent structure, this is a further testimony to the logic of diversity by which the system has to work. The Congress has developed a special internal cohesion of its own, and the organizational and procedural features of that cohesion are implicitly based on the assumption that (despite institutional, societal and personal complexities) almost any issue can be resolved by the fine art of compromise and accomodation. And in times of grave national crisis Congress is capable of responding—especially when adequate executive leadership is forthcoming—with a unity and alacrity that would do credit to a party-disciplined legislature in a far less heterogenous society. Finally, this diffuse process offers an opportunity that few other legislative bodies can equal in permitting a courageous, determined, and skillful individual Senator or Congressman to put together on his own initiative the consensus—both public and legislative—necessary to effect a major innovation. Thus the late Senator George Norris of Nebraska, after ten years or more of relentless effort, ultimately succeeded in securing passage of the act creating the Tennessee Valley Authority, one of the abiding monuments to American ingenuity and public-spiritedness.

QUESTIONS FOR FURTHER DISCUSSION

1. What factors in the representative structure of Congress contribute to the idea that a member of Congress is a delegate of his constituency acting under an instructed mandate rather than a virtual representative of the entire country acting under general mandate?
2. In what ways do the political styles and the method of conducting business differ in the House and the Senate?
3. Outline the major aims of the Legislative Reorganization Act of 1946 and appraise the degree to which these aims have been effected.
4. What are the alternatives to the present seniority system of committee assignments?
5. To what extent have the abuses of the investigatory power of Congress tended to vitiate the utility of congressional investigations, and what have Congress and the courts attempted to do in the way of correction?

V

The American System of Political Parties

THE FUNCTION OF PARTIES IN A DEMOCRACY

Political parties, which are organized to gain control of the government, are present in almost any form of organized society for a reason as simple as that expressed in the fable of the father and sons and the bundle of faggots: there is strength in unity. The purpose which parties intend to realize by gaining access to the machinery of government vary widely from one political society to another, and the means used by a nation's parties to achieve power goes a long way towards explaining a particular political system.

However, the existence of parties in a democratic society—and not just parties but a functioning party system—is more than a useful contrivance; it is a *sine qua non* of democratic order. This is so because political parties are institutions through which the promise of the democratic ideal can be fulfilled, to a greater or lesser degree, in practice. A party in a democracy is dependent on popular support for attaining power and for continuing in office. The primary functions of democratically-oriented parties, in the abstract and therefore undefiled sense which removes them from the greedy hands of the politicians to the elevated realm of ideas, are to develop issues, nominate candidates, and organize the electors. In performing these functions the parties make it possible for the voters to make responsible political choices. And the ability to choose those who govern and the issues that will concern the governors are, after all, the only means available for the exercise of political power which is presumably dispersed among millions of discrete individuals in a democracy.

In view of this situation it further seems clear that the more these party organizations tend to reduce themselves in number, without actually eliminating the possibility of a real alternative in the voter's choice, the more effectively may they be said to be performing their function. If it can be assumed that a monopoly of the party function by a single political organization does not satisfy the demand for effective choice, the major question then centers on the effects of a two-party system as compared with a multi-party system. And most of the literature on political parties indicates that the difference is substantial. First of all, by reducing the voters' choice to a clear-cut either/or proposition, the two-party system compromises and reconciles a broad range of potentially disruptive groups into a relatively stable (albeit temporary and some-times uneasy) consensus. This process of reduction also means that the compromises necessary to arrive at a working majority in the legislative body—or at least many of them—are worked out *before* the election in a two-party system, whereas the adjustments and reconciliations must take place *after* the election in a multi-party system. There is no need to belabor the advantages that the majoritarian proclivity of the two-party system has over a multi-party system in the way of focusing responsibility clearly on the majority party and for imposing on the victor the necessity to redeem its campaign pledges, especially those promises which it has not hedged sufficiently in the heat of oratory.

All the beneficent efforts of biparty government are by no means reserved for the majority party. By affording the minority party a monopoly on opposition the system tends to force a large degree of responsibility on the organization losing an election. This happens be-cause the minority party (if it is large enough to be in anything approach-ing a challenging position *vis-à-vis* the majority party) is constrained to oppose in the light of the omnipresent possibility (and indeed the hope) that it will supplant the majority party and thus assume responsibility for governing in its own right. This imminence of power is a restraining influence on a minority party which might otherwise be prone to excesses in its opposition. Increasing responsibility by concentrating authority and reducing the alternative to the party in power to a single opposing organization may seem paradoxical on the surface, but the method has proved itself pragmatically in political experience.

Finally, there is the moderating effect of a simple dichotomy in the internal politics of a democratic country, an effect which is reckoned by many to be the most important influence of a two-party system. Modera-tion results largely from the simplifying effects of two-partyism that have already been mentioned: the necessity for broadening election appeals so as to encompass a variety of social groups, and the enhanced sense of realism produced by the potentiality of an early accession to power. Politics is still the art of the possible, and parties with an op-portunity to control the government can ill afford to isolate large groups who may be the means to power, or to jeopardize their future existence by appeals based on goals that are impossible to attain. The politics of a two-party state is thus held within the framework of a national tradition which encourages change but at the same time prevents that change from being visionary, radical, and totally unrelated to the unarticulated expectations that grew out of the experience which preceded the change. It is worth noting here that extremist politics within the United States has been most apparent in those areas in which one-party (and frequently multi-factional) politics has predominated. Of course, many commentators are highly critical of the moderation of the two-party system and suggest that what it really means is that there is no difference between the two parties. But this is a superficial view which fails to take account of the tenuous nature of social order and of the stultifying effects of excessively ideological politics. A judgement of this type may be appropriately modified by Lord Balfour's somewhat exaggerated comment that the system works precisely because of the minimal difference between the parties. There are, as a matter of fact, tangible differences between the major American parties which will become more apparent in the succeeding discussion. And what is more important, practical persons within a wide range of the left-to-right political spectrum can agree that both social change and the lack of change can, under different circumstances, involve real threats to the existing order, and that the moderation of the two-party system is a meliorating influence relative to such threats.

ORGANIZATION OF AMERICAN PARTIES

What has been said thus far constitutes an abstract and idealized conception of the two-party system, of course, and the ideal so conceived is rarely approached in reality. In making the transition from the ideal to the historically concrete American party system it may be suggested that, because of the specific conditions which helped to form the system and have maintained it, the structure of American party politics falls somewhere between the extremes of the British system, with its high degree of party responsibility and central party discipline, and a multi-party system with its fragmented parliamentary composition which necessitates uneasy governing coalitions, negates the possibility of positive responsibility, and intensifies ideological as opposed to traditional politics. Despite the fact that American parties are loosely organized and the governments organized by the Republican or Democratic parties depend more on consensus (frequently cutting across party lines) than on a stable majority for effecting programs, the burden of the subsequent discussion will be to show that the American party system has performed its necessary functions surprisingly well in the face of considerable historical and sociological difficulties.

On the one hand, and working against a purer type of two-party politics, is the American system of the separation of powers. The arrangement was deliberately calculated to prevent single organizational control of the entire government, but its main effect (although by no means the sole one) has been to militate against party cohesion and responsibility in the manner often attributed to a two-party system in a framework of parliamentary government. The complete separation of the two "political" branches (Congress and the Presidency), together with certain concomitants of the separation—such as fixed rotating terms of office of the Senate, the House and the President, and the great variations in their respective constituencies—frequently produces governments in which the executive and legislative branches are divided in terms of party control. But even when one party elects a President and majorities in both houses of Congress, the President as party leader has no compelling sanctions, either by way of dissolution or influence over nominating processes, with which to offset the many pressures on individual members of Congress to deviate from the party's position on major issues. Furthermore, the federal system may be said to compound this difficulty by decentralizing party power and thus enlarging the difficulty of establishing discipline at the national level.

On the other hand (and contributing to the realization of two-party politics) there is the important consideration of the continuing existence *in fact* of two major parties which, between them, have a virtual monopoly of national popular support—support which is shared on a basis near enough to equality to make them fiercely competitive. Furthermore, the existence of a single-head, nationally elective Presidency precludes the possibility of sharing executive power among the parties after the style of a coalition government. Finally, the size and complexity of the country, together with the auspicious origins of its party system, have produced and sustained a pronounced absence of absorptive ideology in both major parties. In other words, in order to have any prospect of success at the polls, either party must continue to receive at least partial support from so many different socio-economic groups representing such a variety of interests and aspirations that its program is perforce one of broad and carefully compromised issues.

Before proceeding to examine the historical roots of the somewhat ambivalent two-party system in America, it might be well to outline the main organizational features of the parties, because a sizeable number of the operative principles of the system are implied in the organizations. Since parties are designed to win elections, it is only natural that their organizations should be based on the electoral districts into which the country is divided. Party organizations also tend to be hierarchical in form, with a broad base of party agents at the lower echelons and a gradually diminishing number of individuals and committees playing important roles as the higher levels of party organization are reached. In American parties, however, the hierarchies are not as effectively centralized at the national level as they are in many countries.

The lowest organizational level at which party workers operate is the precinct. An electoral precinct is a small geographical unit which serves solely as a basis for a polling place in which the electors living within its confines cast their ballots. A precinct may thus embrace only a few square blocks of a great city, since it is normally not considered practical to have more than 1500 to 2000 persons vote at a single location. Because of its manageable size, the precinct is the electoral unit at which the *individual* voter may be most directly approached by the party. The parties normally provide for a precinct captain, or in some cases for a precinct committee, to manage their affairs at this level. The captain or the committee has the responsibility for acting as a direct contact between the party and the voters, for seeing that potential party supporters qualify themselves to vote, and for carrying out a variety of routine tasks designed to secure an electoral majority for his party in this small domain. In the days before so many of the social services were public, the precinct captain was often a small-scale welfare or relief worker, using his allocation of party funds for the purchase of food, clothing, coal, or other necessities to be distributed among the needy party faithfuls or even among those who would be likely to remember the party's beneficence on election day. He still acts as a distributor of minor favors in most areas by extending a friendly partisan hand to precinct residents who have received citations for violating traffic regulations, who want a contact with the appropriate municipal government department head in support of an application for a job with the city, or who merely wish to find the proper approach to securing a zoning change or some other minor governmental service.

The next stage in the party hierarchy ordinarily is the ward committee, which in some cases may be composed of the precinct captains or in others may be separately constituted. The ward organization is likely to be little more than an enlarged precinct party instrument, concerning itself almost entirely with the mobilization of the voters, acting as a contact with the next higher party echelon, and maintaining some degree of coordination among the precinct workers.

The next party committee level, however, takes on a broader range of functions. This is the county committee, whose chairman, especially in areas in which party competition is intense, is probably an experienced professional. The county committee has responsibilities for maintaining party effectiveness over an area from which a sizeable number of relatively important public officials are elected (often including members of the state legislature), and which may be a key geographic unit in the party's success within a congressional district or even in the state as a whole. The county committee is therefore concerned not only with getting voters to the polls, but also with recruitment and supervision of party workers, with the screening of potential party nominees to local office or to the legislature, with campaign strategy, and with fund-raising. Particularly in large counties, the chairman and other party leaders will control a substantial amount of local patronage, and in general constitute a force to be reckoned with by office seekers at all levels of government.

A corresponding (or in many cases overlapping) organization exists at the city level. The municipal committee and its chairman are organized and exercise responsibilities for the city that closely parallel the county committee's. In some instances the organizations may be synonymous. The city organizations have a special interest for students of American politics, for it was here that one of the most interesting phenomenon of American politics—the party boss—achieved (and to a lesser degree, maintains) notoriety. The city (and not infrequently the county) boss was formerly the object of much opprobrium, especially in the reformist era at the turn of the twentieth century. The boss was the man who controlled public affairs without assuming popular responsibility, by manipulating party machinery. He and his cohorts largely determined which among the party's office seekers would secure the machine's backing and financial aid; and in return the office holders yielded to the party organization's choice of patronage eligibles in terms of jobs, public works and equipment contracts, franchises, concessions, and other economic favors. The boss was thus a skilled influence broker, informally coordinating and controlling a complex network of public and private individual and group participants in the local system of politics. A substantial number of specific political reform devices have been directed toward weakening his influence: the primary method of nomination in which the rank and file of voters nominate party candidates through direct intra-party election; the development of merit systems for local civil service appointment, stricter budgeting, purchasing, and accounting systems; the city-manager form, and other local government developments owe their origins in part to reactions against the party boss. Yet, in the contemporary era of political "image-making," in which professional public relations firms are able to sell the voters candidates who have been scientifically synthesized to meet the criterion of "positive public reaction," a certain nostalgia for the old-fashioned "natural political man" which the boss represented is frequently apparent.

The next level of party organization above the county and municipal committees is the state central committee (although some other committees such as congressional district committees may supervene in some states). In many ways the state party committees are the most powerful instruments of organized political power in the United States because the national organizations are really loose coalitions of party personnel drawn from the machinery of the various states. This is so because the states largely control the electoral machinery of the country and constitute the major electoral districts, even for national offices. The state central committees of the various states are selected in a variety of ways; their members may be directly elected by party adherents in primary elections, they may be selected by state conventions, or they may be chosen directly or indirectly by county organizations. The state committees may, of course, be subject to domination by one or more powerful county chairmen, or they may tend to fall under the influence of the state governor or some other titular party head. Under any circumstances the central committees are arbiters of the party rules (subject to such legal regulations as may be on the statute books), they are likely to be prime factors in overall party strategy and the coordination of local organizations, they are influential in endorsing aspiring candidates for state-wide elective offices, in large measure they set the tone for the attitude taken by the state party toward the national party organization (in this capacity the makers of presidential candidates must deal with the leadership of these committees), and they are key elements in campaign finance.

The national party committees are composed of members chosen by the various state organizations and confirmed by the national convention. Basically, the national committee of each party is made up of one man and one woman from each state, but the Republicans permit a bonus member (actually the state committee chairman) for each state carried by the Republicans in the preceding presidential election or having a Republican Senator or a Republican majority in the state delegation in the United States House of Representatives. The national committee ostensibly governs the national party between the quadrennial national nominating conventions; in fact its primary function is to make preliminary arrangements for the convention. In some periods the national committee, especially in the Democratic party in recent years, has played a more substantial role in party strategy and attitudes, usually through the work of a policy subcommittee. As indicated in Chapter III (where the composition and main function of the national convention were also briefly described), the chairman of the national party committee is designated by the presidential nominee, and he and his staff (usually referred to as the "national office" of the party) are the campaign work horses of the party in the presidential campaign. Under the general direction of the presidential candidate they plan the itinerary of the campaign, set up the various specialized divisions (women's division, ethnic group divisions, etc.), prepare speeches and press releases, maintain contact with state and local organizations, and otherwise manage the campaign.

One other part of the machinery of party politics—the congressional campaign committee—deserves brief mention. Each party establishes such a committee in each house of Congress for each congressional campaign. These committees are designed to give constituency assistance to party members, especially those who are up for re-election. To this end they provide speakers, assist in planning the congressional campaigns, and in some instances provide limited funds to supplement other sources of campaign finance. The role of these committees, however, is almost always supplementary to the efforts of the congressional district or the state party organization in the particular localities.

From the foregoing it may be correctly inferred that the organization of American parties is loose, decentralized, sporadic, and office-oriented rather than cohesive, disciplined, continuous, and issue-based. The rank and file of the voters are for the most part passive in their relation to party membership, the screening and nomination of candidates is not highly systematized and there are no professional agents to serve in the dual role of local campaign organizers and coordinators of the constituency campaign with central party aims. In this context it should be remembered that party membership is usually very loosely conceived in the United States. Few American voters participate actively in organized affairs of the party, such as local party meetings; and party associations made up of dues-paying individual members are rare indeed. An elector may have to indicate his party adherence when qualifying to vote or affirm it upon challenge in order to participate in a primary election (most state laws call for "closed" nominating primaries in which only members of the party conducting the primary are allowed to vote, although some states hold "open" primaries in which no declaration of party is necessary). But beyond such formal declarations, party adherence is largely a state of mind and entails little in the way of obligation to the party on the part of those who consider themselves to be members.

The financing of American parties and political campaigns reflects these general organizational tendencies. Although numerous attempts have been made to broaden the popular base of campaign funds, these have met with small success. The overwhelming proportion of monies raised by the party committees still comes from large contributions; more than 75 percent of the party contributions exceed $100 and over half of them represent gifts of more than $500. Thus despite the regulations which limit organizations campaigning in more than one state to a maximum expenditure of $3 million in one campaign, set the limits of an individual contribution at $5000, and forbid direct campaign contributions by corporations and labor unions, the party devices for fund-raising and expenditure continue to be directed toward large resources. The estimates of the total costs of recent presidential campaigns range upwards of $100 million. This means, in effect, that a multiplicity of official and unofficial organizations are all engaged in large-scale solicitation and expenditure. It also means that individual stockholders of the corporations and each member of the stockholder's immediate family may be contributing the maximum permissible amounts, sometimes to several different organizations engaged in essentially the same purpose; and that labor organizations have formed separate political action committees which solicit and spend enormous sums. The parties also hold fund-raising dinners which attract the party faithful and others who have to hedge their party bets by a show of generosity beyond their regular gifts. Many questions are raised by these methods of party finance and many hypothetical solutions have been advanced as means of changing them, but in the absence of party cohesion at all levels of American government and without a more widespread sense of party adherence on the part of the electorate the prevailing method is likely to persist in the foreseeable future.

ORIGINS AND CONTINUITY OF TWO– PARTY POLITICS IN AMERICA

Thus far the American party structure and operation has been presented as something of an amalgam of conflicting influences derived from the pluralistic tendencies characteristic of American politics as a whole. For a more penetrating understanding of what these conflicting influences mean and how they came to be what they are, it is necessary to look briefly at some of the historical antecedents of the American party system and then attempt to elaborate its main features.

In the first place, it should be noted once again that the American governmental system is highly legalistic and that this tradition of legalism is closely related to the American revolutionary arguments and to the circumstances attending the drafting of the Constitution. Until very near the actual beginnings of resistance by force, the controversy between the colonists of British North America and the government at Westminster was argued (by the American side at least) in terms of the rights of British subjects under the British Constitution, with particular reference to the Whig constitutional settlement of 1689. Although the radical democrats of the Revolution temporarily overrode the effects of this American tradition of Whig legalism with arguments drawn from the abstract rationalism of the eighteenth century, the Whig tendency clearly predominated in the Constitutional Convention of 1787. The framers of the Constitution were concerned to limit the powers of government by a complex (and tightly binding) legal instrument modelled on what they believed to be the British arrangement of 1689. In the incipient democracy of the eighteenth century, this attempt to nullify the possibility of authoritarian rule by a fixed, superior law was directed more toward the past than toward the possibilities of the future. There was an altogether understandable failure to appreciate how far the politics of Britain were advanced in the direction of an eventual democratic order by the events of 1688–1689, or how far the trend toward such a democratic order had already proceeded in the American experience. And the fundamental aspect of democratic order is its dependence on the possibility of providing an effective means of holding government responsible by political action rather than by a legal negation of positive government.

The upshot of this Whig-Liberal attitude of legalism was the creation of an atmosphere of hostility toward the idea of political parties—a hostility which still manifests itself quite clearly in the American ethos. The basic expressions of this attitude are found in Madison's arguments in Article X of the *Federalist* and in Washington's *Farewell Address*, both of which warn against the evils of the spirit of faction. Madison's comments are more closely reasoned and detailed than those of Washington and are most pertinent to the understanding of certain aspects of the American party system. To be overly brief and therefore overly general: Madison was inclined to think that the danger that some organized "faction" might capture control of the government was offset to some extent by the size and diversity of the country, particularly since this tendency toward political dispersion was enhanced by the legalized decentralization enforced by a constitutionally established federalism. These features of the new country would, in his opinion, fractionize political groups so effectively as to provide a sort of equilibrium of interests which would cancel the possibility of unified control and somehow leave a popularly elected (if hopelessly divided) government free to create a truly independent national policy. Madison thus produced the first—and rather remarkably perceptive—theory of pressure groups, but he failed to see that pressure groups are engaged in something quite different from an organized effort to attain office, which is precisely what political parties *are* engaged in. Government by pressure groups alone is almost inconceivable; what is necessary for governing, especially for governing in a democracy, is an effort to secure the support of a coalescence of individuals and groups sufficient to permit an organization— i.e., a *party* organization—to acquire the offices of, and assume responsibility for, the legally established government. The founding fathers, in short, knew approximately what they did not want government to be; but they fell a long way short of understanding how a popularly based government, composed of representatives drawn from a formidable variety of constituencies, could operate at all. Other than the aforementioned features stressed by Madison, the framers of the Constitution were content to rely on the checks and balances system to prevent any one cohesive segment (social class, economic group, or geographical area) from acquiring control over the government and reverting to rule by or on behalf of a fragment as opposed to the whole of society. In other words, they appeared less concerned with the specifics of governmental operation than with the legal prevention of a recrudescence of authoritarian rule by one, by the few, or even exclusively by the many—if we may use (as the founding fathers certainly did) the classical categorization of the forms of government.

To give Madison full credit, however, it should be pointed out that he recognized, as he put it, that "Liberty is to faction what air is to fire, an aliment without which it instantly expires." He recognized, so to speak, that in an open society an organized effort to capture the offices of government is inevitable, even if he did not quite perceive that the main problem resulting from this situation is to see that the control gained by the effort is temporary and the organization remains responsible for its actions to the popular basis on which its claim to control rests. The fact was, that by reason of the experience of politics, which took precedence over the legal arguments of the Whigs and the *a priori* reasoning of the *philosophes* alike, the social matrix out of which the party system was to develop was subtly shaping the framework of American politics well before Madison wrote his part of the *Federalist Papers*. For the party system, which has been so tenacious in the history of the country, was shaped out of the issues involved in the American Revolution; and the broad divisions established at that time and confirmed in the early constitutional period have continued, with stubborn persistence, to define not only the vague outline of the party bifurcation, but also the bases of support on which each of the two major parties rests.

The fate of the British Loyalists during the Revolution—the removal of the more prominent ones from the United States and the confiscation of their property—effectively destroyed the possibility that a conservative party in the conventional sense might arise. By conservative party was meant a party favoring monarchy, or an aristocratic, High Chuch, Tory party. The forces that were left to contend over the question of what the nature of the new union was to be were the two great liberal elements in the Revolution, the conservative liberals (or the Whigs) and the radical liberals (or the democrats). Although these potentially opposing forces had united for the purposes of the active revolution, they had differed in their reason for revolt, as they differed in social composition and in their respective views of a properly organized society. The historical details are too complicated to go into here, but the main lines can be indicated at a considerable risk of oversimplification. The radicals were in the ascendency throughout most of the Revolution and in the period of the Articles of Confederation, but the Whig-minded conservatives—or as they should be styled, the "Federalists"—dominated the Constitutional Convention. After a vigorous campaign to secure the adoption of the Constitution had overcome an opposition spearheaded by the democrats, the Federalists pulled the democrats into a national coalition in the new and "harmonious" government. However, the rift which soon developed in the Cabinet over Hamilton's peculiarly mercantilist policies; and Washington's preference for Hamilton's views as compared with those of Jefferson, Madison, and Randolph soon spread into the Congress in the inevitable political process of organizing isolated blocs of power into effective support against opposing personalities and their policies. Once this initial breach was made, it was never fully closed and by 1800 the party system was operative in a broad sense.

This apparently simple historical development reveals the first characteristic of the American party system. It is not only a national two-party system, but for practical purposes the same two parties, or at least two distinct nationally organized parties drawing their sustenance from the respective traditions which went into the founding of the two original parties, have continued virtually to monopolize effectively organized political power in the United States. The lines of historical descent are quite clear: The original Federalist party yielded to the Whigs in the 1830s, and the Whigs in turn yielded to the Republicans after 1856; on the other hand, the Jeffersonian Republican party changed its name permanently to the Democratic party after Jackson had fully worked out some of the implications of Jeffersonian democracy in the period from 1828 to 1836. Unexceptionally, the changes in both instances were more in name than in the basic reorientation of a tradition, or even a realignment of issues or of the group coalescences which form the core support of each party. Even so, there have been considerable shifts in the external features of the issues with which each party has concerned itself from era to era in American party history. Furthermore, there has been a constant shifting of peripheral groups back and forth between the two parties, so that many an election has been won or lost by shifts of such groups from one to the other of the major parties. And from time to time some intruding factor has caused an extremely uneasy alliance of certain blocs of voters with one of the major national parties, such as the midwestern farm bloc in the Republican party after the Civil War or the southern conservative bloc in the Democratic party since the New Deal. Even so, the basic spirits of the two parties transcend these apparent aberrations, as is so frequently attested by the historical appeals to the sanctity and purity of the party traditions by one party leader or another. As often as not these appeals to tradition evoke the true image of the effective motivations behind the parties more fully than the party leaders consciously realize.

In view of these sweeping conclusions about the continuity of American parties, it is essential to support the argument by roughly outlining the original division of the parties in terms of issues and bases of support and by indicating some of the accommodations that each party has made in its attempts to retain or to gain the majority position in the government. The Federalists were true Whigs in spirit from the beginning (as they later became in name). The party drew its predominant support from the merchants, manufacturers, and traders from the northeastern states and from the other port towns, along with an occasional admixture of some portions of the well-established farm group. The issues initially evoked by the Federalists were Hamilton's program of the assumption and funding of the public debt and the creation of a national bank. More broadly, they were concerned with the development of a strong central government based on a mixed (i.e., not totally democratic) representation in order to protect property and to stimulate commerce. To this end they supported a high tariff (for the dual purpose of raising revenue and protecting domestic trade and manufacture); a hard currency protected by a national bank financed jointly by private and public capital; some trade with England, particularly in terms of the importation of capital equipment, eventual national self-sufficiency, and a substantial measure of isolationism. By contrast Jeffersonian democracy drew its main support from the southern and frontier agrarian classes, and to some extent (especially after Van Buren's rise in New York politics) from the artisans and laborers of the towns. The Democrats—to give them the name they soon proudly wore—formed a party of radical agrarianism; they were intent on achieving the revolutionary ideal of the political equality of man, except possibly in the case of the growing class of southern Bourbon planters. They advocated a broad distribution of small properties, and emphasized decentralized government (grass-roots democracy). Specifically, they plumped for a soft currency and low tariffs as a boon to the debt-ridden farmers; in the international area the nature of their libertarian radicalism was such that the sympathy of both the leaders and the rank and file of the party went out to the French revolutionists. Finally they opposed national schemes for internal improvement, for a standing army and navy, and for the growth of a great industrial society.

From 1800 until the Civil War the Democratic party maintained itself as the majority party, and with a few temporary and for the most part rather colorless exceptions, it controlled both Congress and the Presidency. Its strength was founded on a regional coalition between the South and the West (or frontier), an alignment which was brought about by Jefferson's skill as a politician and enhanced by the unusual talents of Jackson. Thus regional alliances were a very early feature of the American party system, and they have become a perpetual influence on the party struggle. Even today, when other forms of alignment which are more national in scope probably have a greater effect on politics than regionalism, the vestiges of these geographically-based power structures still play an important role in the functioning of the system.

The Civil War changed the geographic party alignment in such a way as to make the Republican party (heir to the Whigs and through the Whigs to the Federalists) the majority party. The reconstituted majority base depended on a coalition between the midwestern agrarians and the industrial Northeast, leaving only the so-called "solid South" as a dependable regional bloc within the Democratic party. Although this alignment created the uneasiness reflected in the virtually continuous series of inter- and intraparty agrarian protest movements, the Republicans were able to build a substantial national program on its foundations. And this policy of the Republicans during their ascendancy from 1860 to 1932 was remarkably consistent in its aims and spirit with the policies of its Whig and Federalist predecessors. In this case the social policy was aimed (directly or indirectly) at the creation of a large-scale entrepreneural or corporate capitalism. Once again the successful control of Congress and the Presidency was maintained except for rather short interludes of Democratic administration.

The old policies of high tariff and isolation continued to be pursued by the Republicans, but one of those peculiar changes that appear to mark American politics as something special occurred during this period. As is frequently the case, however, the shift of emphasis was more of a surface change than a fundamental alteration, because it reflected an adaptation of doctrine to different conditions rather than a new outlook. The change referred to was the increasing stress laid by the Republicans on laissez-faire as the basis of the national economic policy. Furthermore, the Republicans supplemented this apparent abandonment of the older advocacy of a close tie between the powers of the national government and private capitalism with a heavy emphasis on states' rights. Both states' rights and laissez-faire had, of course, been hallmarks of Jeffersonian democracy prior to this time, but the capital and corporate structure was now such that its executives seemed to feel able to manage without the direct support of government. Ironically, however, the early part of this period coincided with perhaps the most obvious giveaway of national resources of any in history—the immense land subsidization of the railroads. States' rights became, in this context, a powerful defensive force against the occasionally threatened use of national power to regulate corporations in the interest of relieving the plight of the recurrently depressed agricultural sector of society. As a concession to the western bloc that they needed to mollify in order to ensure continued victory the Republicans provided the Homestead Act for the distribution of free land and the Morrill Act for the support of state agricultural and mechanical colleges. Of more direct benefit for emotive purposes at election time was the "bloody shirt" of the Civil War which was used against southern sectionalism and its associations with the Democratic party.

In opposition, the Democrats continued to be an agrarian-based party, although deprived by the causes indicated earlier of support from the western area. The latter party was somewhat anachronistic, too, in its outlook: it never quite came abreast of the prevailing dreams of urban industrial opulence, and this seems to have been the major reason for its continuing minority position. It was still a party of governmental change, as Wilson's incumbency demonstrated, but, except for some of Wilson's innovations, the changes it advocated seemed to relate more to a dream of progress in the past than to the bright future which a governmentally unimpeded industrial economy promised. However, the massive protests which came from a wide variety of sources, including temporary revolts within the Republican party as well as from third parties, were joined in most instances by Democrats and presaged eventual return to power of the Democratic party. For the New Deal was to rely in no small part on programs formulated by the earlier progressive and reform movements when it eventually came to power.

After the Depression of 1929 the next great shift in the American political equilibrium occurred. Once again changes in conditions gave rise to new issues and new opportunities for the "out" party to create an effective basis of popular support. In this case the situation revealed Franklin Roosevelt's genius as a leader of the Democratic party in much the way that earlier events had produced Hamilton, Jefferson, and Lincoln. The power-sustaining dream of a society built on the premise that "the business of America is business" was rudely shaken by the Depression, and the era of unimpeded capitalism was at an end. Henceforth any party that hoped to govern would have to take account of the function that positive government was called upon to perform in redressing the social and individual imbalances resulting from the impersonal forces of a market economy. What Roosevelt produced was not, as some excessive partisans who are rather too free in their language have alleged, a socialist revolution. On the contrary, Roosevelt's program, to the extent that it had an economic aim sufficiently consistent for logical analysis, was capitalistic. But it was capitalistic in a sense which recognized the necessity for governmental intervention in the economy in order to maintain social order and stability in the face of a rapidly disintegrating economic system. It was on this premise, and later on certain premises of international leadership which had been prefigured by Wilson, that Roosevelt built a new national majority coalition in support of the Democratic party.

The one feature of previous major political realignments that was less prominent in the New Deal coalition was pronounced regionalism. To be sure, the South was still solidly Democratic, but that solidity was to prove at least as embarrassing as helpful to the party after the initial momentum of the Democratic victories had slowed down. In the main Roosevelt's coalition cut across regional lines in much the same way that the advent of urban industrialism had done, except with a more pronounced political effect. Roosevelt united the majority of small farmers and laborers in developing a new popular basis for the Democratic majority. Although some of them cut across the urban labor lines, a considerable number of ethnic blocs were also attracted to the revitalized Democratic party, including most of the Negro population, which had previously adhered to the Republicans as the party of liberation. This combination continues to be dominant nationally despite the recent incursion of the Republicans into the Presidency.

THE DISPERSAL OF PARTY POWER

Up to this point the internal unity of the parties and the clarity of the line between them may appear to be exaggerated beyond anything warranted by the facts. If so, the excesses will be offset to some extent by what follows, for the historic consistency and basic coherence of the two parties is certainly muddled by a second major characteristic of the American system—its extreme decentralization. It has often been remarked that the federal nature of the American government has produced a confederated party system. For a variety of reasons the main centers of party power in the United States are not at the national level, but at the state, congressional, county, and city levels. At least two scholars in the field of political parties have pointed out that we really have 51 party systems, a national system and separate systems for each state. Ranney and Kendall in their book Democracy and the American Party System have classified these state systems as (1) two-party systems (in which the two parties are in close, continuous competition for control); (2) one-party modified systems (in which one party is so dominant as to be virtually unassailable but is never without some effective opposition), and (3) one-party systems (in which a single party has a virtual monopoly on organized party activities within the state, but may be characterized by any one of a variety of deviant one-party patterns). If the long experience of national two-party politics has produced some semblances of a responsible party system, this dispersion of party power has done much to fractionize the major parties into a structure that bears more than casual resemblance to a multi-party system.

What are some of the factors in this tendency towards depressing the centers of party strength toward the state or lower levels and thereby producing national parties that are not united and capable of maintaining centralized discipline? The first and most obvious answer is federalism. The national government is in many ways expected to be a coalition of semi-autonomous, locally selected representatives, carefully balanced off against one another in order to preserve a large measure of local independence. This tendency is reflected in specific features of the constitutional arrangement: the election districts (even for national offices) are within the confines of the states, the election machinery and therefore most of the laws regulating parties and elections are left to the tender mercies of the states, and tradition rigorously demands that representatives be residents of the districts from which they are elected. Even the Presidency and Vice-Presidency, which are the only offices in the United States with a national constituency, must be gained by a process which involves securing blocs of state electoral votes based on popular pluralities within each state. And prior to this, the presidential candidate must have been nominated by a process which requires him to line up an effective combination of state and local leaders who control the state delegations to the national convention.

A second and closely related factor in this situation is the grass-roots conception of politics, which is a continuing heritage of eighteenth-century radical democracy. The tradition involves a multiplicity of elective offices and direct representation, that is, representation tied to local opinion and substantially pledged to support that opinion on legislative issues regardless of party commitments on a broader scale. The United States has by far the largest proportion of elected offices in the world. Altogether it has more than 800,000 elected officials, and these are elected from an incredibly complex arrangement of constituencies. But all of these constituencies are localized to a greater or lesser degree and nearly all of them are capable of dispensing a small amount of patronage (or are themselves the beneficiaries of the patronage of some leader not far above them in the organizational echelon). It is small wonder, then, that most of the financial and other means of building effective control over the machinery of the party stops long before it reaches the national level. Even the primary method of nomination, which was certainly an extension of the democratic ideal, added to this localizing effect inasmuch as it centered the nominating processes on local electoral districts, thus minimizing the possibility of increased control by a central organization, although failing at the same time to eliminate the local bosses, as was intended.

Finally, the separation of powers system, particularly in its conjunction of fixed terms of office with a differentiated pattern of constituencies, has further strengthened the association of the Congressman with the district he represents and placed him beyond the disciplinary power of the central organization. The threat of dissolution is absolutely precluded; and since the party needs the support of its locally-oriented politicians more than the politicians need the party, it is rare indeed that a party leader will be bold enough to try to institute party disciplinary action against a member of Congress. The most notable recent case of punitive action in Congress—the censure motion against the late Senator Joseph McCarthy—was a retribution against damage to the special integrity and ethos that has been built up in the Senate as a self-contained body; it has little if anything to do with the contribution of the party system to the process of government.

These features go a long way toward explaining certain apparent anomalies in the American system, such as the characteristic tendency of Congress to vote in patterns that have little or no relation to party alignment, and the cleavage in name to a particular party on the part of sectional or other power blocs who are diametrically opposed to the general issue orientation of the party in question. About the only vote strictly along party lines in Congress is the vote on the organization of Congress, and this is largely explained by the fact that individual members have great stakes in organizational party regularity because of the seniority system, which in itself promotes isolated congressional power centers at the level of committee chairmanships. Thanks to this loose system, southern Democrats, for example, are able to enter into a congressional coalition with right-wing Republicans without losing party identity, and to some extent they even enhance their political power in terms of the opportunities afforded by such a system for bargaining and horse-trading.

The American party system, then, works imperfectly when it is set against the ideal of *party government*. Nonetheless, it has substantial accomplishments to its credit. It has provided the American voters with a considerable measure of choice of both issues and candidates, even though this choice is vitiated to some extent in the sections where two-party politics do not exist—a fact which serves to re-emphasize the value of the system for the country at large. The parties have also overridden in part the unworkable extremes of the separation of powers, and thus have helped to make positive government possible by enabling party leaders to

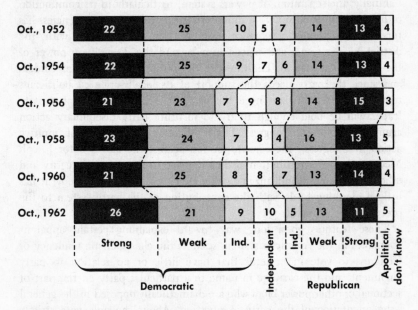

Length of each bar equals 100 percent.

The Persistence of Political Party Identification. *Source:* From Survey Research Center Studies reported in Donald E. Stokes, "1960 and the Problem of Deviating Elections," paper delivered at the 1961 Annual Meeting of the American Political Science Association; 1962 data supplied by Stokes to Fred I. Greenstein, *The American Party System and the American People,* Prentice-Hall, 1963, p. 32.

unify the government sufficiently to deal with major crises in the life of the nation. To this end the party system has played no small part in the shaping of the office of the President, which is the primary source of national political leadership. The party system provided the means for making the Presidency into a popularly elective office; and since this (along with the Vice-Presidency) is the only office in the United States with even the semblance of a national constituency, it is the single agency that is most capable of providing national popular and congressional political leadership in an otherwise deliberately fragmented system. Furthermore, the parties have, in their loose and nonideological form, reflected the pluralism and general tolerance characteristic of American life, while at the same time they have reaffirmed the underlying liberal constitutional tradition. The parties have, in this connection, recognized and accommodated internal differences and have not tried to absorb the entire personalities of their respective adherents into a rigid unity. The result has been the prevalence of moderation over extreme courses of action; and, to a more limited extent, a gradual nationalizing symbolism has been effected within each party which offsets (without eliminating) the latent possibilities of more intense unification along the lines of some class, sectional, or other narrower unifying symbol. In brief, the American party system has been an inseparable feature of the rise and development of the American democracy.

PRESSURE GROUPS AND THE PARTY FUNCTION

And now, despite obvious dangers of excessive compression, it is important to discuss briefly the place of pressure groups in the American system. In the first place, it is not altogether clear that American pressure groups are much more perniciously active than their counterparts in many other countries. A partial explanation of the emphasis on their influence in the literature on American politics lies in the intensity with which they have been studied in the United States. However, this judgement must be somewhat modified by pointing out that in Great Britain, at present the only country in which the empirical study of national politics compares in quantity and quality with that carried out in the United States, the role of pressure groups has not been observed to be quite so compelling as it is in America. And this comparative difference suggests something that is confirmed by other types of evidence; namely, that a completely functioning national two-party system, with central party discipline and cabinet responsibility, acts as a deterrent against the possibility that pressure groups might occupy a dominant place in the political system.

Pressure groups are not political parties in miniature nor are political parties simply an amalgam of great numbers of separate pressure groups. Their respective functions tend to differentiate them not only in degree, but in kind. Pressure groups are organized for the most part in order to effect relatively simple—quite often single—goals. Although more complex types of organizations may play pressure roles, when they do so they temporarily gloss over their complexities in order to present, or claim to present, a united front on behalf of their immediate pressure goal. The nature of pressure groups and their objectives indicate that they are minority interests which seek to gain some special minority benefit, as often as not at the expense of the majority or at least at the expense of other minority interest groups. Pressure groups want some immediate service from government, either directly or in the form of a negation of the application of a positive function of government, and they are prepared to use almost all types of legal (and occasionally illegal) tactics to get what they want, except to try to win a majority in an election. Pressure groups, therefore, are precisely not engaged in fulfilling general democratic objectives and are not prepared to play the game according to the majoritarian rules ostensibly imposed by a democracy.

Of course, one does not usually go so far as to say that pressure groups are undemocratic, for they, too, have their roots in a particular type of democratic soil. The constitutional guarantees of freedom of petition and freedom of assembly—for this read freedom of association for realizing collective goals—are quite clearly parts of a larger conception of freedom of expression, in the absence of which democracy may hardly be said to exist. When the constitutional proscription on interference with the right to an open hearing is combined with the encouragement given to pressure organizations by theories of democracy such as that expressed by Madison, the actual existence of a complicated plurality of interests in the American society is afforded a special ideological impetus. One might say that a state of mind is promoted in which it is assumed that the utilitarian conception of individual interests is the sole motivation of human behavior, and that it is permissible and indeed laudable for an individual to promote aspects of his interests through pressure groups organized for particular purposes, but it is somehow wrong (and possibly dangerous) to compromise and override these groups who are competing for special favors through an organization which holds itself out as the representative of a general interest.

Since political parties quite obviously do hold themselves out as agencies capable of instituting national policy reflecting a general interest and are willing to try to advance that policy by organizing the support of a majority of the voters, they are constrained to pursue democratic objectives and to submit themselves to tests afforded by democratic machinery. And here we come to the crux of the practical manner in which political parties and pressure groups may be distinguished: pressure groups are a means—the most important means in modern democracies —of filling the power vacuum which is left as a result of the imperfect functioning of the parties. To the extent that a majority party is united in the integrity of its commitments to the voters who returned it to power it is able to resist the demands of organized minorities seeking special benefits from government. If the party system worked perfectly any minority would be compelled to seek its objectives by trying to organize a majority; and it is precisely this condition which would force it to moderate its special demands in the articulation of a national policy which would attract a majority of the voters. And this is what pressure groups are not prepared to do, because influence without full governing responsibility is much more suited to their purposes.

Naturally there is no such thing as a perfectly working party system; there are always loopholes between party commitments to the public and the strict accountability of the party in fulfilling these commitments, so every democratic society has its share of effective pressure groups. If the United States seems to have rather more of a problem with this activity than, let us say, most of the other English-speaking countries, this condition may be largely accounted for by the difficulties attending the operation of American two-party politics that we considered earlier. The diffusion of political power among a vast number of officials, the multiplicity of constituencies, and the erosion of central party coordination implicit in the separation of powers and the federal system all contribute to the difficulty of securing control of government by a party united in its obligation to the total body of voters—or national constituency— which brought this nominal party to power. The many points of access to isolated blocs of governmental influence which this diffusion of power produces encourages the vast proliferation of pressure groups in America. And it may be expected that future studies of countries with multi-party sytems and/or complex legal allocations of governmental power will reveal similar developments.

The great number and enormous influence of pressure groups in America may have been the main factor that has led some observers to suggest that the entire process of democratic government is exhausted in the activities of these groups. In the view of several scholars who are inclined toward this conception of politics, a sort of equilibrium is established among these countervailing forces which is productive of such stability as exists in a modern society. With considerable validity it is argued that the activities of various groups engaged in pressure activities tend to offset one another, thereby contributing to the process of compromise and accommodation which are characteristic of consensus government. Further, most individuals are participants in several such groups and are consequently aware of conflicts and compromises among different aspects of personal interest. This interpretation implies, of course, that there can be no majority reflecting a national interest (however tenuous) out of which a national policy can be produced; there are only minorities, special interests, and pieces of policy designed to placate one or another of these groups. The argument advanced here rejects the assumptions on which this formulation is based. The theory that holds group interests to be the sole political reality provides no explanation of the persisting tradition of the American party system, but relies rather on the imperfection of the parties to explain away the obvious existence of such a system. Furthermore, the explanation depends on a *deus ex machina*—the notion of equilibrium—to account for the stability of a well-ordered democratic society. Social order is not so easily achieved; it has its basis in a tradition whose fundamentals override to no small extent the interests which divide men. And the parties play a most important unifying role in preserving that tradition. A government made up of nothing but pressure groups is, as a practical matter, incomprehensible. There can be no doubt that under the special conditions of the American democracy pressure groups will continue to exercise a most important influence. But political parties will do much more than this, for they are among the indispensable institutions through which that democracy works.

QUESTIONS FOR FURTHER DISCUSSION

1. Why has the two-party system in American politics tended to produce the popular dominance of one of the two major parties over the other for long periods of time rather than a fairly frequent alternation of the two parties in office?
2. Why has the phenomenon of the urban political boss largely disappeared despite the fact that the country as a whole has continued to become more and more urbanized?
3. Is it possible to relate the apparent indifference of many citizens to the activities of political parties and the comparatively low voter turnout for elections in America to a general satisfaction with the effectiveness of the political process in this country?
4. How can the looseness with which parties are organized in the United States be reconciled with the ability of the two major parties to turn aside the threat posed by the rise of third (or minor) parties?
5. What are the main techniques used by pressure groups to protect or enhance their interests by obtaining legislative or administrative decisions favorable to them or by preventing decisions deemed to be adverse to them?

VI

The American Experience with Federalism: The States and the Union

UPI

UNITY IN DIVERSITY

Speaking for the Supreme Court in *Texas* v. *White* (1869), Chief Justice Chase said, "The Constitution, in all its provisions, looks to an indestructible Union, composed of indestructible States." Four years after the Civil War the Court was enunciating what the war had already proved, that States could not leave the union. However, as the Chief Justice was at pains to point out, within the Union the states retained their constitutional, geographic, and political integrity. Persons who have not lived under a federated governmental system, and even some who have firsthand knowledge of less intensely federal societies than the United States, have difficulty comprehending the history of American federal relations, the hold that the concept has on the American mind, and the extent and subtlety of its practical influences. Like most of the other major components of the political system, American federalism is characterized by substantial change within a persisting general context of ideas and institutions. Of necessity much has been said about American federalism in the foregoing chapters; but occasion must be taken to consider it as a distinctive aspect of the overall government.

Federalism is a product of intractable social diversities within a geographical area in which the urge toward political unity is clear and the obstacles to closer union are not insuperable. Resolution of the problem is sought through the development of a firm constitutional arrangement which seeks to provide a clear division of powers between a central government and the governments of the constituent units, and to assure that each level of government is independent of the other in the exercise of its own powers. A federal constitution is thus a formal expression of political diversity within the framework of national unity. Since the diversities themselves have not been static in American life, federal relations have changed; and this change has been mainly in the direction of increased national unity. But this has not meant that federalism has disappeared even if one accepts the doubtful proposition that it has become obsolete; for not only do the diversities remain, but the habits and patterns of politics which are associated with the historical experience of a federated system continue to be major influences on the national political life.

American had its beginnings in 13 separately administered colonies strung out along more than 1000 miles of the Atlantic coastline. Local identification was strong among the people living under these units of government and it was sustained by an intrinsic faith in the inseparable connection between freedom and governmental decentralization. But there was also a need of unification for purposes of common defense and trade; and there were bases of unity in a common heritage, language, and law, and in the struggle for independence. Today the social and political variations are still much in evidence; in fact the heterogeneity of American society and government never ceases to astound the observer from abroad. Much, though by no means all, of American pluralism can still be discerned in the great regional divisions of the country, and the individual states—with their tangible boundaries, their separate institutions, and the local identification of their populations—are among the most visible evidences of these differences. It has often been pointed out that the states are historical anachronisms and that their boundaries are artificial inasmuch as they do not conform to any logical divisions that might be made along the lines of geographical characteristics or economic or other functional considerations. While this view may have some validity in the abstract, it overlooks the most persistent influence on political boundary lines—those that are drawn in the minds of men and are accorded visceral reality.

Measured by almost any factor commonly employed as a social standard, the range of the 50 states is vast. The geographic variation is almost universal; there are mountain states, plains states, and transitional states; and many of the larger states have great diversities within their own boundaries. There are states whose rainfall and vegetation patterns are tropical or subtropical and there are states which contain large areas of desert. In climatic extremes there is, on the one hand, the harsh arctic or subarctic state of Alaska, and on the other there is the tropical Hawaii in the Pacific, south of the Tropic of Cancer. In geographic mass the states vary in size from Alaska, with its 586,400 square miles (over twice the area of France) to Rhode Island which covers only 1241 square miles and is territorially smaller than many of the counties in other states. Conversely, in the 1960 census Alaska contained the smallest population of any state—226,167—while New York (now exceeded by California) had 16,782,167 residents. The composition of the populations of the various states is another important indicator of diversity. Vermont, for example, contains a white population comprising 99.8 percent of its residents, whereas Hawaii is 68 percent nonwhite. America as a whole may be a great melting pot, but the ethnic strains are clearly revealed when the mixture is divided into the appropriate state and local moulds. The distribution of forms of economic activity, income, and natural resources are additional measures of the variety of American life as one moves from state to state. And the differences are reflected in the social patterns, the political characteristics, and the administrative practices of the territorial units.

The physical and population growth of the United States has certainly been facilitated by the possibilities that federalism holds out to diversified geographic areas; in fact the capacity to organize new land acquisitions into incorporated territories of the United States and later to admit these areas into full statehood may well be the most important positive contribution that federalism has made to American politics. As the United States acquired new territories by purchase, by cession following wars with Mexico and Spain, and by conquest of American Indian lands, the process of assimilation was begun by dividing these acquisitions into territories with some measure of governmental autonomy. The territories then were developed under conditions which induced them to seek the status of full-fledged statehood within the United States rather than to drift toward or press for some more complete forms of independence. Apart from the original 13 colonies, 5 of the states were carved out of existing states, Texas came into the Union after a brief period of independence from Mexico, and California became a state directly out of the 1848 Mexican cession without going through an intermediate stage of territorial organization. Thus 37 of the 50 states were brought into the system by national action and 30 of these were at one time organized as territories of the United States. Even where sizeable populations of non-British extraction had developed indigenous cultural patterns of their own under the tutelage of the mother country (as was the case, for example, with French Louisiana and some of the Spanish possessions), the transition was fairly easy and carried with it few, if any, of the long-range connotations of imperialism—domestically at least.

As far as admission to the Union is concerned, power rests with Congress; retrospectively, this admission policy can be said to have been one of the great nationalizing features of the 1787 Constitution. The normal procedure for admission has been a petition to Congress on the part of the territorial legislature, followed by a congressional enabling act authorizing the preparation of a proposed state constitution, subject to whatever conditions Congress may care to impose. If, however, these conditions are such that they compromise the normally independent powers of a state, they cannot be enforced after statehood has been achieved. In other words a territory may be constrained to accede to congressional demands in order to become a state, but once it is in the Union its powers are equal to those of the other states, and Congress may exercise no more control over its internal affairs than is possible in relation to any other state. Furthermore, Congress may not erect a state within the jurisdiction of another state or join two or more states or parts of states to form a new state without the consent of the legislatures of all states concerned. Once a territory has received its enabling act it proceeds to draft and ratify a state constitution and then petitions Congress for admission, which Congress may authorize by joint resolution. In addition to the preservation of state territorial integrity, the Constitution imposes certain other obligations on the national government in relation to the states, including protection against invasion and domestic violence and the more nebulous guarantee of a republican form of government. Thus federalism, which is conceived in diversity, ensures the perpetuation of this diversity. However, the diversities exist within a framework of substantial unity which reconciles them to a considerable degree. And by all odds the most important unifying factors have been the constitutional arrangement and the basic uniformity of governmental institutions among the states.

THE LEGAL FORMULATION

It has already been indicated that the explicit formula for the division of powers between the national government and the states is established in the Tenth Amendment. The division is predicated on a national government of constitutionally delegated or enumerated powers, with the remaining unspecified powers (other than those prohibited to the states) being reserved to the states or to the people. Most of the enumerated powers of the central government are to be found in Article I, Section 8, of the Constitution, which establishes the areas in which

Congress may legislate. The main powers so specified include those relating to the fiscal competence of the national government, such as the capacity to tax, borrow, pay debts and to coin money and regulate its value; powers relating to defense and foreign affairs, such as the ability to raise and support an army and navy and an organized militia, and to declare wars; and a variety of other powers of a regulatory, protective and service nature, such as control over interstate and foreign commerce, naturalization, bankruptcy, copyright and patents, weights and measures, the establishment of post offices and post roads, and the punishment of certain types of crimes. The enumerated powers, in brief, were designed to cover those matters which, in terms of the experience in government of the day, needed to be uniformly legislated and administered for the nation as a whole or had to be preempted by the central government to prevent internal conflict.

In establishing the national powers by delegation, considerable scope for flexibility was permitted both through the language of a Constitution and as a result of the omissions of certain items from that document. The capacity to legislate in most delegated areas is not hedged with serious restrictions, and some of the phraseology of the grants—e.g., the authority given Congress to provide for the general welfare—is broadly permissive. Furthermore, the founding fathers saw fit to conclude the list of specific national powers with the sweeping "necessary and proper" clause, which is sometimes referred to as the *elastic* clause of the federal Constitution. This provision grants Congress the power "To make all laws . . . necessary and proper for carrying into execution the foregoing [enumerated] powers, and all other powers vested by this Constitution in the Government of the United States, or in any department or office thereof." These words are the sources of the "implied powers" doctrine, first developed by Chief Justice Marshall in the case of *McCulloch* v. *Maryland* (1819), under which Congress is permitted the widest possible latitude in adapting its statutory means to the realization of the ends for which the national government was established by the Constitution.

Again, when the first Congress yielded to the pressure to include in the Constitution a specific reservation of powers on behalf of the states (the Tenth Amendment), it deliberately refused to accede to the demand of certain strict constructionists that the restrictive modifier "expressly" be placed before the phrase ". . . delegated to the United States . . ."

Thus, while the Constitution specifically delegated to the national government only those powers thought to be essential to national survival and order, it left ample scope for interpretation of central powers when questions affecting these basic conditions of the nation's life were raised.

But, it may be asked, where did this constitutional settlement leave the states? The framers did not undertake to define state powers, apparently under the assumption that the states would continue to function much as they had previously, except for the areas newly marked out for the central government. The states largely retained what later came to be referred to as "police powers"; generally speaking, the police power is the capacity to regulate in the interest of protecting the safety, health, welfare, and morals of the community. At the time of adoption of the Constitution the functions of government were, of course, extremely limited, but even so the main functions of government were embraced by the type of activities left to the states. The states retained primary control over property law and succession, family law, most areas of criminal law, public protection of persons and property, public institutions, welfare, education, public health, roads, and local government.

The Constitution does place specific limits on state powers. Most of these are included in the main body of the Constitution, especially in Article I, Section 10, but others have been added later, most notably the Civil War Amendments. States are prohibited from entering into treaties, alliances, or confederations; and they are denied the capacity to enter into agreements or compacts with other states or with foreign powers without the consent of Congress. They may not coin money, grant letters of marque and reprisal, emit bills of credit, pass bills of attainder, enact *ex post facto* laws, impair the obligation of contracts, or grant titles of nobility. States are not permitted to tax imports or exports, except for those necessary for enforcing inspection laws, without the consent of Congress. Nor may the states collect any duty or tonnage charges or keep troops or ships of war in time of peace except with the consent of Congress. Likewise, the states are not permitted to engage in war without congressional affirmation, unless actually invaded or in such immediate danger that delay cannot be admitted. It should be noted that the Constitution also specifically enjoins the national government from the passage of *ex post facto* laws, bills of attainder, acts providing interstate tariff barriers, and measures granting titles of nobility. The objects of most of these proscriptions on state power obviously were to secure to the central government exclusive control over war, foreign affairs, currency, and international trade; to maintain a system of internal free trade; and to protect individuals against certain types of discriminatory legislation.

The limitations imposed by the Civil War Amendments relate more closely to domestic matters formerly thought to be within the purview of the states. Under these slavery and involuntary servitude, except for the use of the latter as punishment for crimes, are prohibited; citizenship is nationalized and states may not exclude citizens of the United States from state citizenship; and the states are compelled to guarantee all persons within their respective jurisdictions the equal protection of the laws. Furthermore, the due process clause, already binding on the central government by reason of the Fifth Amendment, was included in the Fourteenth Amendment as a protection on behalf of the individual against the states. The clause, which holds that no state may ". . . deprive any person of life, liberty, or property, without due process of law . . ." has both a substantive and procedural connotation. As heretofore mentioned, the provision has been broadly construed not only to require that the states operate in good faith within all of the limits, remedies, and procedures afforded by the law in criminal cases, but that the substantive guarantee of individual freedom—especially the First Amendment freedoms of speech, press, assembly, petition, and religion—may be enforced against the states by the federal government on behalf of individuals. However, the substantive connotation of the clause in the area of civil liberties was not developed until fairly recently: in the case of *Gitlow* v. *New York* (1925) the United States Supreme Court held that the fundamental personal liberties of the First Amendment are "protected by the due process clause of the Fourteenth Amendment from impairment by the States"; and the case of *Near* v. *Minnesota* (1931) was the first in which the Court held a state statute invalid on the ground that it violated substantive provisions of the First Amendment. These are among the earliest examples of the trend (later manifested so strongly) toward federal judicial protection of personal liberties against the actions of state governments. The Fifteenth Amendment denied the states the power to use "race, color or previous condition of servitude" as a basis for excluding persons from suffrage. This amendment (followed later by the Nineteenth, or women's suffrage, Amendment) placed stringent limits on an area of action hitherto almost exclusively within the purview of the states, although in the case of Negro suffrage the full promise of the guarantee has only recently been made good in the broadest sense and in specific instances has not yet been fully realized.

Neither the constitutional grants of power to the federal government nor the limits placed on the powers of the states come near to establishing the precise point at which the line is drawn between federal and state powers. Much of American constitutional history has been conspicuously concerned with this very problem. Although the legal standard of federalism may be that each of the two levels of government should be limited to its own sphere and independent of the other in that sphere, in practice even in a federal system government is a "seamless web" of activity in which the powers, influences, decisions, and execution of programs are so intermingled as to be almost indistinguishable.

The most apparent form of interplay between central and local units comes about because many of the powers of government do not belong *exclusively* to the states or to the central government, but are held *concurrently*. Of all the recognized concurrent powers of the states and the nation, undoubtedly the most important is the power of taxation. The extent of its taxing power is a basic factor in establishing the degree of a particular government's independence in relation to the other units in the overall political system, because not only is accessibility to revenue an indispensable condition for governing at all, but the capacity to generate tax revenues on its own initiative is the mark of the original as opposed to the derivative power of a government. And in relation to the fundamental category of taxation, the United States Constitution places very few restrictions on either the states or the central government. To be sure the states are precluded from the levy of tariff charges, from taxing federal property, or from passing a tax measure which conflicts with a valid federal law or a treaty, and the national government is not permitted to levy direct taxes except in proportion to the population of the states (for a time this reservation prevented the imposition of a federal graduated income tax), but by and large the bulk of both states and federal tax revenues today come from essentially the same sources, these being mainly individual and corporate income taxes and excise taxes. As a practical matter the major sources of revenue vary somewhat among the jurisdictions. State governments have tended to move out of the field of real property taxation and the federal government does not levy this form of tax (taxes on land having been construed by the courts as direct taxes); in consequence, property taxes provide the main fiscal support of local government. Similarly, the federal government assesses proportionately high income taxes and does not apply a general sales tax, with the result that state income taxes are set at a fairly low rate where they are utilized, and more and more states have found it necessary to resort to general sales taxes. What makes the state and federal power of taxation concurrent is the fact that each government has access to overlapping sources of revenue through its independent powers of legislation. There is no denying that the respective taxing powers of the dual jurisdictions affect one another practically, especially insofar as the central government has the fiscal advantage which results from a tax system covering the entire country, but it is still true that neither level of government is legally dependent on the other for its supply. In other words, neither level is excluded from implementing programs in response to politically ascertained needs by dependence for tax legislation on the other.

Concurrent powers are by no means restricted to fiscal affairs. Even in the instances in which the central government is given clear authority over a specified area of governmental action, the states are often permitted to act in the same area if the Congress has not legitimately preempted the field. In the legal field of bankruptcy, for example, which is within the province of the delegated powers of the national government, there have been several periods in which no generally effective national legislation has existed on the subject and the states have proceeded to fill the hiatus. Since 1898, however, comprehensive federal laws have been operative in relation to bankruptcy, with result that the former functions of the states have been superseded. In other areas the fusion or overlapping of power and responsibility has been more complicated. The regulation of interstate commerce presents about as many difficulties of interpreting the rough line of division between state and nation as any problem that has confronted the courts. Not only is a workable distinction between interstate and intrastate commerce practically impossible to establish, but in matters on which the federal government has not acted the courts have been reluctant in recent years to preclude state action altogether, even where interstate commerce is clearly involved. In such instances the courts have attempted to weigh the public benefit of the regulation against the public interest in preserving commercial intercourse among the states from undue burdens, obstruction, or discrimination. Thus it may be possible for a state to refuse permits for certain types of inter-state motor carriers in order to avoid hazardous congestion on the high-ways, but the power to regulate in this fashion may be denied a state if it can be demonstrated that the action was taken in order to restrict out-of-state competition.

In the field of foreign affairs, the Supreme Court has repeatedly per-mitted the national government broader latitude than would be permis-sible in domestic matters, and has sanctioned the invasion of the reserved powers of the states in the fulfillment of treaty obligations. However, even here, where federal powers would appear to be plenary and exclu-sive, a number of cases might be cited in which the states have used their independent powers in such a way as to affect the implementation of the national foreign policy, albeit indirectly.

THE FEDERAL CONCEPT IN APPLICATION

The foregoing discussion points to the conclusion that the legal divisions are probably less effective than is political experience in establishing the balance between the states and the nation. However, this is not to deny that the legal expression of the division acts as an important determinant of the nature of the political struggle. Almost every exercise of national power has had to run the full gamut of the considerable restraining tests —both legal and political—that federalism imposes. The assumption of a new responsibility by the national government has invariably been challenged in the courts, even after it has received the sanction of a political decision within the framework of national political institutions that are federated rather than unified. The latter characteristic, as has already been demonstrated, holds true especially for the Congress and the party and pressure organizations which play so important a role in congressional composition and behavior. At the same time, state powers have not been held in check nearly as much as the repeated use of phrases such as "the march of power to Washington" or the more sinister-sounding "usurpation of state powers by the federal government" would imply. To the extent that there has been a diminution of state powers as a consequence of the enlargement of national government activity (and even this contention may be contested on the grounds that both state and national powers have been enhanced in recent years), the alteration has been produced by political responses to the changing structure and functions of American society. A good case may be made to support the notion that at least some (and perhaps a majority) of the founding fathers intended to create a constitutional basis for national supremacy. The supreme law of the land clause, the generous language of delegated powers, and the later evolution of the United States Supreme Court as the arbiter of central versus state powers all lend support to this interpretation. Yet it is the pragmatic shaping of the national-state relations—and often with the tacit or direct consent of the state governments—rather than reliance on legal formula that has led to the present situation.

Even the creation of a "more perfect union" in 1787 did not undermine the tacit assumption that the states would continue to exercise the lion's share of governmental functions and would consequently be the main focus of civic attention. In the *Federalist Papers* Madison noted ". . . that the first and most natural attachment of the people will be to the governments of their respective states." The reasons for this were clear: more offices, greater emoluments, and more people would be involved in state than in national administration, more of the domestic and personal interests of the people would be regulated and cared for at this level, the public would be more conversant with the operations of the state governments, and their personal and political ties with the states would be closer than they would be with the central government. Almost 50 years later Tocqueville offered proof of the accuracy of Madison's prediction when he noted, "The Americans have . . . much more to hope and to fear from the States than from the Union; and, according to the natural tendency of the human mind, they are more likely to attach themselves strongly to the former than to the latter. In this respect, their habits and feelings harmonize with their interests." And such was the case until well after the Civil War. In a predominantly agrarian society with an abundant and easily accessible supply of land and a tradition of local self-rule involving minimal governmental functions, the domestic activities of government were naturally few and highly decentralized. The consequence was that most of the internal functions of government were carried out by the state and local governments, even during the period when Chief Justice Marshall was laying the constitutional groundwork for expanded national powers.

During the first few years under the new Constitution the supporters of state as opposed to national authority attempted to consolidate the position of the states by providing for state administration of federal law. Particular proposals were advanced in Congress to have the states collect federal customs and excise taxes (on liquor) and for the state courts to maintain jurisdiction in federal cases other than those which the Constitution entrusted to the original jurisdiction of the United States Supreme Court. All of these attempts were defeated and American federalism has always operated through a dual system of administration and courts. Although this duplication is unquestionably expensive and has perhaps produced undue conflicts of laws, it has left each of the two levels of government with the capacity to exercise its functions independently of the other (without, of course, excluding cooperative action), even when there has been something of an imbalance between the two in the extent and importance of their activities.

The great expansion of central governmental functions began in the closing years of the nineteenth century and the change is attributable as much to the industrial revolution which occurred in America after the Civil War as to any other factor. By the latter half of the nineteenth century many parts of the economy had grown beyond the capacity of the individual states to regulate them effectively. Beginning with the Interstate Commerce Act in 1887, the central government entered the field of regulation in areas heretofore largely occupied by the states. The Act was passed in response to the demands of railroad users (mainly the farmers) that the federal government intervene to control excessive rates, selected (and privately worked out) rebates to some shippers, and other abuses which the states could not control because in crossing state lines the railroads reached beyond the jurisdiction of the individual states. Although the Act was passed largely as a hollow concession to reform groups, with little accompanying indication that Congress and the courts were prepared to deviate very far from a laissez-faire basis of national economic policy, the Act inaugurated a trend in national regulation that has since been incontrovertible. State powers of regulation were not drastically affected by the action at first, and the power to regulate surface transportation remained a concurrent one. However, the changing structure of the economy meant that the dominant responsibility would shift more and more toward the central government because effective regulation depended on the exercise of power on a national scale against nationally organized railroad corporations.

In the meantime the need for other regulatory adjustments made themselves felt. Early in the twentieth century, as the frontier receded and the illusion of a "magic pitcher" abundance was dispelled, the conservation of natural resources became a *cause celebre* of American politics, and the government at Washington tentatively embarked on a national program of controlled use of resources, replacement of natural products where possible, and area protection and rehabilitation that was eventually to loom large indeed. In other fields, too, the combination of *caveat emptor* and inadequate capacities of the states were giving way to national action. The Pure Food and Drugs Act of 1906 (providing federal standards and inspection of these commodities), the Federal Trade Commission Act of 1914 (designed to control unfair trade practices which threatened the market economy), and the Federal Reserve Act of 1913 (laying the regulatory basis for elasticity in the supply of money) were pragmatic responses to problems of such moment that they could not be totally ignored. Interspersed with these changes, or in some cases arriving somewhat later, were other national governmental programs enacted almost entirely in response to changes in technology; the rapid transition from horse to automobile, for example, led directly to federal interest and participation in highway planning and construction and to the regulation of the transportation of oil through pipelines in interstate commerce. Aviation and the radio produced similar incursions on the part of the central government. In some of these instances, of course, the problems bore no relation to state lines and simply could not have been met within the geographically constricted jurisdiction of the states regardless of the real or presumed formal allocations of power between state and nation.

Although the trend toward national action was dimly visible after 1887, the collapse of the national economy in 1929 revealed the extent to which economic and political interdependence had moved across state and local boundaries. Reluctantly, but with a firmness of political response, the public relinquished some of the major points of what Kenneth Galbraith has called the "conventional wisdom" in order to face the dual reality that an industrial economy was not inevitably self-correcting and that the states were neither administratively nor financially able to cope with the problems of an economic system that was national in its organizational scale and area of interdependence. National regulatory action was undertaken for activities which had formerly been untouched by government or, in some few instances, had been only limitedly affected by state or local policies. The stock market was made subject to national regulation through the establishment of the Securities and Exchange Commission in order to reduce the uncontrolled speculation in stocks which had been in no small part responsible for the unwarranted inflation in stock prices and the eventual collapse of the market in 1929. Legislation in the areas of business, agriculture, and labor was greatly expanded in the effort to bring the basic elements in the economy into a new equilibrium. Much of this legislation was experimental and did not survive, but other parts of the program were continued as experience proved their usefulness in preventing or slowing periodic disturbances in the economic order.

During the depression years of the 1930s the federal government also vastly expanded its activities in the area of public works. In large measure these programs were designed to provide employment and thereby stimulate economic activity. Some of the agencies created, such as the Works Progress Administration (WPA), the Public Works Administration (PWA), and the Civilian Conservation Corps (CCC) were obviously stopgap organizations. Even so, the work they did pointed to the piled-up needs for public construction in the fields of education, governmental buildings, and recreation facilities; and some of the projects carried out (especially in the development of public parks and natural recreational sites) remain as testimonials to the possibilities for improvement of the physical environment of many sectors of the country. In the great regional rehabilitation effort carried out through the Tennessee Valley Authority and in the generally expanded attention to multi-purpose flood-control and conservation works, continuing programs have been created which have had an increasingly important effect on the physical safety, economic welfare, and leisure activities of the residents of local areas, as well as the country at large.

Undoubtedly the greatest permanent expansion of federal governmental functions growing out of the conditions of the 1930s was in the social services or, to use the more common American designations, social welfare and social security. Public assistance programs were brought into effect either directly by the central government or through federal financial assistance to the states in order to cope with economic disabilities over which the individual had little or no control. An old-age assistance program, aid to dependent children, aid to various categories of disabled persons, and general assistance programs were instituted through grants to the states. In large measure these clearly established, rationally administered, and adequately financed programs replaced the haphazard programs of relief to the needy which formerly had been left to county (and sometimes city) governments. In addition, two insurance programs were put into effect under the Social Security Act of 1935: one was retirement insurance in the form of old age and survivors benefits (OASI), and the other was an employment insurance plan (Employment Security) designed to provide unemployment compensation to covered persons under prescribed circumstances and during a stipulated time period. The Old Age and Survivor's Insurance program is a wholly federal activity, while the unemployment compensation plan is a combined activity of federal and state governments. The latter program is now merged for purposes of administrative supervision with the previously existing employment service, which was designed to bring prospective employees and employers together through a placement service which is able to deal with labor supply and the job market on a comprehensive rather than a piecemeal basis.

As the foregoing discussion implies, one of the most important means by which the federal government has expanded its activities in functions once thought to belong almost exclusively to the states has been its general power to appropriate money for promoting the "general welfare." For this purpose the "grant-in-aid" from the federal treasury to the states (and to local governments) has proved to be a most useful device. The grant-in-aid arrangement is by no means the recent innovation that many of its critics imply. Even prior to the adoption of the Constitution, the central government provided, through the Northwest Ordinances of 1785 and 1787, for the granting of sections of land in the Northwest Territory for the support of the common schools. Throughout the nineteenth century the granting of public lands was the most common form of federal support for various state activities. Included among these were grants to support a variety of internal improvements (such as roads, canals, and railroads) and for education at all levels, but most notably for the support of agricultural and mechanical colleges in every state and territory through the Morrill Act of 1862. Some of these grants were unconditional, but (again contrary to the representations made by some critics of later direct monetary grants) many of them were extended under the stipulation that their use by the states conform to specifications laid down by federal statute.

In the twentieth century, monetary grants have tended to supersede land grants as a form of federal stimulation of state activity. Simultaneously with the closing of the frontier and the limitation of available public lands there came changes in the need for services and methods of administration which required fiscal resources not readily available to the states or available in such unequal proportions as to impede the implementation of services on a uniform basis throughout the country. Although small sums had been spent for these purposes earlier, the first major use of monetary grants-in-aid was in 1916 in the form of grants to assist the states in highway construction. Since that time, the expansion in the number and amounts of grant-in-aid programs has been enormous.

In 1900 only slightly over $7 million was distributed in the form of federal grants-in-aid. By 1920 the amount had risen to more than $43 million, in 1935 the figure had jumped to $2¼ billion, and at present the estimated amount exceeds $7 billion. Leaving aside the costs of defense, which eats up about two-thirds of the federal budget, grants-in-aid to state and local government now represent approximately 20 percent of federal expenditures. A recent congressional committee report listed 35 major grant-in-aid programs, most of which were further subdivided into several parts. Public welfare assistance programs (over $2¼ billion) and federal aid to highways (now enlarged to almost $3 billion with the recent establishment of the long-range interstate system) represent by far the largest areas of expenditure, but large amounts also go into such programs as public health, housing, and urban rehabilitation. The continuing growth of the grant-in-aid program is indicative of the fact that solutions to problems with which the state and local governments are unable to cope independently can be achieved through political and governmental action in which the states administer functions coordinated from a policy standpoint by the national government.

The functional changes in American federalism are primarily related to the changing sociological and economic structure of the country. In the past 50 years the United States has become overwhelmingly and irreversibly urban-metropolitan and industrial. This rapid change, which one observer refers to as a movement "from agriculture to urbiculture," was well under way before any real political adjustment to the changing pattern of American life was attempted. In consequence, there remains among the American public a great nostalgia for the supposedly less complicated mode of life of the agrarian period and a tendency to resort to political nostrums of the earlier era to solve the problems of a massive, industrially-based democracy. American federalism, with its emphasis on divided and narrowly defined powers of government, decentralization of policy formation and administration, and a strong sense of local identification, assists in the preservation of this somewhat anachronistic outlook.

The outlook is, in fact, more apparent than real. Pragmatic adaptation of governmental powers and functions to changing needs and conditions

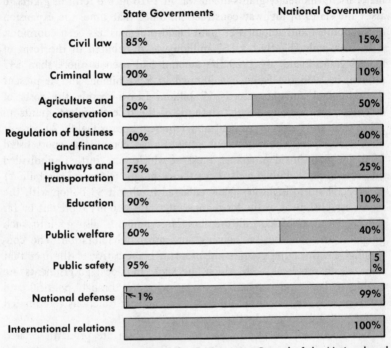

	State Governments	National Government
Civil law	85%	15%
Criminal law	90%	10%
Agriculture and conservation	50%	50%
Regulation of business and finance	40%	60%
Highways and transportation	75%	25%
Education	90%	10%
Public welfare	60%	40%
Public safety	95%	5%
National defense	←1%	99%
International relations		100%

An Impressionistic Representation of the Comparative Control of the National and State Governments over Selected Phases of American Life

of American society has been far more extensive than many persons realize. Furthermore, and contrary to the frequent representations of American states-righters and anti-governmentalists, the growth of government has not been overwhelmingly at the national level and solely the result of a steady and deliberate intrusion on state and local powers. Since the middle years of the depression decade of the 1930s, the federal government has spent more than the combined state and local governments;

in the last ten years, however, the difference has narrowed considerably. Despite the continuing large national expenditure on defense, the central government today accounts for about 60 percent of total governmental expenditure in the United States (approximately $165 billion annually) as compared to 40 percent for the state and local units. For some time prior to the mid-1950s the ratio was nearer 75:25, but both state and municipal units more than doubled their outlays during the past decade. Although inflation accounts for part of this increase, most of it was a result of a great upsurge of interest and activity in such functional areas as education, highways, health programs, parks and recreation facilities, and the development of public works and rehabilitation programs to meet the challenge of the so-called "metropolitan explosion." Public employment at the state and local levels has also grown substantially in recent years and is now more than 2½ times the 2,400,000 persons in the civil employment of the national government.

The volume of domestic functions of government carried out by the states and localities has thus grown at a faster pace than that of the national government in recent years. It may be argued, of course, that much of this growth has been stimulated by national action through grants-in-aid or other devices which give the federal government a large share of policy control in areas not specifically delegated to it by the Constitution. But even this contention loses much of its vigor when it is considered that the power of the central government to spend in the interest of the general welfare is virtually unrestricted, that state participation in joint projects is voluntary, and that the policy decisions for planning and implementing the functions are made within the framework of a political system whose power structure is characterized more by its diffusion among the federated units than by its centralization. In a practical sense, the United States is now practicing what many observers refer to as "cooperative federalism," as opposed to the earlier notion of "dual federalism" based on a system of mutually exclusive powers manifesting themselves in a complete division of functions between the nation and the states.

THE GOVERNING OF THE STATES

The internal governments of the states might be said to extend the characteristic of diversity in unity ascribed to the United States as a whole.

Their constitutional forms and institutional structures tend to show a uniform pattern, but the internal operations of the various state systems are highly individual. All of the states have written constitutions that conform to the arrangements characteristic of American constitutionalism in general. Power is explicitly or implicitly found to inhere in the people and legitimate power is specifically bestowed on the government through a constitution and within a framework of popular consent. The government is further limited by the incorporation into the constitution of a bill of rights guaranteeing freedom from governmental interference in matters of individual privacy, ensuring duly prescribed legal procedures, protecting property and contracts against arbitrary seizure or dissolution, and reinforcing the idea of uniformity in the application of the law. As in the case of the United States Constitution, the state constitutions provide the means for their own piecemeal amendment; and even though some of them prescribe specific methods of complete revision, the absence of such a provision is not taken to preclude the possibility of a complete rewriting of the state's basic law.

All of the state governments also base their governmental institutions on the tripartite separation of powers principle. All but one state (Nebraska) have bicameral legislative systems, all have popularly elected governors as chief executives, and each maintains a system of state courts which normally consists of a lower level tier of courts of original jurisdiction, intermediate courts of appeal, and a court of final jurisdiction called (or corresponding to) a supreme court.

Within this broad institutional framework, the variations are enormous and the overall political style of each of the 50 states has unique features. Every state has its separate history and local traditions, as well as a common participation in the whole or a part of the overall history of the United States. All of the variations of political background, public personalities, economic and social structures, and the presence, absence, or degree of intensity of one or more central political issues combine to vary the precedents and styles of politics from state to state. In an institutional sense the degree of party competition, the effectiveness of executive leadership, and the representative quality of the legislature are among the factors most likely to influence the main locus and methods of utilization of political power within a given state. As in most political systems, the sources and uses of power are subtle, complex, and variable in flexibility, so that generalizations about groups of states or comparisons and contrasts among states must depend on a close knowledge of the actual practices within each state under consideration.

The relations among the states are, like the intergovernmental relations between the states and the nation, broadly covered by the United States Constitution. The major constitutional stipulations in this area include the "full faith and credit clause," the "interstate privileges and imunities" clause, an extradition provision, and provisions governing the settlement of controversies between states.

The full faith and credit clause (Article IV, Section 1) requires that each state give full faith and credit to the ". . . public acts, records, and judicial proceedings of every other state." This provision is designed to give nationwide validity to civil matters such as wills, contracts, conveyances, etc., which are executed in a particular state. The provision does not extend to criminal matters. In civil proceedings such as divorce, the specific circumstances under which one state is obliged to accept the actions of another have been brought into question, but generally it may be said that the principle has been closely adhered to.

The interstate privileges and immunities clause (Article IV, Section 2) enjoins each state to extend the same privileges and immunities to citizens of other states that it affords its own citizens. Obviously designed to prevent the states from imposing the disabilities of alienage on emigrants or transients from other states, this provision has not prevented such actions as the imposition of out-of-state tuition fees on students from other states enrolled in state-supported universities. Disabilities of this type may be considered not to deny interstate privileges and immunities inasmuch as they are imposed to help defray costs that are regularly met by taxes on the permanent residents of the state. Since state citizenship now consists solely in meeting the state residence requirement (provided one is a citizen of the United States), political disabilities such as exclusion from the right to vote are ordinarily short-lived when persons move from one state to another. However, in a number of cases federalism does impose serious barriers on relocation of persons. This is especially true in matters such as license to practice the professions of law and medicine, or other occupations; unless the states concerned have reciprocal arrangements a person may be confronted with the necessity for qualifying himself anew when he moves across state boundaries with a view to establishing a professional practice or engaging in a licensed occupation.

The interstate rendition or extradition provision (Article IV, Section 2) clearly requires a state to deliver a person fleeing from a criminal charge to the state in which the charge has been levied upon the demand of the executive authority of the latter. Ordinarily, the states are cooperative in such matters; however, since the Supreme Court has refused to intervene in cases in which extradition has been refused by the governor of the state to which the person has fled, the constitutional stipulation must be deemed to be within the discretionary powers of the state governors.

At least two provisions of the federal Constitution relate specifically to the settlement of controversies or adjustment of problems among the states. In Article III, Section 2, the judicial powers of the United States is extended to controversies between two or more states and the Supreme Court is given original jurisdiction. This assignment of juridical responsibility conforms to the idea of the Supreme Court's position as interpreter of the Constitution of the governmental system as a whole, and its use in this connection has been extensive.

The second constitutional provision is more closely related to the solution of mutual problems. Although Article I, Section 10, of the Constitution is negative in providing that no state shall enter into an agreement or compact with another state without the consent of Congress, the provision has been given something of a positive turn in practice through the development of interstate compacts for the resolution of a number of interstate difficulties. More than 100 compacts have been executed; at first these tended to be confined to boundary agreements, but more recently they have been used for a variety of regulatory or service functions. One of the most important public corporations in the United States, the Port of New York Authority, was established by a New York-New Jersey compact in 1921 and now operates a vast network of terminal and transport facilities in the greater New York area. A number of interstate compacts, frequently involving several states, have been developed in the field of natural resources regulation, perhaps the most prominent of these being the interstate oil compact. The Supreme Court long ago held that congressional consent is required only if the compact increases the political power of the states in a manner which may encroach upon or interfere with the just supremacy of the United States, and some compacts (e.g., the Southern Regional Education Compact) remain in operation even though attempts at securing congressional approbation for them have failed. Some observers hold that the inter-state compact offers a broader latitude for solving public problems of a nature peculiar to federal systems than their somewhat limited use in America indicates. In particular, it is often suggested that compacts might be extensively applied to the problem of interstate metropolitan areas, to the development of regional planning authorities, and to the use of water resources and hydroelectric power facilities.

The states have also cooperated in ways other than those prescribed or implied in the Constitution. As early as 1892 the states organized the National Conference of Commissioners on Uniform State Laws. Although many model statutes have been devised by this organization to ease interstate transactions and lessen the conflict of laws among the states, the organization's success in securing state adoptions has been somewhat limited. In only three or four areas of legislation have the model laws been adopted by all states; and only a dozen or so more uniform statutes have been enacted by as many as three-fourths of the states. In addition to this device, a number of organizations of state officials have been created on both regional and national bases with the object of maintaining communication on problems in which the officials are mutually concerned; the most widely publicized of these has been the Conference of State Governors. The Council of State Governments, in operation since 1935, coordinates many of the activities designed to improve interstate cooperation. Its monthly periodical, *State Government*, and its biennial *Book of the States* maintain a current flow of in-formation relating to the organization and activities of the individual states and their various interrelations.

Federalism is so deeply rooted in American experience that we often overlook its legal complications, the duplications and conflicts of organ-ization and functions which it produces, and the financial burden that Americans apparently are willing to incur to maintain it. Very often the idea of federalism is sustained by boasting of attributes that the system may not possess. It is doubtful, at the very least, that American consti-tutionalism and democracy are as heavily dependent on the decentral-izing effects of federalism as the practicing politicians avow, although in terms of securing the desired voter response the politicians are on sound ground. On the other hand, there can be no question but that American federalism originally was an invention necessary to the estab-lishment of a "more perfect union." It is equally valid to suggest that the nature of federalism as the concept has developed through experience in the United States has enabled the country to stretch and adapt its original form of government from one for a small agricultural country to one suitable for an urban-industrial colossus. And in the unlikely event that it should really be superseded by a unitary government, the size and diversity of the country make it probable that something like it would have to be invented to take its place.

QUESTIONS FOR FURTHER DISCUSSION

1. What were the main arguments for and against the recent admission of Alaska and Hawaii to the Union, and what underlying reasons existed for and against admission that were not brought out in a specific manner?

2. How valid is the argument that many of the centralized activities of American government (that might otherwise be decentralized) cannot be transferred to the states unless the states improve their political and administrative structures?

3. What are the main strengths and weaknesses of a federal system as compared to a unitary system of government?

4. Would it be desirable to replace the present system of grants-in-aid for specific programs with a single large grant to each state on the basis of some overall calculation of the state's needs and resources?

VII

Local Government in America

NATURE AND ORIGIN OF THE SYSTEM

The American system of local government is not a single system so much as it is 50 systems, because the units of local government are primarily creatures of the states and not of the central government. In the face of the growing complexity of interrelations among the levels of government (and in the horizontal relations among governments at the same level), some observers have suggested that the categorization of governments in terms of "levels" is, in itself, more misleading than helpful for understanding contemporary politics and administration. However, despite the fact that federal, state, and local administrators who are engaged in cooperative intergovernmental projects or who are operating in complementary functional areas may in one sense form a subgovernmental system of their own, each is responsible in the final analysis to a separate legal jurisdiction with its separate policy-determining political authorities. And even though there are some direct functional relations between the local units and the national government, mainly in the form of grant-in-aid programs, even these cooperative relations are sanctioned by direct or implied state consent. For example, in more than one state cities have found themselves unable to take advantage of federally sponsored urban renewal programs because the state constitution or state laws were held to contain provisions which denied the municipalities the necessary authority to enter into these agreements. Thus American local government is almost exclusively a product of the determinative authority of the political and legal system of the state.

The legal bases of local government authority are frequently quite complicated. The state constitutions usually contain general provisions for local government organization and powers; and some of the more detailed state constitutions go into such extensive details of local government powers, limitations, and relations to the state as to establish a virtual federal relation between the state government and the local units. The latter analogy should not be pushed too far, however, because the states are conceived to be internally unitary, and the local units are therefore jurisdictions which are subordinate to the powers of the state.

In spite of the wide variations produced as a result of individual state control over their respective local governments, there is some degree of uniformity on a national scale, and an even greater degree of homogeneity is apparent in the forms, powers, and practices of local government when considered on a regional basis. The prevailing forms of local government in the United States are the county, the incorporated municipality or city, and the special or *ad hoc* district. In some states, notably in New England, the importance of county government tends to be superseded by smaller geographical entities called "towns." In some sections of the country other than New England the counties are subdivided into subdistricts or townships, some of which exercise some local government powers in their own right.

For the most part the forms of local government in use in America have a long historical background. Colonial local government was in large measure an adaptation of English local government modified by local patterns of settlement, economic activity, and other social adjustments necessitated by the new environment. Thus in New England the "town" became the typical colonial form of local government and has continued to this day to be lauded as one of America's great contributions to the idea of local direct democracy. The New England settlers tended to congregate into small villages, with farming being carried on in the immediately surrounding countryside. The pattern of settlement resulted from a combination of factors, including the need for defense against Indian attacks, the problem of the severe winter climate, the development of diversified small farms as the major economic units of the region, and the convenience of the village form of settlement for the practice of tightly-knit Congregationalism in religion. Many of the local government decisions in such communities could be made directly through the participation of all male heads of families; as a result the town meeting evolved into a hallowed symbol of direct popular government.

In the southern colonies, on the other hand, the settlers tended to occupy larger tracts of land in a pattern of more isolated farms or plantations; in consequence, the county form of government tended to predominate. The counties covered a much broader geographic area than the towns; they consequently tended to become more of an administrative district corresponding to the older English counties. These early county governments, like their British counterparts, were often dominated by important landholders who held the traditional offices of sheriff and justice of the peace. In the colonial period the middle Atlantic states, between New England and the South, found that their needs were best met by forming both county and township governments, the counties performing some functions, and the townships carrying out those activities which needed to be administered close at hand. Simultaneously with the development of these forms, the practice of incorporating boroughs or cities developed among the colonies. Thus, broadly speaking, the basic forms of American local government go back about 300 years.

COUNTY AND TOWN GOVERNMENT

In geographic terms county government may be said to be the most comprehensive form of local government in the United States, since county jurisdictions cover the entire areas of all but three states. Rhode Island does not use counties for local government purposes, Connecticut abolished its counties in 1960 following a long-term decline in the functioning of counties, and the newly organized state of Alaska has authorized the formation of boroughs for local government purposes, presumably in an effort to provide greater flexibility in the extension of local government powers and to avoid the impression that these local units are simply administrative districts of the state. The state of Louisiana, it should be noted, uses the term "parish" rather than "county," but the parish units in that state may be equated with the counties in other states. In most states which use the county, the counties overlay any city or the parts of cities that may be incorporated within them geographically. In a few instances, the governments of cities and counties have been consolidated in whole or in part into a single government. In some other places, most significantly in Virginia, examples of city-county separation may be found, in which cases the city governments affected may be vested with all the powers normally assigned to counties in addition to the powers delegated through their municipal charters to cities. During the past 40 years there has been very little change in the total number of counties in the United States; today there are slightly more than 3050. Although the size and number vary widely from state to state, the average number of counties is approximately 65 per state.

Counties serve two primary governmental purposes. First of all, they are administrative units or districts of the state; as such they serve as decentralized centers for the administration of a variety of state functions. Included among these are such important matters as the administration of election laws, the maintenance of law and order, the keeping of public records in such matters as conveyances, mortgages, wills, and marriages, and the provision of direct governmental services in fields such as welfare, education, public health and others. In a great many instances the counties also furnish the boundaries of state legislative representative districts (combinations of counties also constitute United States congressional districts), areas of judicial administration, and the confines of other administrative entities such as local school districts. The county units are thus interwoven in numerous ways, both political and administrative, with the state governments and the other forms of local government. In addition to serving as administrative subdivisions of the state, the counties perform some localized functions of their own. These vary considerably from state to state, but for the most part they relate to such activities as the maintenance of local roads, drainage, and bridges. Although the counties are not incorporated and are not ordinarily vested with general police powers, some states have conferred upon their governing bodies executive powers of a regulatory or service nature. For instance, in some states, they may be permitted to license and/or regulate certain types of business activity and in a few instances they may have comprehensive powers of planning and zoning.

From the foregoing discussion it may readily be seen that the counties were originally conceived as governmental units designed to serve a predominantly rural population. In point of fact the organization of county government and its method of functioning is still closely related to its rural origin, and the counties have come under considerable criticism for the part they have played in maintaining a predominantly rural outlook in local government long after the country has become highly urbanized. As indicated above, the number of counties tends to remain firmly fixed and county boundaries have tended to remain sacrosanct even in the face of the vast changes in the sociological structure of the communities which they govern. County boundaries were originally drawn in such a manner that the people who lived in them could conveniently travel to the county seat, transact business, and return to the outlying farm all within the span of a single day. Although conditions of transportation and local government needs have changed so drastically in recent years as to make this concept largely outmoded, the sense of local identification with the counties remains very strong, particularly in predominantly rural areas. In consequence little in the way of reform has been forthcoming in county government, either in relation to boundary adjustments or to their organization or methods of administration.

For the most part county governments tend to be somewhat loosely organized, with governmental powers being disseminated among a wide variety of elective and appointed officers. The main governing body is usually a council of popularly elected officials, with some such title as the county board, court, commission, or police jury. The number of members of such a board varies from state to state and their duties are similarly diffused. However, two types of county governing authorities predominate: one of these tends to be small in size (3 to 9 members), is usually elected from the county at large, and is ordinarily called the "county commission"; while the other tends to be large, is normally elected from the subdivisions of the county (or is an *ex officio* body composed of township supervisors), and is often designated the "board of supervisors." In some states in which county governing authorities are selected by wards or townships, the administration of the local functions of government may be divided up among these members and carried out largely on a ward or township basis. Most of the county governing authorities have responsibility for the preparation of the county budget, for the levying of tax rates and assessments within the framework of legal controls established by the constitution or state law, for the maintenance of local buildings, roads, bridges and other facilities, and for the administration of such regulatory powers as are confided to them.

In addition to the general governing authority, the counties ordinarily have a wide variety of separately selected county officers and agencies. Such officers or agencies usually function with a degree of independence that might seem surprising to outsiders. A county may, for example, have a popularly elected sheriff who is primarily responsible for local law enforcement, for the maintenance of the county jail, and for serving processes or otherwise carrying out the orders of the state district court having jurisdiction in his county. Other separately elected officials may include the tax assessor, the tax collector, the coroner, the clerk of court, the county surveyor, and the county attorney. In many instances the primary duty of such officials will be outlined in the state constitution and further elaborated by state statutes. In many of the southern states the local school districts are coterminous with the counties, in which cases there usually is an elective county school board and an elective or appointed superintendent of county schools.

Much of the criticism that has been directed toward county government relates to the absence of any authority that may be said to be collectively responsible for the maintenance of county functions as a whole. A plethora of elective officials, each performing distinctive functions and in many cases having separate sources of revenue for their individual functions, creates many isolated sources of political power and prevents the sort of coordination that is vital to contemporary professionalized administration of governmental functions. The system also tends to make for highly personalized management of public affairs, leaves access to government open mainly to personal influence, and otherwise inhibits the development of rationalized, objective methods of administration. It is worth noting in this respect that of all the different units of government in the United States the county tends to make less use of modern tools of management than any other type. To cite but one example: merit systems of personnel management are much less extensively used in the counties than in the federal government, the states, or the municipal governments.

In New England, town government is the comprehensive form of local government, thus leaving the counties as traditional geographical areas, but usually with a few functions such as the administration of justice by the courts and responsibility for activities normally handled as part of the court's administrative responsibilities. The town in these areas usually means a geographical entity that is ordinarily much smaller than the average county, and which includes one or more built-up settlements as well as some surrounding rural areas. The distinctive characteristic of the New England town remains the town meeting of all qualified voters (though in some cases the town meeting has become representative rather than direct by substituting a system of electing a certain number of voting delegates for universal participation). The town meeting is usually an annual event, with the possibility of some special meetings at other times if circumstances require them. At the annual town meeting the townsmen or the voting delegates set the tax rates, approve or disapprove major appropriations, establish major policies, and elect the selectmen and the town clerk who will supervise the routine administration of the town government functions. Some towns also elect a variety of other officials. Although the towns may or may not be incorporated,[1] even where they are not incorporated state law may confer extensive functions of a municipal type on them. Again, like the county governments, the towns were created mainly for village and rural purposes and have not always adapted very well to the rising tide of urbanization. Some of them, however, have managed to shift to town managers or other forms of local administration designed to secure a higher degree of efficiency and to formulate policy recommendations to be presented at the town meeting. Much, of course, depends on the size of the town. If it is large enough and sufficiently heavily populated to furnish the tax base and clientele for effective administration, it can often furnish a model of local government integration and comprehensiveness. However, many towns are small and contain scattered populations; as a result the tax burdens that local citizens are called on to bear for local roads, drainage, schools, etc., may be much heavier than they would be if the functions were administered over a broader area. At the same time, local residents are usually reluctant to consolidate even the most obviously uneconomical services with those of the adjacent town units. Local community identity by no means follows the "natural" areas of economic and administrative integrity or convenience, especially in America where local separation is so much a part of the political folklore.

MUNICIPAL GOVERNMENT

Municipalities ordinarily are organized upon application for a charter by a group of persons who are living in sufficient population density to feel a need for the services provided by this particular form of government. The constitutions of the states and the laws regulating the forms of the city charter and the powers which may be extended under the charter vary considerably from state to state. In some cases the state legislature will approve charters on an individual basis, in which instances they are referred to usually as "special act" charters. In other cases the states will provide general laws regulating the matters which may go into a municipal charter and the charters will be drafted in

[1] In Massachusetts, for example, all towns are incorporated and are, in effect, the exclusive local government entities throughout the state, except for those larger cities which are incorporated as municipalities. The county functions in that state are quite limited.

accordance with these enactments and approved by the state when they are found to conform to the prescriptions of the general municipal government laws. For a long time, and especially from the reform era of the 1890s until World War I, proponents of municipal reform argued against the special act charter and the narrowly constricted general act charter in favor of "home rule" charters. A home rule charter system is based on the provision by the state of broad general laws covering matters pertinent to municipal charters, with the actual drafting of the charter and the choice of the permissive powers that may be included in it being left to the charter commission of the city which seeks incorporation or an alteration of its existing charter. Municipal home rule, which thus gives a city the power to draw up, adopt, and modify its own charter within the framework of a state's general laws, was often advocated as an antidote to the repeated interference in municipal affairs for political purposes by state leigslatures and other governing officials of the states. In a number of cases charters may be classified according to the size of the municipal unit, with varying powers and restrictions being extended to cities of different sizes. There is also available to the cities of some states an optional charter arrangement, whereby a city may select—from a variety of possible charters predrafted by the state—the particular form of municipal government which seems most suitable to it. Most students of American local government regard the local self-determination arrangements of a home rule, classified, or optional charter as being without full effect unless some constitutional protection is given to the system which will prevent the legislature from making discretionary changes in the laws, the classifications, or the optional organic laws available to the cities.

In recent years the entire concept of home rule has been subject to increasing scrutiny because it has not proved to be the universal solvent of municipal problems that it once promised to be. The states can never divest themselves of responsibility for maintaining a system of local government, and as the needs of municipalities change with the changing structure of the society it often becomes more important to secure broader legal concessions from the states than merely to maintain the right to frame charters within the sometimes narrow limits of the general law. And if the state legislature is controlled by a rural majority with little sympathy for the plight of the cities, the financial and other disabilities which may affect municipalities become more important as practical considerations than the simple right to frame patterns of organization and political powers according to a prescribed legal arrangement. Home rule without adequate attention to the needs of urban life can be only limitedly effective.

The rapid transition from a predominantly rural to an overwhelmingly urban population in the United States has exacerbated these problems. A substantial amount of rural-urban conflict has long been discernible in those states which contain very large cities, and the tension has mounted as small cities and towns have burgeoned into metropolitan areas. Much of the resulting controversy has been most clearly visible in the state legislatures, where the rural areas have been substantially overrepresented in proportion to population. The desire to maintain their favorable power position, together with a distrust of the mode of life and style of politics in the cities, has produced numerous examples of legislative discrimination against the urban areas in terms of distribution of certain types of tax resources, location of major access roads and other public facilities, and reluctance to provide legal authority for planning and other programs essential to life in the city. This lag in the adjustment of political institutions to the changing patterns of life is in process of radical alteration as a result of the 1964 Supreme Court decisions on reapportionment. In some states the disabilities of the cities in the face of rural-dominated state legislatures have already been partially overcome by the massive scale of urbanization; in others, the reallocation of legislative seats now taking place gives rise to the expectation that at least one barrier to the assumption of local initiative in solving metropolitan problems will soon be breached.

Although the details of the organizations vary quite broadly, there are really only three general organizational forms of municipal government in use in the United States. These are the mayor-council, the commission, and the council-manager forms. The mayor-council form is the oldest and is still the arrangement used by more cities than either of the others. All of the largest cities in the country—that is, those with populations in excess of a million—use this system and many others in all size categories are also governed under this form.

In mayor-council cities the usual practice is to have a popularly elected council which acts as a legislative body, and an elected mayor who serves as the chief executive. In some cities councilmen run at large while in others they are elected on a ward basis. For the most part membership on a city council is considered to be a part-time job, with the council holding regular meetings no more than once or twice a month, or at most once a week. Although a city council may be divided into a few committees for specialized functions, as a general rule the use of committees in American local government is much less pervasive than in England. For one thing, with few exceptions the American council tends to be much smaller than its English counterpart, so its policy functions tend to be exercised in plenary sessions, with detailed information and recommendation reports originating in the office of the chief executive or in one of the municipal departments. Again, the presence of an elected chief executive in the person of the mayor lessens somewhat the necessity for using council committees as coordinating instruments of local government functions in America as compared to England, where the mayor is usually ceremonial and the clerk is appointed.

The standard practice of assessing the office of mayor in mayor-council cities is to regard the mayor as either a "weak" mayor or a "strong" mayor in terms of the institutional powers of the office. In the strong-mayor system the mayor will have the power of appointment over most of the department heads and will ordinarily have the power of suspensive veto over ordinances passed by the council. The weak mayor, on the other hand, is usually regarded primarily as a ceremonial figure, with limited powers of appointment and with no veto. In the latter type of mayoralty the executive powers are usually dispersed among a variety of elected executive officials, boards, and commissions, or among similar individuals and groups appointed mainly by the council, although even the weak mayor may have the power of appointment over some offices. As in all other separation of power systems in the United States, the formal allocation of powers is frequently less important in determining the actual manner in which the government operates than is the use which a mayor may make of the office in terms of his political strength, his personal capabilities, and other subtle factors pertinent to effective government. Even in cases in which a mayor's formal assignment of powers may appear to make him a "weak" mayor, executive leadership may still be exercised through budget preparation and presentation, the authority to make recommendations on policy, and the skillful use of public relations. Here again description is always limited to generality, and a knowledge of the individual city is necessary in order to clothe these bare bones of power in the living flesh of government.

The commission form of municipal government is something of an anomaly in American political life, since it is based on an unusual merger of the administration with the policy-making or legislative body. This form of muncipal government began in Galveston, Texas, in 1901, following a destructive tidal wave which inundated massive amounts of property, took many lives, and threw the city's finances and services into chaos. Following the catastrophe, a group of businessmen took charge of the public affairs in the city in an effort to avert an impending anarchical situation. On the basis of their experience, these community leaders applied for a charter from the state to embody the form of government which they had developed and the charter, which legally inaugurated the commission form, was granted. Under a commission system of government, the city commission consists of three, five, or seven members, ordinarily elected at large. In standing for office each potential commissioner designates a specific administrative post which he will fill if elected. One commission position is that of the mayor, who presides over the commission's meetings and, in addition, heads one or more of the municipal government departments; another commissioner is elected to assume the responsibilities for finance, and he administers any department or departments of fiscal affairs which may be included under the charter. Other commissioners are elected to assume various administrative duties, such as heads of the departments of public works, public safety, utilities, or others, depending on the particular organization of the city. Collectively, the commissioners (including the mayor) serve as a legislative body; in this capacity they are responsible for framing policy, approving the budget, and presumably for holding the government as a whole accountable to them. In their separate administrative capacities they supervise the programs which come under their respective departments. The system has been criticized by many governmental purists as tending to lead to lack of coordination because each commissioner becomes more concerned with the affairs of his own department than with the operation of the government as a whole, and thus tends to evade such coordination of overall governmental functions as may affect his department in a manner that he considers adverse to its interests. It is often charged that dissension, deadlock and trading of votes results, and that these conflicts and compromises are detrimental to the whole or to certain phases of the city's program. Whether attributable to these criticisms or not, it is true that there has been a noticeable decline in the number of cities using the commission form of government since 1920, when the form reached its peak of about 500 municipalities with populations in excess of 5000. Even Galveston gave the plan up in favor of the council-manager system in 1960.

The council-manager form of government originated as an outgrowth of the general reform era prior to World War I. Under this form a municipal council, again varying in size from city to city, is elected to carry out the legislative responsibilities of the muncipal government. The council in turn appoints a professional city manager who acts as chief administrative officer under the direction of the council. The manager is responsible for all the functions of city government, he ordinarily has the power to hire and fire personnel subject to rules and limits of the merit system, and he usually is protected in the exercise of his adminis-trative duties by a charter guarantee of some type against council inter-ference with ordinary day-to-day administrative affairs. The council-manager system was deliberately designed as an analogue of the board of directors and general manager arrangement charcteristic of corporate business management. The manager plan has had a rather remarkable success in medium-sized American cities, and has also made considerable inroads into small cities. It has the advantages of simplicity, profession-alized management, effective coordination, and a strict responsibility and accountability. It is not, however, a panacea for municipal problems, as a good many cities have discovered. In addition, the sources of political leadership in council-manager government are not always clearly discern-ible and some cities seem never to be able to adapt themselves to its use; in these cities the manager system is usually characterized by a great deal of turmoil in the council and a high rate of turnover of the managers themselves.

Of the more than 3000 cities in the United States with populations over 5000, approximately 1600 (54 percent) are governed under the mayor-council arrangement, about 250 (8.4 percent) utilize the com-mission form, and more than 1150 (over 38 percent) operate under the council-manager plan. The council-manager system has had a greater vogue in recent years than either of the other two forms among cities that have changed their systems. After an initially rapid development in the 1920s, city-manager government developments slowed down during the depression years of the 1930s, but picked up again very rapidly in the 1940s and 1950s. Today some 1800 cities of all sizes utilize the city manager and a good many others use some variation of the form. The commission type of government has declined more or less in proportion to the rise of the city-manager system.

Municipalities are designed to render services that are essential when people live in great population agglomerations. City governments are expected to provide directly, or to supervise and regulate the provision of, a variety of complex services. Many of these services are costly, yet the public is not always able to understand that the advantages of urban life may be maintained only at a certain price. Problems of transportation, sanitation, recreation facilities, protection of persons and property, and the provision of water and public utilities are but a few of the broad general categories of services which a city is normally expected to cope with. These are not services that can be postponed or provided in a haphazard or irregular manner; they are urgent necessities, and at the same time they are the type of services of which little notice is taken until one or more of them breaks down. Since one of the most important sociological developments in recent years has been urbanization and suburbanization, the problem of municipal government—and particularly metropolitan municipal government—has become one of the critical areas of American government and politics. Being a compact area, the effects of governmental services (or the lack thereof) are more immediately visible at the level of the city than in any other governmental jurisdiction. In past years the cities were afflicted with the problem of domination by political bosses who ruled through spoils and virtually without responsibility, and other political liabilities; today the plight of the cities is related much more to inadequate consideration by the governments of the states and by the lack of far-sightedness on the part of individual citizens or groups within the cities who are unwilling to plan for or properly finance the present and future needs of the expanding population. American cities are often pointed out as being amorphous in both governmental and community structure, as lacking in proper attention to aesthetic qualities or possibilities, and as encouraging the type of uncontrolled growth which creates far more problems than can be solved in the foreseeable future. Unfortunately, a good many of these charges are true. At the same time great efforts have been made by reformers as well as by some of the states and the national government to meet these discernibly bad conditions. For the most part such efforts have been directed toward solving the distinctively metropolitan problems rather than the problems of local government as a whole.

THE PROBLEM OF METROPOLITANISM

The growth of metropolitan communities in the United States has been phenomenal in recent decades. Although census bureau definitions of metropolitan areas have varied in detail from decade to decade, the general approach is to define a metropolitan area as a local geographic unit which includes a core city with a minimum population of 50,000, together with the overlying or contiguous county or counties which forms a continuation of the core city's urbanized pattern and which has a high degree of economic and social interdependence relative to the core city. The 1960 census revealed 212 such areas in the United States. These 212 areas contained more than 112 million persons, or about 63 percent of the total population. This fact is all the more striking when it is realized that the 168 metropolitan areas identified by the census of 1950 contained a little over one-half of the American population at that time. The nature and rapidity of growth of these areas is further indicated by the fact that about one-half of the metropolitan area populations now live outside the boundaries of the core cities. The population movement represented in this expansion of the metropolitan community, and especially its mushroom growth outside the core cities, is symptomatic of the increasingly obvious fact that large-scale urban growth has far outstripped the governmental capacity to deal with the situation within the framework of the existing structure. The main response thus far has been to try to handle the problems on a piecemeal or patchwork basis, and the results have often been a paralysis of the central or core city, leading to a deterioration of the central section of the area and a further flight to the suburban fringes by formerly urban residents.

Observers have characterized the local government situation in such variously derogatory terms as chaotic, hopeless, and even nightmarish. A multifarious collection of local government units have sprung up to try to cope with these problems; a recent survey indicated that there were more than 15,000 separate units of government in existence in the 212 metropolitan areas. Many of these metropolitan agglomerations spill over county and state lines; and the outlying local governments are strangled by the tentacles that shoot out from the once-compact body of the core city. The New York metropolitan area (covering parts of several states and numerous counties) alone embraces more than 1400 separately organized governmental units. Service levels, public accountability, and tax rates vary within these governmental entities in a manner that makes comparison seem almost completely futile and the possibility of adjustment virtually hopeless. Among the most striking developments is the proliferation of special or *ad hoc* tax districts in the areas outside the core cities. These special districts ordinarily are designed to perform single functions, usually of a municipal nature, and the functions that they undertake are often totally unrelated to the performance of other local government functions which need to be carefully integrated and coordinated with them. Some segments of the public who seem to fear the cost of municipal services under a united metropolitan government often do not realize that they are paying premium prices for substandard public facilities and services through the maintenance of a highly proliferated organization of local service units. And when it is realized that the New York City budget alone (which by no means covers the local government costs of the New York metropolitan area) exceeds the expenditures of any one of the state governments of the 20 smallest states, the scope of the proliferation of urban governments is amply underscored. The American frontier attitude of self-help, limited public activity, and narrowly constricted areas and functions of government and administration is more apparent in local government than at any other level, and at the same time the inadequacies of this traditional response to a modern technological society should be more easily apprehended and corrected at this level than any other.

A great many alternative solutions to the metropolitan problem have been suggested, but none thus far has managed to secure general acceptance, and only in a few areas has a particular answer been successfully worked out. On the surface, annexation by the central city of surrounding territory would appear to be the most direct and effective solution. However, annexation laws are difficult to apply because they frequently depend on a favorable popular response both from the central city and from the area proposed for annexation, with the result that the cities frequently want to take in only the more desirable types of outlying communities and these are precisely the types that do not wish to be caught up in what they regard as a power and tax grab on the part of

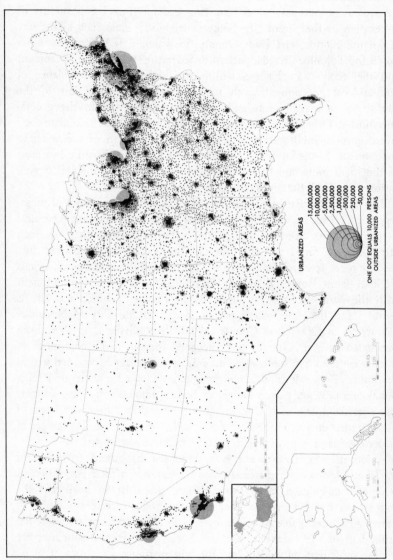

Population Distribution: 1960. Source: Department of Commerce, Bureau of the Census.

urban politicians. Again, many of the built-up areas outside the core cities are separately incorporated and are thus exempt from the possibility of annexation by the parent city. Some metropolitan areas such as the city of Miami, Florida, and Dade County, in which it is located, have followed the Toronto, Canada, pattern in federating the county government and the many municipalities within their areas into a semblance of unified local government, with specified functions being left to the continuing municipal units and the others transferred to the general government. Other cities and counties have attempted to consolidate their entire governmental system into a single unified plan of metropolitan government. In the latter cases an attempt is made to abolish all or most of the small units and to create a comprehensive governmental organization vested with functions of both city and county.

This brief explanation of attempts to deal with the problem of megalopolis by no means exhausts the efforts—both wholesale and piecemeal —that are going on in the United States, but more often than not such attempts have failed and the examples of successful metropolitan consolidation are few and far between. Two successful recent consolidations are the Baton Rouge, Louisiana, consolidation of its city government with the parish (county) of East Baton Rouge in which the city is located, and the more recent partial merger of the City of Nashville, Tennessee, and Davidson County, in which Nashville is located. Both Baton Rouge and Nashville had the good fortune to be core cities of smaller metropolitan areas whose urbanization was largely confined within the limits of a single county, and both cities adopted a compound functional consolidation (i.e., a merger of certain administrative departments and a partial amalgamation of the governing bodies without total loss of identity of county or city government) rather than a complete merger of all local units of government into one comprehensive system.

American local government is a somewhat haphazard collection of traditional forms, with extremely broad variations in their adaptation or attempted adaptation to changing circumstances. In no small part the states have failed to realize that governmental structures created 150 years ago are incapable of taking care of local government needs in the latter half of the twentieth century. Local government boundaries are for the most part outmoded, and the administrative structures of many sectors of local government are manifestly cumbersome and diffuse. Even in those instances in which local leadership has been heavily concerned with the problems (and there are many such places), the state governments have not been in a position or have been unwilling to offer more than piecemeal assistance to individual communities in arriving at a solution. State governments, for example, do not ordinarily maintain departments of local affairs which could maintain surveillance over the local government system and appraise its operations and needs. Yet this hiatus is one that could easily be filled if the state governments could be made to realize that the local units within their borders are among the most crucial problems that the states have to face. Finally and most importantly, American urbanization has now come of age and it is crucial that the inhabitants of the urban communities begin to realize what has happened to the character of those communities and to take the sort of remedial public action which is available to them in a democracy.

QUESTIONS FOR FURTHER DISCUSSION

1. What general conditions of American government and politics encourage the resistance to a general improvement of county administration and a consolidation of county units that are too small to perform their main functions in a comprehensive and economic manner?

2. To what extent are physical, social, and long-range capital planning necessary for the development of the services, conveniences and aesthetic qualities of the emerging metropolitan community?

3. In what ways does a charter for a municipal corporation differ from a Constitution?

4. What are the advantages and disadvantages of the special district as a means of procuring local government services?

VIII

America's Role in World Affairs

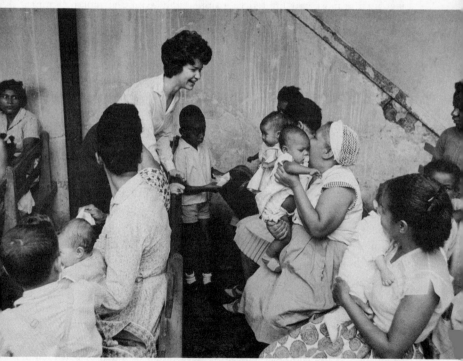

Peace Corps, Washington, D.C.

THE IMPACT OF INTERNATIONAL COMMITMENT

Few events in American political history can be said to equal, either in dramatic impact or in external and internal consequences, the entry of the United States into full-scale participation in international affairs. Little more than 25 years ago the country still clung to the predominantly isolationist state of mind out of which American foreign policy had been framed for more than a century. The permanent military establishment was negligible, external commitments were minimal, and concern with the emergent totalitarian dictatorships and their expansionist tendencies was for the most part limited to a unilaterally expressed moral disapprobation.

Yet by 1940 the United States had begun to mobilize its manpower and resources in a great effort to become, in President Roosevelt's words, an "arsenal of democracy." In the year the first peacetime conscription in the country's history was inaugurated, a commitment of aid by all means short of war was made to the allies, and 50 destroyers were exchanged with Britain for the use of naval bases in the Caribbean. Even before America's active entry into the war as a result of the Japanese attack on Pearl Harbor in December, 1941, the government had gone far toward committing the country to a long-range policy of collective international action through the development, with Britain, of the peace aims embodied in the Atlantic Charter. And well before the end of the war these intimations of a reversal in the national attitude toward international politics were being confirmed by America's leadership in the preliminary stages of the creation of a new international organization to replace the League of Nations. As early as 1943 the work of drafting the principles that were to culminate in the Charter of the United Nations was under way—an effort which was to be substantially completed at San Francisco in the spring of 1945, shortly before the German surrender. Under the impact of these events, together with America's massive economic and manpower contributions to the war effort, the postwar exhaustion of the European allies, the devastation of much of continental

196

Europe, and the rapid expansion of communism as a result of the policies of the newly invigorated Soviet Union, the United States not only became heavily involved in foreign affairs but found herself in a position of leadership in international politics.

The effects of this new role are by no means confined to the foreign policy machinery of the United States and to international organizations and governments external to America; it reaches into almost every aspect of domestic government and politics. Although foreign affairs could hardly be said to have been a minor aspect of government even in the heyday of American withdrawal, its former place on the public agenda bears no comparison with the position it occupies today. Foreign policy now interacts with, and tends to dominate, all but a few issues in American politics. The federal budget has been vastly swollen by the necessity for maintaining an enormous national and international defense machinery, by the underwriting of military forces in other countries, by an elaborate program of foreign economic aid which serves as a major adjunct of policy, by disproportionately large contributions to international organizations, and by the need to maintain a host of new information and intelligence services as instruments of foreign policy.

The impact of this rapid expansion of activities and expenditures on the organization of government and the exercise of political power has been pronounced. The traditional burden of the Presidency in the field of foreign policy has been enlarged to the point of adding an entirely new dimension to the office. The administrative machinery through which the President exercises his function as the country's chief diplomat has grown in geometric rather than arithmetic proportions, thus leading to the necessity for creating an apparently permanent "inner cabinet" in the form of a National Defense Council for developing and coordinating foreign and defense policies. The President's role as popular and congressional leader has also been affected by the central place of international affairs in contemporary American politics. Every presidential election since 1940 has reflected the rising influence of foreign policy questions on the nominating process and in the campaign. And the attempt to hold a majority congressional coalition in line on defense, foreign aid, and the space aeronautics programs (and especially to secure the appropriations to underwrite them) has occupied a steadily increasing share of the President's time and energies.

More and more congressional time, too, has been devoted to foreign affairs and closely related issues; new committees have made their appearances in areas such as atomic energy, space, and government operations, the impact of international political competition with the Soviet Union has been directly or indirectly responsible for broad new programs (e.g., the National Defense Education Act) which go far beyond the immediate problems of defense, and several new fields of legislative investigation have been opened up or broadened, including especially internal security, defense contracts, and foreign aid programs.

The courts have also had a hand in shaping the law as well as governmental and public reactions to the changing course of events produced by the new internationalism. Tensions have developed between the demands of domestic security and the fundamental individual freedoms guaranteed by the Constitution, a host of questions has arisen involving the meaning of and appropriate methods for dealing with subversive activities, and a sharpening of the always thorny problem of congressional investigations has occurred, all of which have opened the way to litigation requiring the elaboration or alteration of applicable judicial doctrines.

A more subtle, if no less general, change may be discerned in the broader reaches of the American political mind as a response to the new international commitment. The ramifications are so numerous and so complicated that they can only be sweepingly suggested and cursorily illustrated in this context. One of the more important manifestations of this phenomenon has been the unfolding of an elaborate national symposium on the symbols which give meaning to American life. Scores of books, reams of periodical literature, and hours of radio and television tapes have been produced in a renewed effort to interpret the American political tradition, the national destiny, the strengths and weaknesses of a democratic society, and the functions and qualities of the United States as preceptor of the noncommunist world. From its beginnings as a new nation in the eighteenth century America was both self-conscious and self-assured about its national destiny, but the self-consciousness has now been forced to take full account of relations with other national states, old and new, and the self-assurance about the inevitability of national success has been called into question by the combination of failures and successes and the apparently unending state of crisis that have attended the country's wholesale intervention in world politics.

Some practical consequences of this self-analysis are of the utmost importance to America and to the world. One of the most prominent examples is the area of race relations, which is beyond question the most intense domestic issue in American politics today, but which also has close ties to the new American posture in international politics. The rapid and irreversible steps which are being taken by the President, the Justice Department and the federal courts toward guaranteeing American Negroes full legal and political rights, freedom from discrimination, and equality of economic opportunity may be attributed in large part to a heightened awareness of the contradiction between the promises of American life and the single most conspicuous failure to make good on those promises. This awareness is very much a part of the renewed quest for self-understanding, and it is inseparably connected with a strong sensitivity to the effects of the issue on American influence abroad, and particularly in the uncommitted and increasingly important nonwhite sectors of the globe. The United States, as an avowed opponent of colonialism, has had to recognize the embarrassing ambiguity involved in supporting the movement for independence of African countries while the status of a very large portion of its own Negro minority remains inferior to that of the society at large. Secretary of State Dean Rusk pointed up the interrelation of this domestic problem with the American position in international politics succinctly when he remarked, "We fight with one arm tied behind us."

FROM WITHDRAWAL TO INVOLVEMENT

The magnitude of these changes must be set against the traditional bases of American foreign policy prior to World War II in order for their full implications to be understood. Although the British colonies of North America owed their successful development in large part to England's effective role in international power politics in the seventeenth and eighteenth centuries, and although American independence was both fostered and maintained in its initial period by the complicated workings of the European-dominated system of international politics, the United States early demonstrated a tendency to withdraw as much as possible from any commitment to the prevailing system of diplomacy.

Concern with keeping the western hemisphere free from the exercise of major influence by European powers was manifested long before an official policy along these lines was proclaimed. Both Jefferson and Washington warned against the dangers of "entangling alliances," and the

revolutionary alliance (1778) with France—which was ostensibly permanent—was terminated at the Franco-American Convention of 1800.
Paradoxically, the American posture of isolation did not prevent American involvement in almost every major European power struggle in the
nineteenth century. And ironically, the troubles of Europe almost
invariably redounded to the benefit of the United States in terms of the
consolidation of her predominant position in the western hemisphere
and the annexation of vast expanses of territory. The diplomatic history
of the United States during its first hundred years of independence is
largely a play on the theme of a seemingly uncalculated exploitation by
America of the international crises in Europe. Two important consequences may be discerned in this situation. In the first place, both the
policy of isolation and the self-righteous tone of American nationalism
seemed to be completely vindicated by the country's continuing success,
despite the apparent designs and connivances of European powers whose
governments were looked upon by most Americans with moral disapprobation. In the second place, the American propensity to geographic
expansion received an enormous impetus from these events; the idea of
America's "Manifest Destiny" to expand the republic westward all the
way to the Pacific and beyond came to be accepted almost without question as the young nation seemed to meet each new test with increased
vigor.

The continental expansion of the United States in the first half of the
nineteenth century illustrates the interplay of European crisis and American territorial aggrandizement. The purchase of the Territory of Louisiana in 1803, which was the largest single land acquisition in American
history, was made possible by a combination of the failure of Napoleon's
policy in the western hemisphere and by the financial difficulties accruing
from his imperial ambitions. In 1819 Florida was ceded to the United
States by Spain, which was beset by colonial revolutions in Latin America.
Although less directly related to European affairs, the annexation of
Texas in 1845 (following Texas' separation from Mexico) and the
absorption of California and most of the present American Southwest
as a result of the Mexican War (1846–1848) tended to confirm the
validity of the American policy of isolation from the European power
struggle and the fulfillment of territorial ambitions in North America.
As a result of the compromise settlement of the dispute with Great
Britain over the Oregon Territory in 1846 and the Gadsden purchase of

1853 from Mexico of the territory which now comprises the southern portions of the states of Arizona and New Mexico, the continental expanse of the United States was complete.

The first formal pronouncement of the doctrine of isolationism and the "sanitation" of the Western Hemisphere was the Monroe Doctrine of 1823. The doctrine was embodied in the annual message of President James Monroe to Congress; it was intended as a response to the threat by the concert of continental European powers (the Holy Alliance) against the new republics which had been created in South America as a result of revolts against Spain. The doctrine warned the European powers that henceforth the American continents were not to be considered as subjects for colonization. It further enunciated the principle that the political system of the allied powers was essentially different from the political system of America, and that any attempt to extend the European system to any portion of the western hemisphere would be regarded as dangerous to the peace and safety of the United States. Finally, the pronouncement stipulated that the United States would not interfere with existing colonies or dependencies of any European power, and that the United States would refrain from interference in the internal concerns of any of the powers of Europe.

The original proclamation of the Monroe Doctrine, which was an affirmation of an American policy that was already clearly in effect, was far less important than its subsequent influence. In the first place, any intention that the powers which made up the Holy Alliance might have had of restoring Spain's position in the Western Hemisphere had been effectively stayed at least two months prior to the Monroe Doctrine as a result of British pressure on France. Furthermore, although the President's statement received a favorable popular reaction in the United States as well as among many groups in Britain (where it comported with British policy), elsewhere it was regarded as a rather audacious and perhaps ineffectual pronouncement of a somewhat brash newcomer to the community of nations. In fact, it was not until the 1850s that President Monroe's name became firmly attached to the doctrine and it began to be recognized as a major basis of American policy. Its importance, therefore, is related less to its initial impact than to its availability for application in later controversies, and for the insinuation that the United States was determined, as the strongest power in the Western Hemisphere, to thwart any possibility of a European hegemony in the New World, if indeed it did not intend to establish a hegemony of its own. The doctrine thus formed the point of departure for the gradual movement of America in the direction of great power status, a condition which was not to be fully realized until after the Spanish-American War (1898). Even more important, perhaps, was the fact that the Monroe Doctrine was to become the strongest bastion of the isolationist spirit in the United States, a spirit that was, paradoxically, to increase in intensity at each stage of America's development as a world power prior to World War II.

Again somewhat paradoxically, the American Civil War (1861–1865) strengthened America's claims to recognition as an equal-status power. The capacity of the United States to mount a great military machine and to wage an internal war that was, in strategy and advanced weaponry, a forerunner of the wars of the twentieth century, indicated a hitherto unrecognized potential in the New World. In the midst of the Civil War, the United States was able to force capitulation on the part of the British Government to the demands that the construction of ships for the Confederacy in violation of neutrality be halted. At the conclusion of the conflict, the United States thwarted French ambitions in Mexico by tacitly supporting the overthrow of the puppet Emperor Maximillian, whose installation was undoubtedly prompted in part by America's time of troubles and whose very presence constituted a major challenge to the ability of the United States to enforce the principles set forth in the Monroe Doctrine.

Although the posture of isolation continued to be made, American tendencies toward expansion did not cease with the realization of the American dream to span the North American continent from the Atlantic to the Pacific. As a consolidated nation-state with a large territory, growing population, and an expanding and rapidly diversifying economy, the United States was subject to the same internal political pressures to extend its influence beyond its own territorial limits as any other national state in the nineteenth century. A major difference was that while the European powers were engaged in a global competition, the United States restricted its horizon to a view westward across the Pacific. In the 1850s and 1860s the United States was the leader in opening China and Japan to western trade; in the last quarter of the nineteenth century the American government also became involved in an imperial dispute with Germany and Britain over Samoa, and after a long period of interest in

Hawaii (fostered by missionary and trading activities) the islands were finally annexed to the United States in 1898 following Admiral Dewey's victory at Manila. In the meantime, in 1867, the United States had purchased Alaska from Russia, a step which not only fitted into the pattern of Pacific expansion but also acted as a means of thwarting the possibility that the territory might be annexed by Britain if the hostilities between Britain and Russia had eventuated in war.

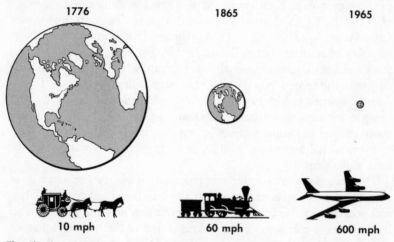

The Shrinking World—Comparative Sizes of the Globe Expressed in Travel Time for the Prevailing Modes of Transportation

The ambivalent attitude of America toward foreign affairs reached its apogee in the Spanish-American War of 1898. By engaging in this war with a declining imperial power, ostensibly for the liberation of Cuba, the United States found itself in the position, contradictory to its own professed aims, of itself becoming an imperial power. As a consequence of the war the United States annexed Puerto Rico, the Philippines, and the islands of Guam and Wake. During the course of the war the United States also acquired Hawaii and part of Samoa, and Cuba was made an American protectorate.

Under the leadership of President Theodore Roosevelt, the newly acquired prominence of America in international politics continued to be developed primarily along the lines that had been set for it by the foregoing events; however, Roosevelt reversed the practice of refusing to admit to playing the game of power politics and entered into the competition openly and with gusto. In 1903 he completed the steps necessary to secure the long-awaited inter-oceanic (Panama) canal across the isthmus between North and South America, and in 1905 the President announced as a corollary of the Monroe Doctrine that the United States asserted the right to regulate the internal affairs of Latin American states in the event that these had consequences which cut across American foreign policy. Even earlier, at the first Pan-American Conference of 1889, the United States had assumed a protectionist attitude toward Latin America. In the Far East the United States continued to foster its policy of an open door in China, thereby generating certain hostilities from another rising international power, Japan, which were to culminate only with the Second World War. Thus despite the fact that the United States purported to withdraw from active participation in the world power struggle, to eschew territorial ambitions beyond the North American continent and to assume a somewhat superior moral posture with respect to international actions, its position in all these matters was, to say the least, ambivalent.

Theodore Roosevelt's active role provoked strong reaction from those who recognized the extent to which the traditional policy of isolation had been controverted by deliberate intervention in world politics. This reaction was to culminate in the striking revival of the spirit and practice of isolationism at the conclusion of World War I. At the outset of the war, the United States strongly reasserted its traditional neutral position *vis-à-vis* the European struggle. Once again America's position seemed to have been vindicated as the balance of power system failed and the whole of Europe became embroiled in a catastrophic upheaval. As the debilitating war continued, and particularly as developments took place that were gradually drawing the United States into the conflict, some of the underlying ideals of American independence began to be expressed as the justification for American intervention. Americans have always tended to regard themselves as generically republican and as having a specific obligation to promote the political and economic ideals which apparently have been so productive for American political life. Woodrow Wilson articulated these ideals precisely in setting the goals for concluding the war and effectuating the peace. The world was to be made safe for democracy, first by defeating an autocratic and aggressive power, and then by the establishment of an international order based on the principles of national self-determination, the development of a practice of open covenants openly arrived at in international diplomacy, and the creation of a League of Nations to serve as a forum for world opinion, with that expression of opinion forming the basis for collective decisions among the independent nation-states.

Although Wilson's idealistic position was in many respects related to the moral outlook that had produced isolationism (especially as that outlook developed into the notion of hemisphere "sanitation"), Wilsonian conceptions of appropriate action in world affairs tended to contradict the doctrine of isolation by committing the United States to a permanent, clearly recognized role in international politics. Consequently, Wilsonian idealism confronted two implacable opponents: the cynical "realists" among the European diplomats who were not prepared to accept his magnanimous proposals for establishing the peace, and the "irreconcilables" among the members of the United States Senate, a group led by Wilson's unrelenting personal antagonist, Senator Henry Cabot Lodge. When Wilson's health failed during the course of his attempt "to take his case to the country" the proponents of the treaty (with membership in the League of Nations "riveted in") were without effective leadership, and Wilson's unwillingness to compromise over the terms of the treaty threw the entire matter into such confusion that the Lodge forces were able to emerge victorious. With the defeat of America's proposed entry into the League of Nations by the Senate, the isolationist position was reaffirmed as the basis of American policy and Wilsonian idealism was rudely shunted aside. Although the United States took part in the various negotiations for peace and disarmament in the 1920s and continued to press its special claims as benevolent protector of Latin America, the withdrawal was as complete as it had been prior to the era of Theodore Roosevelt. Japanese aggression in China in the 1930s, the Italian invasion of Ethiopia in 1935, the Spanish Civil War (1936–1939), the Munich crisis, and even the open declaration of war in Europe in September, 1939, did little to shake the American spirit of neutrality.

Despite the fact that Franklin Roosevelt's New Deal revived much of the spirit and many of the specific solutions to problems characteristic of the domestic reform program of Wilson's New Freedom, the attitudes of the New Deal administration in foreign policy appeared to be more closely related to traditional patterns of isolation than to the high-minded involvement envisioned by Wilson. Even the one outstanding accomplishment of Franklin Roosevelt in foreign affairs during the early days of the New Deal—the development of the "good neighbor" policy in Latin America—harked back to the old principle of the sanctity of the Western Hemisphere above all other considerations. Even when the country began to move rapidly into a major program of defense mobilization in 1940, the Neutrality Acts of the mid-thirties, which were prime examples of the American preference for unilateral as compared to collective efforts to maintain peace, were still on the statute books. In fairness to President Roosevelt, it should be said that his state speeches after 1935 clearly indicate a growing concern with the deteriorating conditions of world politics; however, the prevalence of the isolationist mood in the country apparently urged him to caution in his efforts to build a strong popular consensus in support of a redirection of American foreign policy. And the forcefulness of the President's leadership from 1940 onwards in preparing the nation psychologically and militarily for inevitable involvement in the global conflict and for its postwar commitments can hardly be overestimated.

THE NEW STRUCTURE OF INTERNATIONAL POLITICS

By the end of World War II the lines of the future which were laid out in the early part of this chapter were already being clearly drawn. No one doubted that the United States was irrevocably involved in international politics. One question that did remain was whether the United States was going to follow Wilsonian idealism to the bitter end or whether it was going to attempt to play the game of power politics in the sense in which it had been played in the nineteenth century. As it turned out, this country was to make a valiant effort to apply as much of Wilson's idealism as possible; at the same time, it soon became apparent that a realistic sense of power play would have to be developed if the United States, Western Europe, and many other parts of the world were to survive under conditions that would enable them to preserve their liberal constitutional systems. Indeed, many of the difficulties in the period since 1945 have revolved around the problem of reconciling Wilsonian idealism with realism in international affairs. The Atlantic Charter (with its four freedoms), the assumptions about peace and cooperation that the United States delegations took to the conferences with the allied powers before and immediately after Germany's surrender, and the enthusiasm with which the United States participated in the creation of the United Nations, all were strongly flavored with the ideals for which Wilson had stood. At the same time the rapid consolidation of a new and greatly expanded Soviet empire, the shaky economic and political basis of western Europe, and the responsibilities that the United States had to assume for occupying parts of Europe and the East pointed strongly to the necessity for the United States realistically to appraise the political and military possibilities for effecting its purposes in international affairs.

In place of the old balance of power among a multiplicity of European nation-states, there was now a bipolarization of power between two massive nation-states—the United States and the Soviet Union. The Soviet Union moved aggressively and realistically to consolidate its control over the areas that it occupied. In those countries into which Russian power did not reach directly, the instruments of propaganda could be skillfully applied to foment discontent, which could in turn be exploited by the locally organized revolutionary party. The major powers of Western Europe, hitherto the focal area of international politics, had suffered such enormous physical destruction and, except for the United Kingdom, such demoralizing military defeats that their economic recovery was problematic and their potentiality for resumption of leading roles in world politics appeared inconceivable. The system of colonies, protectorates, and spheres of influence fostered by the "great" powers was already in a process of ferment which might erupt chaotically at any time unless some orderly approach could be made to its liquidation. If the process of deterioration was to be halted, and the long-range American aim of a peaceful world made up of independent, pluralistic nation-states capable of collective action through international organizations was to be realized, America had to assume the initiative as the leading *power* dedicated to such ideals.

The United States possessed a number of natural advantages in the new situation. The American economy was far and away the most productive in the world, and this productive capacity had been substantially increased during the course of the war. The United States shared with western Europe, which still constituted the potentially strongest third force in international politics, virtually all social, religious, cultural, and political values. To the small states already in existence and to incipient states which were soon to emerge from colonialism, the United States could hold itself out as having never been an imperial power and having always promoted the concept of the self-determination of nations. Indeed, the United States had itself emerged from colonial status by way of revolution, and had served as an example for many of the states which had come into existence since the eighteenth century.

In its confrontation with the Soviet Union, however, the United States was at a disadvantage in several respects, some of which bore a close relation to the very sources of its advantages. The Soviet Union had at its disposal a comprehensive ideology and a political system which permitted it much more flexibility of means than was the case with the United States. Although the question of the real motivations of Russian foreign policy may be open, there can be little doubt but that the justification for Russian action is offered in terms of Marxist ideology. By taking the standard position that the Soviet Union is the potential victim of a hostile, war-mongering collectivity of capitalist nations surrounding it and bent on its destruction, the Soviet government can rationalize the use of any means whatsoever to combat this threat. In the occupied areas satellites could be deliberately created and held in line by strong political, and even military, action. Elsewhere revolution could be encouraged and invasion of adjacent "capitalist" states by communist countries in support of domestic revolution was deemed legitimate. Ideologically speaking, peace is not possible until capitalism has been destroyed and the harmoniousness of universal communism is substituted for the inevitability of war among capitalist nations. By contrast, the United States was bound by its moral commitment to assist in the realization of a plurality of open societies and to pursue its policies in a much more limited and indirect way. At the same time, the nature of Soviet government put Russia in a position to change and adapt its foreign policy and to justify such changes propagandistically without the necessity of becoming involved in a long internal political debate in which the party in power is faced with the type of opposition that is characteristic of a democratic society.

Given the distinctions among the advantages and disadvantages accruing to the United States and the Soviet Union in a bipolarized world, it is only natural that the United States should be placed in the somewhat negative position of responding to communist tendencies to expansion rather than developing the primary initiative in international affairs. In a democracy the capacity to make effective decisions is necessarily limited by the extent to which the public is prepared to support the policies of government, and public opinion is frequently amorphous. This point has been only limitedly understood by the American public, with the result that a great deal of criticism has been directed toward the lack of a more positive approach to the settlement of international problems. This is especially characteristic of the more inflammatory periods of international politics. In some respects American public opinion reflects a tendency to waver between Wilsonian idealism at its most impractical extreme and an antithetical position of a suspicion, hostility, and distrust of even those powers aligned with the United States in opposition to communism, as well as toward the idea that anything of consequence can be achieved through international diplomacy. And the flux of public opinion in these matters certainly contributes to the observed ambiguities on foreign policy in official circles. However, despite these uncertainties and tendencies to impatience—many of which indicate the survival of the spirit of isolationism—a large measure of consistency may be discerned in the main aims of American policy as well as in the efforts that have been made to effect these aims. To no small extent this development can be traced to the capacity of the American public (acting in response to persuasive leadership) to broaden its political horizons. The ideal objectives of American foreign policy since World War II have been the maintenance of peace, the containment of communist imperialism, the creation of conditions which would enable the self-determination of nations to become a viable principle, the reduction of tensions among major powers, and the collective restraint of overt conflict among nation-states in all parts of the globe.

Regardless of whether the Soviet Union (and in more recent years, Communist China) is motivated almost entirely by the ideology of world revolution or whether the Soviet Union's expansionist tendencies derive from more complex motivations that relate to nationalism and historical factors going back far beyond the communist era in Russia, the United States clearly operates from the premise that the imperialist tendencies of the Soviet Union are very much a part of the realities of contemporary international politics. The American government further regards these efforts to expand the Russian and Chinese spheres of influence as decided threats to its own ends. The pragmatic approach to meeting these threats has been the doctrine of containment. Thus despite a great deal of discussion about the possibilities of rolling back communism and/or freeing the countries behind the Iron Curtain from satellite status, the main efforts of the United States have been directed toward preventing the physical expansion of the Soviet sphere of influence and providing support for noncommunist regimes in those areas which are threatened with internal communist revolution supported by Russia or other communist powers.

In terms of the direct power struggle, the United States has relied on building up its own military defense programs, primarily in the form of the so-called "strategic weapons," the extension of military assistance to powers with which America is allied, and the development of a series of security pacts which are aimed at securing collective action against communist threats in various parts of the world. In this connection the United States has entered into four major regional security organizations: the North Atlantic Treaty Organization (which is the main bulwark of defense for western Europe and is perhaps the most important of all the organizations of this type), the Southeast Asia Treaty Organization, the Organization of American States (composed of the Latin American countries other than Cuba), and the Australia-New Zealand-United States Pact. In addition the United States cooperates with the Central Treaty Organization (United Kingdom, Turkey, Iran, and Pakistan) and maintains a number of bilateral treaties with other powers such as Japan, Korea, Nationalist China, and the Philippines, who are not members of the other collective organizations. All told, the United States has, through these various mutual commitments, taken the initiative for bringing into being a multilateral defense arrangement involving more than 40 national states. In addition, the United States has extended military aid to a sizeable number of other countries as part of the overall strategy of defense against communist aggression.

The vast program of economic and development assistance that the United States has carried on since World War II constitutes the second major aspect of American foreign policy. The first step in this direction was the development of the Marshall Plan in 1948. The Marshall plan aimed at providing the economic basis for European recovery; during the four years that it was fully in operation the United States provided approximately $17 billion of economic aid to Europe in support of plans for economic redevelopment which were worked out for the most part by the participating countries themselves. The economic debilitation of Europe following the war was regarded as the most immediate danger to the American interest in maintaining noncommunist governments. The unquestioned success of the Marshall Plan was a major factor in pushing the idea of economic aid and technical assistance into other areas of the world. President Truman built on the Marshall Plan when he enunciated the notable Point IV proposal in his inaugural address in 1949. In the proposal the President suggested that long-range economic development programs supported by United States funds could provide the economic underpinning for underdeveloped and newly emerging states to build their economic strength sufficiently to prevent the communist powers from capitalizing on social discontent to the point of subverting existing regimes, and thus preventing free choice of the governmental systems by which such countries would be ruled. Since the war, the United States has spent approximately $90 billion on economic assistance of this type. The great debate in Congress and among the American public over the effectiveness of these expenditures is a continuing thing, which reaches a new crescendo with each federal budget. A vocal congressional element, drawn in large part from the old isolation-minded regions, but drawing support from others among the economy bloc and the outright cynics, continually chops away at the idea of the program on the grounds that it is wasteful and ineffective as a means of halting the spread of communism. Other critics, both inside and outside the United States, have leveled the charge against the program that it smacks too much of the type of interventionism carried on by the United States at the turn of the century under the rubric "dollar diplomacy." On balance, the American aid program has to be reckoned a success in helping to realize the major goals of foreign policy, despite some notable examples of failure. By underwriting a portion of the European recovery the United States derived incaculable benefits toward the realization of its desire to preserve the traditions of liberal constitutional democracy among the Western powers. In helping to pull Europe out of the economic doldrums, the foreign aid program contributed to the reconstruction of the most important power bloc outside the direct control of either of the two great powers. In other areas the gains have perhaps been less obvious, but as the country has grown in experience with aid to underdeveloped countries fewer mistakes are apparently being made in the methods by which aid is extended, the uses to which the investments are put in the recipient countries, and in the propaganda opportunities which grow out of the program. In this connection it might be noted that technical assistance has tended to supersede the direct transfer of goods and funds as the major method of pursuing the goals of economic assistance. Organizations such as the Peace Corps, which were looked upon with widespread skepticism at their outset, have now apparently proved to be of greater long-range value than many of the more direct forms of monetary aid, and at a much lower cost to American taxpayers. In addition to its vast programs of unilateral aid, the United States has also cooperated with, and to a considerable extent underwritten, such international bodies as the World Bank, the International Finance Corporation, the International Development Agency, and the Organization for Economic Cooperation and Development.

The United States has not neglected the traditional methods of diplomacy, although the changed conditions which attended the bipolarization of power and the Cold War have placed much more emphasis on the effective use of propaganda and on the attempt to forestall the growing strength of a single great opponent in the struggle than would be the case in a multi-power situation. Although the Soviet Union has seemingly been able to utilize general propaganda techniques somewhat more effectively than the United States, in at least one forum—and that perhaps the most important one—the United States has been able to maintain a considerable advantage over its great rival in mobilizing world opinion. In the United Nations the United States has been in the fortunate position of being aligned with the majority bloc and has thereby forced the Soviet Union to make an excessive use of such dubious implements as the veto power. In the one great test of the capacity of the United Nations to apply the sanctions of collective security—the Korean conflict—the United States achieved what appeared to most observers to have been a notable victory by securing collective support to stabilize the existing balance of geographic spheres of influence. However, the decision was taken during the absence of the Soviet representative from the Security Council, so that the unanimous front presented by that organization in the Korean crisis can hardly be said to have brought the two great power blocs any closer together on the issue of collective security. It is worth noting also that the United Nations has been an important means of maintaining at least an overt show of world support for the application of the doctrine of limited warfare, a concept which in itself gives some cause to hope that breaches of the peace may be confined to those areas in which the confrontation of the communist and noncommunist states is most immediate.

Although the United States has at times shown considerable impatience with the politics of neutralism which has increasingly manifested itself among the newly independent states, the development of a neutral bloc can in some ways be seen to fit better into the American policy of containment than into the Soviet policy of exercising an out-and-out imperial power in its sphere of influence. Increasing tensions, for example, between Communist China and the Soviet Union have certainly proved more of an embarrassment to the ideologically impregnated pattern of Soviet aggrandizement than the neutral countries have to America. The latter development has also worked the beneficial effect (from the standpoint of the United States) of lowering the level of tension between the United States and the Soviet Union by reducing Soviet pressures on some of the areas in which the United States influence has been most pronounced.

THE MACHINERY OF FOREIGN POLICY

The machinery through which the United States conducts its foreign affairs is a highly complex one; many of the complicating conditions, in fact, have already been pointed out in the chapters on the branches of government. The President obviously has the leading function in the conduct of foreign affairs. He has the primary duty of developing major foreign policies and directing their execution. However, the constitutional arrangements under which the Senate shares in the treaty powers and the Congress as a whole provides the necessary appropriations for supporting foreign policy, together with the naturally divisive tendencies between the two branches, make for serious conflicts in areas such as the mobilization of public opinion, the economic support which can be generated for foreign affairs, and the high degree of partisanship which frequently develops over issues of foreign policy. Despite these limiting factors, it is generally expected that the President will maintain the initiative in this field and will effectively control its processes, both through the practice of personal diplomacy and through his power to appoint those immediately responsible for overall foreign policy as well as the personnel which represents the United States abroad.

The central unit of that part of the machinery of foreign affairs under the President's immediate control is, of course, the Department of State, which acts under the direction of the Secretary of State. The Secretary of State is chief foreign policy adviser to the President and is responsible for the administration of the affairs of the Department. Like the other executive departments of the government, the Department of State is organized in hierarchical form, with the most important subdivisions being directly under the authority of the Secretary of State. The principal bureaus are broken down into geographical sectors for dealing with problems of the various parts of the world. Within each of these bureaus further subdivisions take place until one reaches the so-called "desk officers," who are responsible for channeling information to the higher policy echelons and for maintaining a reciprocal channel for transmittal of policy to their counterparts in the country or countries with which they are concerned. In addition to the bureaus based on geographic areas, the Department also contains certain functional bureaus such as the Bureau of Administration, the Bureau of Security and Consular Affairs, the Bureau of Intelligence and Research, the Bureau of International Organization Affairs, and several other related functional units. Another part of the Department which has varied in importance at different periods in recent American history is the Policy Planning Council and its chairman, who is sometimes in the position of exercising major advisory influence on the central direction of policy. In recent years, as the program of economic assistance has grown into one of the two or three most important tools of overall policy, the Agency for International Development and the Peace Corps have also assumed major functional roles within the Department.

Outside the Department of State a number of staff and/or line agencies have important influence in the construction of foreign policy and the administration of foreign affairs. In some cases, the staff agencies are of prime importance for coordinating the vast apparatus which has a direct or indirect impact on the conduct of foreign affairs. As previously noted, the most comprehensive of these staff agencies is the National Security Council, which brings together at the highest level the administrative officials most immediately concerned with the broadest questions of national defense and international commitments. Since so many of the American aims are dependent on the status and functions of the military establishment, the Department of Defense is a singularly important co-operating agency in the overall conduct of foreign affairs; the National

Security Council is therefore a crucial agency for coordinating the activities of the Departments of State and Defense. The Central Intelligence Agency, which was established to coordinate the wide variety of tasks involved in the collection and analysis of overall intelligence data, acts as the eyes and ears of the National Security Council.

Some other independent agencies are engaged in functions which are essential outgrowths of the new American participation in international affairs. The United States Information Agency, for example, is organizationally independent, but acts within the framework of State Department policy as the major means of disseminating information about the United States in the broadest sense. The USIA is concerned with interpreting cultural, social, political, and economic aspects of American life to the various countries of the world; it is also involved in evaluating the impact made by American customs and actions on the peoples of other countries and in developing reciprocal methods of informing Americans about social and political life abroad. If the term propaganda may still be used in a nonpejorative sense, the USIA is the most important propaganda medium through which the United States attempts to create mutual understanding and build a basis of support for American policy in world opinion. At least two other new independent organizations which must be accorded a place in any broad outline of administrative organizations involved in foreign policy decisions are the Atomic Energy Commission and the National Aeronautics and Space Administration. Although both are fundamentally concerned with national defense, their functions are so broad and the implications of their activities are so far-reaching in terms of international negotiations and the struggle for prestige within the context of the Cold War that they must be included in the highest level councils responsible for hammering out decisions that affect international diplomacy.

THE DILEMMA OF INVOLVEMENT

The United States moved from an apparently unassailable position of isolation to one of unprecedented leadership in world politics in less than a decade. The assumption of this burden involved changes in the organization and processes of American government, the total effects of which are incalculable. It is only natural that the rapidity of these changes should have placed heavy strains on a political experience which had been conditioned for so long to such different attitudes and modes of action in international relations. Probably the most notable—one is tempted to say notorious—consequence of the shift away from isolationism that has characterized recent American thinking is the tendency of the American public, and often supposedly responsible leaders, to assume that it is possible to produce a policy which will permanently settle the outstanding issues of world affairs. Americans have long been accustomed to dealing successfully with their internal problems without having to give too much consideration to the external world and are likely to exhibit signs of frustration in the face of the intractability of world politics. They tend, therefore, to be reluctant to see that diplomacy is a continuing thing and that some problems must be lived with and adjusted to rather than solved. This is one source of the insecurity which has given rise to such apparently diverse peculiarities as McCarthyism and the popular susceptibility, with reference to the Korean conflict, to such catastrophe-evoking slogans as "There is no substitute for victory."

The isolationist spirit is closely connected both as cause and effect with a moral tendency of the people of the United States which is best designated as puritanical. With some exaggeration it may be said that a strong sense of national rectitude has fed upon the belief, enforced by observation of the series of internecine European wars from Napoleon to Hitler, that America has been providentially elected as the superlative national state. This position, it is felt, derives from the rigor of her individualistic moral code, and its truth is clearly demonstrated, in a worldly sense, in her economic supremacy. By the same token her refusal to submit herself to the corruption of continuing close association with other national states has preserved her pristine purity and enabled her, when events elsewhere are out of hand, to intervene in and settle international disputes in order to make the world safe for democracy.

Although part of the isolationist *rationale*, this puritan outlook has proved easily adaptable to the new era of active participation in international politics. It accounts in large part for the tendency to look at foreign problems in terms of a simple black and white dichotomy. The frontier puritanism of the western movie, with its clear division into the good men and the bad or the cowboys and the Indians, is transmuted into a categorization of foreign powers into the mutually exclusive and exhaustive classes of those "for us" and those "against us." This is the attitude so much complained of by the Eastern powers who insist that

Americans are incapable of appreciating the subtleties of neutralism. In replying to charges of misunderstanding, the moral forces behind the American spokesman practically compel him to insist not only that there can be no neutrality in the conflict between communism and the free world, but that partisanship towards freedom must be overtly demonstrated. Good works as well as faith are necessary for salvation.

Even more galling in its effect on the American sense of moral rectitude is the fact that the motive behind foreign aid is brought into question. It is frequently charged abroad that aid is offered solely and simply on the expectation that the recipient will immediately submit to American leadership in foreign affairs and will be bound to participate unquestioningly in the realization of the aims of American policy. This suggestion immediately puts American opinion on its moral high horse and encourages it to ride off and leave the accuser to his just fate. Nothing is calculated to provoke the puritan more than questioning his motives, and few things are more likely to afford a better excuse to deny or to place restrictive conditions on economic aid than such an allegation. What frequently is not clear to American opinion in this debate is that America's supreme moral assurance produces behavior which belies its true motives. One of the main characteristics of the puritan, other than his facility at self-justification, is the unfortunate inflexibility of means which sometimes frustrates movement toward his ends.

It is not the least of America's difficulties as a leader of the free world that the political institutions available for coping with the problems resulting from the country's former isolationism and her moralistic propensities are more calculated to increase the effects of these influences than to restrain them. The facts of American political life are such that there appears to be no way to keep the discussion of American foreign policy, and even authoritative pronouncements on it by men in high office, within the bounds of responsibility and free from entanglements with extraneous issues which make possible the exploitation of foreign problems for partisan purposes.

In the first place, the expectation that the conduct of foreign affairs will be completely in the hands of a responsible executive is not applicable to the American system. The constitutionally embodied principle of the separation of powers of government among three distinct branches (and its concommitant protection of such separation by a complex system of checks and balances of each branch against the others) provides for a sharing of the conduct of foreign affairs between the President and Congress. Although the evolution of the administration of foreign affairs in the United States has, by virtue of necessities long recognized in other countries, been in the direction of responsible executive autonomy, the ambiguity of the basic legal arrangement has not been overcome. There is still ample scope for contention between the President and Congress over their respective areas of operation in this field. Unfortunately these conflicts are stimulated by crises; the Bricker Amendment debate of a few years ago, for example, which represented a serious congressional attempt to limit the President's powers in foreign affairs, occurred at a time when the Republican party was in power and badly needed unity and solid congressional support for the program that it was attempting to carry out.

At the root of this matter is the disintegrated structure of political parties in the United States. There is no procedure within the parties for channeling discussion upwards to the central party organization, which might then be responsible for the execution of policy as a collective entity and might be expected to develop the necessary techniques for imposing a measure of discipline and restraint on its adherents during the course of the execution of policy. To the contrary, in the United States the center of party gravity is much lower down; effective political party control is exercised at the level of the states, and in some cases even at the level of the big city. This decentralization of party political power has the effect of allowing all of the conflicting views on foreign problems of both parties to come unresolved into the national forum, there to become the object of constant and uncontrolled disputation. The task of reconciling the confusing agglomeration of locally dominated thinking about foreign affairs even within one party has thus far been beyond the capacities of the party leaders, and the effort at bipartisanship in most periods has amounted to little more than a verbal tribute to an ideal. The forces of disintegration are most strongly suggested by recalling that a former Republican leader of the Senate, William Knowland, earned himself the title "the Senator from Formosa" by reason of his highly personal views—views which have a much more definite source in the politics of the ex-Senator's home state of California than in the accepted policy of his party.

Despite the irreconcilability of the disparate opinions of the various decentralized power groups within the parties, it is still necessary for the national organization to try to appease each of them for purposes of electoral unity. The most effective way to accomplish this is by a diversionary attack on the other party, and these attacks are apparently predicated on the idea that the more strenuous the blow struck at the opposing party the more effective the diversion. Such tactics are dangerous because the overcommitment of the forces of criticism may leave no flexibility for maneuver when the party is called upon to conduct its own policy. This plight clearly beset the Eisenhower administration of 1953–1961: the uninhibited attack by the Republicans on the Democratic administration's foreign policy during and preceding the 1952 election campaign made it necessary for the new Republican administration to appear to break completely with the policy of its predecessor. A real dilemma was created because a full assessment of the situation seemed to offer no alternative but to continue the policy of containment along lines laid down by the Democrats. Hoist in this way by its own petard, it was necessary for the new administration to invent a succession of slogans such as "agonizing reappraisal" and "massive retaliation" in order to create the impression that a redirection of the entire policy was underway. The conduct of American foreign policy in recent years is explained to some extent by reference to the definition of the function of a political party platform given by a distinguished politician of the last century. It is the purpose of a platform, he said, to give the impression of moving steadily onward and upward while warily standing still. Unfortunately for American prestige, the strident words of the politician, framed mainly for home consumption, have often made more of an impact on America's allies than the more restrained deeds which accompanied or followed them.

Despite these handicaps the American record in international politics over the past twenty-odd years has been impressive. American independence had been forged in an atmosphere which gave strong impetus to the idea that the United States was a unique experiment in constitutional republicanism, and during more than 150 years the success of that experiment was deemed to be dependent on keeping the country free from involvement in international politics. Within the space of a remarkably brief period Americans discovered that the assumptions on which noninvolvement had been based were no longer tenable and that leadership among the Western community of nation-states had been thrust on the country under conditions that had no historical precedents in a modern epoch. In the light of American experience the response to this state of affairs has been little short of remarkable.

The pragmatic success of the internal governmental system of the United States has produced a national consensus which expresses itself in a strong commitment to the major symbols of American life. These symbols have provided much of the basis for the idealism which America has displayed in international politics, including the concept of the self-determination of nations; an emphasis on egalitarianism; and a deep-rooted commitment to the notions that democracy is the sole practicable basis for government, that international peace depends on the broadest possible extension of viable democratic systems among the nations of the world, and that a workable political system must be undergirded by a strong economic system which will provide a decent standard of life for the local citizens as well as the possibility for individual social and economic mobility. American entry into world affairs was to impose a severe test on the basic features of American idealism both at home and abroad.

In this connection, the domestic problem has centered largely on the question of whether the ease of American life and the habit of success had so affected the American government and people that the strains imposed by the continuing international tensions would produce serious aberrations. On the whole, however, the country has been willing to make the sacrifices and to face up to the crises and failures of postwar international politics. The attitude of national self-sufficiency has occasionally taken a xenophobic turn, and some tendencies have been exhibited toward a rigid closure of American society around the symbols of the American consensus to the detriment of the flexibility needed to cope with world affairs realistically. But if the nation has experienced McCarthyism and other forms of witch-hunting, it has eventually found the means for coping with such movements, and has apparently learned something from such experiences. And although apprehensive about and impatient with the intractability of international politics the government and the public have generally performed well under conditions of crisis. Despite its inexperience, American leadership acted vigorously and from strength in its unaccustomed role; yet it has simultaneously demonstrated a capacity for restraint when circumstances called for moderation. From the first postwar threat to expand Soviet power in Greece through the Berlin airlift, the Korean conflict, the pressures and counterpressures in the Far East and on into the more recent Cuban crisis, the response has generally been prompt, vigorous, and appropriately conceived; where failures have occurred or mistakes have been made, they have not produced precipitate and irresponsible corrective action.

In relation to its allies, to the communist bloc, and to the states outside either of these spheres of influence the United States has managed to develop realistic policies without compromising its idealistic premises. The policy of containment has been effective, especially in Europe, but also to a considerable degree in Latin America, and in portions of the Middle East, other parts of Africa, and some areas of the Far East. The government has resisted the strong pressures to seek a quick solution to problems through massive use of force, by and large it has avoided the urge to give aid under conditions which would prejudice its stand against interfering with the independence of the recipients, and in building a system of defense alliances it has generally abided by its commitments to free negotiation, equal status among nation-states and national independence. The United States has supported the activities of the United Nations and other international organizations, has accepted their defined principles, and has been generous in its fiscal contributions to them. At the same time, it has neither neglected the other avenues of diplomacy nor has it foregone the possibilities of unilateral action.

Like most national states, the United States displays a complex intermingling of idealism and realism in framing and executing its foreign policy. Very often the two become hopelessly confused, with the result that at some times expedient actions are justified through the rhetoric of high morality and at others an overindulgence in idealism imposes heavy burdens on the possibility of realizing long-range interests. Given the adjustment that the United States had to undergo in foreign relations and the scope of the problems since World War II, the American record of leadership probably compares fairly well with that of most other great powers in previous eras.

But the task is far from complete. Not only do many of the problems which gave rise to the post-World War II tensions persist, but the changing structure of the international community and the altered interrelations of its components have contributed to the emergence of new difficulties out of the partial reduction of the old ones. In many respects the world has moved away from the conditions that characterized the postwar era. The nation-states of western Europe have been reconstituted on a basis of unprecedented prosperity, and in the development of various cooperative arrangements culminating in the Common Market they have achieved a degree of unity that exceeds all but the most optimistic predictions of a decade ago. At the same time the intransigence of France both in refusing Britain's admission to the Common Market and in insisting on an independent development of nuclear armaments poses a serious threat to the broader aspects of Western unity and creates another major burden on American leadership. The ideological split between the Chinese and Russians adds a totally new dimension to the problem of containing communism and controlling the omnipresent threat of a disastrous nuclear war. The rapid rise of a multiplicity of new non-Western nations, with a strong insistence on national and individual human comity, has had a pronounced effect on American internal politics (especially in the area of race relations) and has already begun to reshape America's role in the United Nations. All of these and other factors, some as yet undetected, will continue to test the viability of American goals and the flexibility of its policy-making institutions in the still new and still unaccustomed place that the country has occupied in world politics for the past 25 years.

QUESTIONS FOR FURTHER DISCUSSION

1. Can an "objective" national interest be said to exist apart from the ideals and aspirations set for themselves by the residents of a national state in the conception they hold of their existence as a nation?

2. Is there any validity in the charge that American membership in the United Nations has resulted in a relinquishment of national sovereignty?

3. In what ways has the development of a large (and apparently permanent) military establishment placed a strain on the translation of American democratic ideals into reality?

4. Was the recent Nuclear Disarmament Treaty affected directly or indirectly by the growing rift between the Soviet Union and Red Chinese and by the attitude of General DeGaulle on the development of France as an independent nuclear power?

5. How has the Castro revolution in Cuba altered the problems of American relations with the Latin American countries?

IX

Epilogue

United Nations

[The United States has often been cited as a country which has displayed a genius for politics.] Despite this characterization it is only recently, if at all, that certain intellectual circles in Europe have ceased to think of America as a relative parvenu among nation-states. And in some respects the latter attitude has validity. [The country has been independent for less than 200 years, its population is conglomerate and a large portion of it has only recently been assimilated to American nationalism. It rose to a position of affluence and international power in a relatively short period of time, and (like most "other" societies, both old and new) it continues to reflect uncertainties about the meaning of its particular political experience. [Measured by other criteria, however, the continuity of the American system places the United States among a select list of modern political states whose political orders have shown remarkable stability over a period of time.]

[It sometimes seems strange to Americans to reflect on the fact that the country has become something of a prototype of modern constitutional democracy, the main forms of which emerged from the liberal ideas of the seventeenth and eighteenth centuries. In almost all respects the United States was the first national state to give practical effect to those ideas, and it has continued to measure its practice largely by their standards.] At the time of the French Revolution, for instance, the United States had already inaugurated the new government under the Constitution of 1787, and the constitutional order established in that era has not only survived into the latter half of the twentieth century, but has been substantially strengthened, while France has passed into its fifth republican era. [The United States may also lay a plausible claim to being the oldest federated republic continuously in existence; as such it has been a prime example for the many experiments in federalism that have taken place all over the world in the intervening period. The country was among the first, if not the first, modern nation-states to accept without equivocation the idea that governmental power is derivative solely from those over whom the government exercises authority, and it had already produced a representative structure of government before the idea of direct representation of the public had been fully articulated as a theory in the early nineteenth century. The continuity and adaptability of American institutions are equally noteworthy. The system of political parties in the United States through which so large a part of the democratic ideal has been translated into action is unquestionably one of the oldest in the world, especially when it is considered that essentially the same two parties which emerged from the political struggles of the late eighteenth century continue to dominate American politics today.

The tenacity of its ideals and institutions is illustrated above all by the fact that the country survived one of the most devastating civil wars in history without sacrificing the essentials of its political order, and indeed engaged in the Civil War largely because of the incompatibility of the institution of slavery with the political ideals on which it had justified its revolution and built a new political order.

In moving from the position of a new liberal nation-state of the eighteenth century to its present situation as a great power, while preserving the basic ideas and institutions to which the country was originally committed, the United States has made the transition from a radical experiment in new political forms and institutions to a status which might well be described as a traditional liberal state exhibiting overtones of a conservative disposition to protect and enhance its particular political heritage. During this course of historical development the ideas and institutions comprising that heritage have frequently had their utility and adaptability rigorously tested, and some of the central problems of contemporary American politics represent continuing and possibly even more stringent tests of their viability.

A voluminous amount of social criticism, both domestic and foreign, has grown out of the effort to interpret the meaning of American society and politics. Much of the commentary has been esoteric and some of it has been puerile. However, a common thread of interpretation runs through the best of this literature from Tocqueville to the present. The thesis that has probably been most widely accepted is that the American political system is what it is largely because of the persistence of liberal ideas and liberal traditions in America. The United States did not have a feudal period; it was almost entirely a product of modernity, despite the fact that certain of its constitutional forms can be traced to earlier periods. The absence of a feudal experience, with its emphasis on fixed status and a society which was organic in its structure and purposes, made America an "open" society in the sense in which such a society came to be visualized in the period during and after the Renaissance.

As more than one interpreter has noted, the United States was affected more strongly by the liberal ideas of John Locke than by any other single source. And Locke is preeminently the exponent of the liberal national state. Furthermore, the American environment was peculiarly susceptible to experimentation along the lines of Lockean liberalism. Locke's psychology led to a conception of radical individualism which was fostered by the rude state of naturalistic equality characteristic of the early American settlers. The material basis for the application of the individualistic property doctrines of Locke were present in the New World in the form of the seemingly endless bounties of nature with which man could mingle his labor and impress into his exclusive use without encroaching on the resources already appropriated by others. The great distance from the existing seats of government authority, the legal instruments by which settlement was authorized, and the necessities of life in the new environment gave a particular sense of reality to the abstract idea that society and government are formed by the establishment of a contractual relation among discrete individuals previously living in a state of nature. The doctrine of majoritarianism, too, was a fitting adjunct to a society conceived in terms of the primacy of the individual, a sense of natural equality, freedom of acquisition and contract, and an implicit assumption that the range of issues to be settled publicly rather than privately was quite narrow and subject to resolution without an elaborate apparatus of government.

Thus it was that the two abstract ideals of liberalism—freedom and equality—were given specific content in the American political experience. Or, as Professor Hans Morgenthau has put it in his book, *The Purpose of American Politics*: "The American purpose, from the Charter of James I to the contemporary racial revolution, has been the achievement of equality in freedom." But as Professor Morgenthau and others have recognized, the translation of this idealized purpose into concrete political experience raises many practical questions which have not always been answered consistently, and some of which undoubtedly cannot be answered in any definitive sense. In the first place, the concepts of liberty and equality are not only not patently complementary, they are in many respects antithetical. Emphasis on the freedom of the individual carries the logical implication that certain individuals may rise above others by virtue of natural talent, diligence, or sheer good fortune, and thus negate the principle of equality. And many controversies in American politics and public policy have turned on this theoretical difficulty, even though the problem has not usually been posed in this precise form.

A problem which is related to, but not identical with, the tension between liberty and equality is the failure to ask the sort of questions that might throw light on the concrete meaning of these great abstractions. Unless the terms "liberty" and "equality" are to be used as emotional rallying symbols on behalf of some ideological cause, common sense compels us to ask, "Freedom from what?" or "Freedom for what?" or "Equality in relation to what?" The questions have become more important as American society has moved away from the social conditions which contributed to the emphasis on radical individualism, governmental negativism, and extreme decentralization. In the Jacksonian era the attempt to forego virtually all differentiations of education and experience as criteria for political and administrative competence gave a dubious meaning to equality in a democratic society and left problems for the public service which still plague the country. Similarly, the justification of unimpeded capitalism and the vast inequalities in wealth arising in the "age of enterprise" in terms of social Darwinism gave a narrowly materialistic, puritanical meaning to freedom which still hovers around most of the movements of the radical right. The simplicity of society which characterized the early period of American life, the continuing success of the American experiment in democracy, and the general economic affluence of America have fed the widespread American belief that all social problems have simple solutions (a concommitant of the notion of progress), and these solutions for the most part depend on a return to the elemental ideas and forms with which the country originated. But America today is a technocratic, urban society whose frontier has long since disappeared, whose pluralism has much more of a group basis than a ruggedly individual one, whose economic interdependence bears no comparison with the earlier frontier independence, and whose conditions of economic and social mobility are largely institutional rather than personal. The necessity of adjustment to the conditions of a mass society has forced both American ideas and institutions in the direction of a new complexity, but both have also exhibited symptoms of social lag, especially in crisis periods.

Nevertheless, the American political experience has been richly varied and complex, despite the apparent desire of many Americans to conceive of it as relatively undifferentiated and simple. In fact, one of the major ambiguities of American politics (and one which may well contribute to the stability of the national consensus) is that the practice of American politics has a tendency to adjust to new conditions more rapidly than does the ideological component of the national life. In the face of the massive interpretative and critical literature on American society and politics, it would take a bold observer indeed to end a brief survey of the origins and functions of the principal institutions of American government and politics on anything other than a note of contingency. There can be little doubt but that the institutions of American politics have served the country well in the past, despite certain built-in difficulties. But what are the prospects for adaptation to the problems that are emerging in the present and foreshadowed in the future?

Can a political party system made up of parties whose internal compositions are so diffuse and whose centers of power are so unintegrated as they are in the United States provide a connective between public opinion and governmental policy sufficient to support the increasing tendency for major issues to be national rather than local in scope? Or will the divisive potentialities in a confederated and checked and balanced party system result in the "deadlock of democracy" so skillfully analyzed by Professor James M. Burns in his recent book by that title? Can the United States Supreme Court continue to maintain the enormous prestige on which its function as arbiter of the Constitution depends so heavily, now that it has forsaken its role as the custodian of economic orthodoxy for that of protector of civil liberties? Can the enormous burden of the Presidency continue to be managed by a single man, especially if neither the Congress nor the political parties accommodate themselves more to the national constituency?

The answer to these and other questions cannot be given in terms of the institutional structure alone. Much depends on the adaptability of the corpus of ideas by which Americans interpret their society and government and their individual places in it. And as more than one commentator has pointed out, the apparent political success of the past may cause the American public to rely upon outworn orthodoxies in its confrontation of new and confusing issues, and thus close the society against the pragmatic adaptation of the going system to changing conditions.

Domestically, the country is having to confront some problems to which attention may be long overdue, while others are still in the incipient stage. One of the most critical long-standing problems is the racial situation, in which (in terms of the interplay of ideas and institutions) the fundamental issue is whether or not America can fulfill its commitment to the ideal of equality. In the economic sphere America is still faced with the classic problem of securing full employment in a free society. President Johnson's recent declaration of war on poverty dramatically pointed up the contradiction between the American promise of material abundance for all and the prevalence among some segments of the population (and in certain sizeable geographical areas) of economic distress comparable to that in many of the underdeveloped countries. Even after the 1929 depression and the experience of the New Deal, and even in the face of the inescapable growth in size of the corporate units of the private economy, many Americans are still not reconciled to the necessities for collective action implied by an urban, technocratic, mass society, but would prefer to resort to a naturalistic order in which big government would have little or no role to play. In the matter of community life, the rise of the metropolitan area has raised serious questions about the capacity of Americans to achieve sufficient cohesiveness of purpose even at the local level to solve some of the most obvious problems of a mass society. The habitual response of individual Americans to an environment considered incompatible has been to move to another environment, preferably one which was new and undeveloped. This attitude, with its notions of freedom rooted in the near anarchism of the frontier, carries over into the pattern of the flight to the urban fringes, where it is apparently hoped that the problems of the city can be avoided in a new form of insularity.

In the preceding chapter the impact of certain well-worn orthodoxies on American foreign policy was discussed at some length. Here, too, the tests of the political system and the ideas which inform it are being made in terms of the consistency with which America is capable of fulfilling its own larger purposes. Can a society which is almost 200 years removed from its own revolution, and which in the intervening period has maintained an unassailable national independence and achieved a remarkable internal stability, have much patience with the tumultuous aspirations of newly emerging nations and the efforts of older states to improve their economic and political lots? As Professor Arnold Toynbee has put it in the title of one of his lectures, "Can America Rejoin Her Own Revolution?"

All of these and a great many other issues appear on the agenda of American public life and will have to be resolved or at least alleviated by means of the governmental machinery and processes outlined in the foregoing chapters, if at all. And in the process of resolution or alleviation, the problems themselves will subtly but surely reshape the major political institutions and provide the historical background from which future problems will emerge. And whether explicitly or implicitly acknowledged in relation to the flux of events, the questions which Tocqueville perceived as essential ones for the American democracy will still be present: Can a society which places so much emphasis on freedom avoid the extremes of anarchy, on the one hand, and social conformity on the other? By the same token, can the ideal of equality be realized more completely without the parallel abandonment of all standards by which a differentiation of social rewards on the basis of merit would be justified, or without the imposition of majority tyranny? The capacity of constitutional democracy to make the pragmatic accommodations necessary to cope with the enormous complexities of contemporary life will go a long way toward determining the extent to which the ideal of equality in freedom can continue to be implemented. And while the United States may be the prototype of a society founded on such a purpose, it is by no means the only national state with a stake in the future of the ideal of liberal constitutional democracy.

Bibliography

The following books are only a minute fragment of the vast literature on American government and politics. In this instance the process of selection was necessarily highly subjective; but in general an attempt was made to secure a balance between those books that have worn well over a longer period of time and those contemporary works that are most provocative in interpreting America's political past and identifying the essential problems of the present. A number of these volumes are now available in paperback. Fortunately, many of the books cited and the periodical literature on the subject contain enough bibliographic items to permit an indefinite follow-up on materials available for consultation.

GENERAL WORKS

Brogan, Denis W., *An Introduction to American Politics*, London, 1954.

Bryce, James, *The American Commonwealth*, first published in 1888, available in numerous editions.

Hamilton, Alexander, James Madison, and John Jay, *The Federalist*, available in numerous editions, some with extensive commentaries.

Hartz, Louis, *The Liberal Tradition in America*, New York, 1955.

Hofstadter, Richard, *The American Political Tradition and the Men Who Made It*, New York, 1948.

Parrington, Vernon Louis, *Main Currents in American Thought*, New York, 1927–1930.

Rossiter, Clinton L., *Seedtime of the Republic*, New York, 1953.

Tocqueville, Alexis de, *Democracy in America*, first published in 1835–1840, available in numerous editions.

CHAPTER I

Beard, Charles A., *An Economic Interpretation of the Constitution of the United States*, New York, 1913.

Brown, Robert E., *Charles Beard and the Constitution*, Princeton, 1956.

Corwin, Edward S., *The Constitution and What It Means Today*, rev. ed., 1958.

Farrand, Max, *The Framing of the Constitution of the United States,* New Haven, 1913.

Harbison, Winfred A., and Alfred H. Kelly, *The American Constitution: Its Origin and Development,* New York, 3rd ed., 1963.

CHAPTER II

Beth, Loren P., *Politics, the Constitution, and the Supreme Court,* Evanston, 1962.

Freund, Paul A., *On Understanding the Supreme Court,* Boston, 1949.

Gelhorn, Walter, *American Rights: The Constitution in Action,* New York, 1960.

Mendelson, Wallace, *Capitalism, Democracy, and the Supreme Court,* New York, 1960.

Warren, Charles, *The Supreme Court in U.S. History,* Boston, rev. ed., 1932.

CHAPTER III

Binkley, Wilfred E., *The Man in the White House: His Powers and Duties,* Baltimore, 1958.

Johnson, Walter, *1600 Pennsylvania Avenue: Presidents and the People,* Boston, 1960.

Neustadt, Richard E., *Presidential Power,* New York, 1960.

Rossiter, Clinton Lawrence, *The American Presidency,* New York, 1956.

White, Leonard D., *The Federalists,* New York, 1948; *The Jeffersonians,* 1951; *The Jacksonians,* 1954; and *The Republican Era,* 1958.

White, Theodore H., *The Making of the President 1960,* New York, 1961.

CHAPTER IV

Bailey, Stephen K., *Congress Makes a Law,* New York, 1950.

Burnham, James, *Congress and the American Tradition,* Chicago, 1959.

Burns, James M., *Congress on Trial,* New York, 1949.

DeGrazia, Alfred, *Public and Republic: Political Representation in America,* New York, 1951.

Galloway, George B., *Congress at the Crossroads,* New York, 1946.

Gross, Bertram M., *The Legislative Struggle,* New York, 1953.

CHAPTER V

Agar, Herbert, *The Price of Union*, Boston, 1950.

Binkley, Wilfred E., *American Political Parties, Their Natural History*, New York, 3rd ed., 1961.

Burns, James M., *The Deadlock of Democracy*, Englewood Cliffs, 1963.

Key, V. O., Jr., *Politics, Parties and Pressure Groups*, New York, 5th ed., 1964.

Lubell, Samuel, *The Future of American Politics*, New York, 2nd ed., 1956.

Schattschneider, Elmer E., *Party Government*, New York, 1942.

Truman, David B., *The Governmental Process: Political Interests and Public Opinion*, New York, 1951.

CHAPTER VI

Anderson, William, *The Nation and the States: Rivals or Partners*, Minneapolis, 1955.

Graves, W. Brooke, *American Intergovernmental Relations*, New York, 1964.

Key, V. O., Jr., *American State Politics*, New York, 1956; *Southern Politics in State and Nation*, New York, 1949.

Thursby, Vincent V., *Interstate Cooperation: A Study of the Interstate Compact*, Washington, 1953.

White, Leonard D., *The States and the Nation*, Baton Rouge, 1953.

CHAPTER VII

Baker, Gordon E., *Rural Versus Urban Political Power*, New York, 1955.

Jones, Victor, *Metropolitan Government*, Chicago, 1942.

Mumford, Lewis, *The City in History*, New York, 1961.

Sayre, Wallace S., and Herbert Kaufman, *Governing New York City*, New York, 1960.

Wager, Paul W., *County Government Across the Nation*, Chapel Hill, 1950.

Wood, Robert C., *Suburbia: Its People and Their Politics*, Boston, 1958.

Chapter VIII

Almond, Gabriel A., *The American People and Foreign Policy*, New York, 1950.

Bailey, Thomas A., *A Diplomatic History of the American People*, New York, 6th ed., 1958.

Herz, J. H., *International Politics in the Atomic Age*, New York, 1959.

Kahn, Herman, *On Thermonuclear War*, Princeton, 1960.

Kennan, George F., *American Diplomacy, 1900–1950*, Chicago, 1951.

Morgenthau, Hans J., *Politics Among Nations*, 3rd rev. ed., New York, 1960.

Schuman, Frederick L., *International Politics*, 6th ed., New York, 1958.